A Community for Children?

Children, Citizenship and Internal Migration in the EU

LOUISE ACKERS
University of Leeds

HELEN STALFORD
University of Liverpool

ASHGATE

Published by
Ashgate Publishing Limited
Gower House
Croft Road
Aldershot
Hampshire GU11 3HR
England

Ashgate Publishing Company
Suite 420
101 Cherry Street
Burlington, VT 05401-4405
USA

Ashgate website: http://www.ashgate.com

British Library Cataloguing in Publication Data
Ackers, Louise, 1960-
A community for children? : children, citizenship and internal migration in the EU. - (Research in migration and ethnic relations series)
1.Children's rights - European Union countries 2.Children of migrant laborers - Civil rights - European Union countries 3.Citizenship - European Union countries 4.European Union countries - Emigration and immigration
I.Title II.Stalford, Helen
323.3'52'094

Library of Congress Cataloging-in-Publication Data
Ackers, Louise, 1960-
A community for children? : children, citizenship and internal migration in the EU / Louise Ackers and Helen Stalford.
p. cm. -- (Research in migration and ethnic relations series)
Includes bibliographical references and index.
ISBN 0-7546-1858-7
1. Children's rights--European Union countries. 2. Citizenship--European Union countries. 3. Children of migrant laborers--European Union countries--Social conditions. I. Stalford, Helen. II. Title. III. Series.

HQ789.A25 2003
305.23'094--dc22

2003058284

ISBN 0 7546 1858 7

Printed and bound in Great Britain by
Athenaeum Press Ltd., Gateshead, Tyne & Wear

Contents

List of Cases

European Court of Justice and Court of First Instance

Aissatou Diatta v Land Berlin (Case 267/83) [1986] 2 CMLR 164
Anita Cristini v. Société nationale des chemins de fer français (Case 32/75) ECR 1085
Baumbast and R v. Secretary of State for the Home Department (Case C 413/99) Judgment of the Court of Justice of 17th September 2002, 2002/C274/03
Belgium v. Humbel (Case 263/86) [1988] ECR 5365
Bernini v. Minister van Onderwijs en Wetenschappen (Case C-3/90) [1992] ECR I-1071
Brown v. Secretary of State for Scotland (Case 197/86) [1988] ECR 3205
Burchell (Case 377/85) [1987] ECR 3329, 3 CMLR 757
Casagrande v. Landehauptstadt München (Case 9/74) [1974] ECR 773, [1974] CMLR 423
Commission of the European Communities v. Belgium (Case 42/87) [1989] 1 CMLR 457
Commission of the European Communities v. Federal Republic of Germany (Case 249/86) [1986] ECR 1263
D and Sweden v. Council (Case T-246/97) [1999] ECR II-1 para.26.
Dzodzi v Belgium (Cases C-297/88 and C-197/89) [1990] ECR 3783
Echternach and Moritz v. Netherlands Minister for Education and Science (Cases 389 and 390/87) [1989] ECR 723
Francesco Reina and Letizia Reina v. Landeskreditbank Baden-Wurttemberg (Case 65/81) [1982] ECR 33
Grant v. South West Trains (Case C-249/96) [1998] IRLR.
Gravier v. City of Liege (Case 293/83) [1985] ECR 593
Hauer v. Land Rheinland Pfalz (Case 44/79) [1979] ECR 3727
Hessische Knappschaft v. Maison Singer et Fils (Case 44/65) [1965] ECR 965
Hoever and Zachow v. Land Nordrhein-Westfalen (C-245/94 and C-312/94) O.J. C 370, 7.12.1996
Hofmann v Barmer Ersalzkasse (Case 184/83) [1984] ECR 3047
Humer Reported 5th February 2002 (Case C-255/99) O.J. 2002/C 84/09
Landesamt fur Ausbildungsforderung Nordrhein-Westfalen v. Lubor Gaal (Case C-7/94) [1996] ECR 1-1031

Maria Teresa Fernandez de Bobadilla v. Museo Nacional del Prado & Others (Case C-234/97) OJ 1999/C 366/01
Martinéz Sala v. Freistaat Bayern (Case C-85/96) [1998] ECR I-2691
Matteucci v. Communauté Français de Belgique (Case 235/87) [1988] ECR 5589, [1989] 1 CMLR 357
Michel S. v. Fonds national de reclassement social des handicappés (Case 76/72) [1973] ECR 437
Ministère Public v. Even (Case 207/78) [1979] ECR 2019
Morson and Jhanjan v Netherlands (Cases 35 & 36/82) [1982] ECR 3723
Office National de l'Emploi v. Deak (Case 94/84) [1985] ECR 1773
P v. S and Cornwall City Council (Case C-13/94) [1996] ECR I-2143
Pietro Pinna v. Caisse d'Allocations Familiales de la Savoie (Case 41/84) [1986] ECR 1
Prais v. Council of the European Communities (Case 130/75) [1976] ECR 1589
Raulin v. Minister van Onderwijs en Wetenschappen (Case C-357/89) [1992] ECR I-1027
Rutilli v. Minister for the Interior (Case 36/75) [1975] ECR 1219.
R v. IAT and Surinder Singh ex.p. Secretary of State for the Home Department (Case C-370-90) [1992] ECR I-4265
Safet Eyup v. Landesgeschaftsstelle des Arbeitsmarktservice Vorarlberg (Case C-65/98) [2000] 3 CMLR 1049
Stauder v. City of Ulm (Case 29/69) [1969] ECR 419
Van Den-Boogaard v. Laumen (Case C-220/95) [1997] 2 FLR 399
Vito Inzirillo v. Caisse d'Allocations Familiales de l'Arrondissement de Lyon (Case 63/76) [1976] ECR 2057.

National Case Law

C v. C (Divorce: stay of English Proceedings) 11 May 2000, [2001] FLR 624
Gillick v West Norfolk and Wisbech Area Health Authority [1985] 3 All ER 402 (HL)
Grewal [1979-80] Imm.A.R. 119 (Immigration Appeal Tribunal)
Hemain v. Hemain CA [1988] 2 FLR 388
I v. I [2001] 1 FLR 913
Irvin [2001] 1 FLR 178
M v. M (Financial Provision After Foreign Divorce) FD [1994] 1 FLR 399

R v Secretary of State for the Home Department (ex parte Amarjit Singh Sandhu) [1982] 2 CMLR 553

R v Secretary of State for the Home Department (ex parte Amarjit Singh Sandhu) [1983] 3 CMLR 131

Acknowledgements

We are indebted to a number of individuals without whom the publication of this book would not have been possible.

First of all, we would like to thank the children, young people, parents and key informants who gave up their time to be interviewed for the research. We would also like to acknowledge the support of the European Commission (the former DGXXII) and the Nuffield Foundation who funded the original project on which many of the findings reported in the book are based.

We are privileged to have worked with such dedicated and rigorous research partners in Portugal, Greece and Sweden. Our thanks go to Heloísa Perista at the Centre for Studies in Social Intervention (CESIS), Lisbon; Martha Blomqvist and Vera Gustaffson at the Centre for Feminist Research, University of Uppsala; and Poppy Giannaki at International Social Services in Athens.

We are grateful also for the academic input of Sonia Morano-Foadi to the legal framework on family breakdown and to Mark Redmond for his much-valued contribution at all stages of the research process.

The rigorous efforts of Simon Prideaux and Keleigh Groves in preparing this book for publication are particularly appreciated.

This book is dedicated to our brothers and sisters,
migrant children in their own right

1 Introduction

This book considers the nature and extent of children's citizenship status in the context of the European Union (EU). It is based essentially on the findings of a three-year European Commission and Nuffield Foundation-funded research project[1] evaluating the impact of EU law and policy upon the legal status and experiences of the children of EU migrant workers. The research was cross-national and socio-legal in nature and focused primarily on the free movement provisions as the primary source of entitlement for this community of children. The importance of social entitlement under these provisions to the emergence of a concept of 'Citizenship of the Union' places the study at the centre of some very important developments, the consequences of which potentially encompass a much broader field of interest.

Previous academic research on the free movement of persons provisions has identified the economic nexus underpinning access to and ongoing enjoyment of this entitlement and the derivative nature of migrant family members' rights (Meehan, 1993; Wallace, 1993; Ackers, 1998). The research findings reported in this book represent an attempt to develop this analysis within the specific and commonly overlooked context of EU migrant *children*. By filling this apparent research void, the intention is, ultimately, to address an identifiable policy vacuum. The following chapters thus consider the extent to which the important body of European social rights now available to migrant children serve to both secure their stake in EU citizenship and provide an important springboard for more wide-reaching developments in favour of children more generally.

It is important to clarify from the outset, however, what we mean by 'citizenship' in order to establish how the concept might be advanced and applied to children in the EU. On the one hand, a traditional analysis of children's material rights under EU law and, specifically, under the free movement provisions, provides a useful barometer for evaluating their citizenship status in a formal legal sense. This, however, only reveals part of the picture. Through conducting in-depth empirical research involving children and drawing upon children's rights discourse, our aim is to consider European citizenship more holistically in terms of children's

---

[1] Project reference number 96-10-EET-0122-00, Youth For Europe Programme (DGXXII), 1997-2000.

active participation in decision-making, and in terms of how EU law and policy consider, promote and impact upon children's well-being and autonomy.

Defining Citizenship in an EU Context

'Citizenship of the Union' has commonly been interpreted in terms of the formal rights it yields as articulated in Articles 17-22 EC. In addition to the extension of modest political rights for all European citizens, these provisions consolidated a platform of social rights for EU migrant workers that have progressively evolved since the Treaty of Rome under the free movement of persons provisions.[2] Indeed, it has been argued that the interpretation of free movement secondary legislation by the European Court of Justice (ECJ) has elevated the principle of free movement of persons into one of the fundamental rights of Community law, thus marking a trend towards the realisation of an overall European citizenship (Ackers, 1994; Nielson and Szyszczak, 1994; Scheiwe, 1994).

The evolution of these provisions has been very much influenced by 'common sense' presumptions about family relationships, gender roles and social and economic barriers to mobility. Initially, the provisions focused quite narrowly on labour market measures, but later shifted to a more holistic interest in workers as members of families and to aspects of family policy as the key to 'facilitating mobility' (Ackers and Stalford, 1999).[3] The formalisation of the status of 'Citizenship of the Union' thus marks a step in a long process that has tied the development of citizenship to intra-Community migration. To this end, as D'Oliveira (1995, p.65) asserts, mobility has become 'the central element around which other rights crystallise'. The rationale for the ECJ's incursion into areas of family policy in this area of Community law is based firmly on a conceptualisation of women and children as the non-productive appendages of male workers.[4] Scheiwe (1994, p.250) suggests that:

---

[2] A range of secondary provisions have substantiated the basic right to free movement, most notably, Regulation 1612/68. Its provisions will be considered in detail in chapters four, seven, eight and nine. See also Ackers, 1998 and Ackers and Stalford, 1999.

[3] The facilitating mobility test was first introduced in Case 207/78 *Ministère Public v. Even* [1979] ECR 2019 and is discussed in more detail in chapter four.

[4] Despite the fact that women form a significant proportion of all EU migrants moving, in the main, as single women for work – see Ackers, 1998, and Moebius and Szyszcak, 1998 for a critique of the ECJ's distinction between productive and 'unproductive' work. This point is further illustrated in chapter five.

> Provisions on the free movement of workers allow interventions into the family sphere ... to augment the male migrant worker's mobility. In this model, a (male) worker's family is clearly a market-related issue that matters.

The importance of the economic nexus in justifying the extension of workers' rather than citizens' rights is further reinforced by Pringle (1998, p.134): 'Put simply, children are not workers and are themselves not a primary focus for European Union attention'.

This oversight (in both EU *and* migration law, policy and research) reflects, in the first instance, the primacy attached to paid work and to economic roles within debates around both European citizenship and intra-Community migration. Similarly, the literature on international migration typically takes a very narrow view of migration motivations. Specifically, the literature tends to construct the majority of 'voluntary' (as opposed to 'forced') migrations as economically-motivated profit-maximising behaviour in much the same way as the EU policy-agenda is based around the notion of labour mobility and the free movement of 'workers'.[5] Kofman (2000, p.46) makes an interesting and relevant point, albeit relating to the lack of attention afforded to the involvement of women in migration, when she argues that 'theoretical and methodological perspectives and the choice of research agendas have played a major part in rendering them invisible'. She particularly alludes to the dominance of methodological individualism in international migration research which, she argues, implies a focus on the 'international migrant as a single person, usually assumed to be male, disembodied and disembedded from contexts such as familial or household relationships or the wider society in which he lives' (Koffman, 2000, p.52). Our own work has also highlighted the overemphasis on the male breadwinner model in migration theory which tends to subsume the interests of family members, a practice which is mirrored at EU law and policy-level.

To the extent that children have been recognised within these debates, the concern has, again, typically been with the wider family as a potential barrier to workers' mobility. Issues of family reunification as part of the economic impetus, intensifying the need for flexibility in trans-European labour markets, have, not surprisingly, constituted a further major catalyst underpinning the development of free movement policy. On other, more recent occasions, the recognition of the family as a relevant unit in its own right reflects more ideologically-driven concerns. A report by the High

---

[5] These issues are developed in chapters three, four, six and seven.

Level Panel on the Free Movement of Persons (Veil, 1997, pp.42-54), for example, argues for the extension of social rights to the families of migrant workers on the grounds that, 'access to those advantages is a means of achieving the objective of the preservation of family unity and of fostering integration in the host state'.

Whilst this justification for intervention in the family sphere has proved quite effective in extending rights to the non-working partners and children of migrant workers, it reinforces a functionalist approach to families and tends to conflate the interests of children with the wider interests of their parents and, in particular, the 'worker-parent'. As such, it has had little effect in encouraging policy measures designed to deal with the practical reality of family breakdown[6] and has largely failed to identify children both as policy recipients and as policy actors in their own right. The concept of 'Union Citizenship' has been invoked only insofar as to extend entitlement to the family as an indivisible entity with the result that the interests of the child continue to be eclipsed by more (adult) economic and labour market concerns or subsumed within a more general European 'family policy'.

This is not to undermine the significant advancements to children's entitlement under the auspices of workers' families' rights and the operation of the free movement provisions, but it does raise several important considerations. Firstly, as chapters four, six and seven will demonstrate, current provision relating to the family fails to take into account changing patterns of family life across the EU which have generated increasing diversity in family forms and shifted boundaries of authority and responsibility for children (often from the parent onto other adults or the children themselves). Secondly, as chapters eight and nine will illustrate, it fails to adequately account for forums other than the family unit which engage with and facilitate the development of children's sense of personal and public identity.[7] Furthermore, it ignores the significant strides made within the international and national children's rights movement towards acknowledging that children – migrant and otherwise – do have independent interests and needs to those of their parents and, indeed, have a valid contribution to make to the life of the wider Community.

---

[6] A point developed in chapter seven.

[7] Education, for instance, provides a crucial example of one such forum although, as the case law demonstrates, children's educational rights are largely coterminous with their familial link with the migrant worker parent.

Children as EU Citizens in Their Own Right

Having described how children's rights under the free movement provisions have been largely incidental to the developments in respect of their worker-parents' rights, a similar oversight is evident within the context of more general interpretations and advancements of the concept of citizenship. Citizenship, in a broad sense, is traditionally allied with notions of rights and responsibilities which are earned according to the extent of an individual's engagement with society in an economic, social and/or civil capacity. Involvement in the labour market has, in the past, been widely regarded as providing the primary forum within which this process takes place. More recently, however, there has been a concerted effort by academics and, latterly, policy-makers, to advance the concept of citizenship beyond traditional notions of economic contribution and labour market value towards a more inclusive interpretation which accounts for variables of gender, race, ethnicity, class and disability (Ackers, 1996; Wallace and Fine 1996; Lister, 1997; Lewis, 1997). In particular, recent feminist critiques have focused on the need to widen the concept of social contribution to encompass unpaid caring work as the legitimate basis of a claim to social rights.

While developments in citizenship discourse to incorporate previously marginalised groups are to be welcomed, it is only relatively recently that the citizenship status of *children* has been seriously considered (Roche, 1992; Franklin, 1995; Freeman, 1996). Yet even these attempts to widen the concept have failed to significantly dissipate the common association between the 'active', 'good' citizen and those who at least have the potential to pay taxes, undertake paid work and take on civic responsibility (Hill and Tisdall, 1997, p.37). Children's rights advocates have thus identified the common tendency to either locate children's citizenship rights within the framework of their parents' or family rights or to focus on their future potential as 'citizens-in-the-making.' (Mnookin, 1981; Eekelaar, 1986; James and Prout, 1995; Bainham, 1998; Stalford, 2000).

The tendency to overlook children as active citizens is particularly pronounced in an EU context. This is in spite of a recent, more genuine endeavour to bridge the gap between Member States' nationals and the Community institutions by promoting a more meaningful, universal engagement with EU citizenship. Such endeavours are attributable partly to the emergence of a more distinct European social agenda which has gradually extended the remit of Community competence beyond the exclusively economic market-oriented objectives that previously underpinned Community life, towards a more embracing interest in promoting citizens' well-being and quality of life. The concern to activate and substantiate the concept of EU citizenship is also fuelled by concerns relating to the democratic deficit that has so far served to exclude nationals' input in EU policies and decision-making processes. Children have yet to be acknowledged within this process, however, as either the recipients of policy or as potential agents of European policy-formation.

One explanation for the lack of EU provision targeting children as autonomous citizens lies in the issue of legal competency, domestic sovereignty and the application of the principle of subsidiarity as enshrined in Article 5 EC. Certainly, theoretical and political arguments which delineate the boundaries between the EU institutions and Member States to regulate domestic social and civil affairs have routinely justified the exclusion of children from the EU policy agenda. As Ruxton (1997, p.16) points out:

> The primary emphasis on economic over social matters in the European Treaties leads to children's interests being largely ignored in EU policy development. In fact, the legal competence relating to children is limited in precisely those areas which should be seen as a priority. As a result, the EU is more concerned with, for instance, the free flow of goods and services to do with children than with children themselves! There is not a single mention of children in the Treaties of the European Union.[8]

The arguments around limited competency and the importance of subsidiarity, as a break on supra-national intervention in family policy matters, have been increasingly called into question on the grounds that EU policy may itself have an impact on children. In other words, the EU may be responsible for the creation of policy spill-overs which operate to the detriment of children. Concerns around environmental policy are a case in point but so too, arguably, is labour migration policy. Ruxton (1997, p.16) continues:

> The impact of the European treaties on children is very difficult to assess. There are issues arising from the Single Market's emphasis on the free movement of goods, services and people which may have a significant negative impact on children, but at present there is no competence to take the necessary remedial action. Specific examples include the legal and

---

[8] The 1997 Treaty of Amsterdam has since introduced two new legal bases for action which offer some potential for policy development: Article 13 refers to measures to combat discrimination based upon age and Article 29 allows for inter-governmental action to combat offences against children.

> social consequences for children when their parents increasingly choose [and are encouraged by EU policies][9] to live in different parts of the EU following family breakdown.[10]

These concerns, around the unintended consequences of mainstream EU policies on children, have manifested themselves in pressure for policy-impact studies or forms of child-audit, built very much around the arguments developed in relation to gender-audit and the commitment to 'mainstreaming' within equal opportunity policies (Ruxton, 1999; EFCW, 2002; Stalford, 2003). Ruxton's statement in particular reflects an important concern over the lack of knowledge and inadequacy of statistical and empirical data on children, which arises, in part at least, as a consequence of limited legal competence.[11]

These concerns are complemented by pressure from the international children's rights movement. They point to the invisibility of children within EU law and policy-making and the lack of effective mechanisms to actively promote and protect children's rights in the evolving European social arena. The disparity between EU law and international and European human rights law is particularly evident in the light of Member States' ratification of the 1989 UN Convention on the Rights of the Child (UNCRC) and implementation of the European Convention on Human Rights and Fundamental Freedoms 1950. For example, Article 3 of the UNCRC enunciates the 'best interests' principle:

> In all actions concerning children, whether undertaken by public or private social welfare institutions, courts of law, administrative authorities or legislative bodies, the best interests of the child shall be a primary consideration.

The implementation of Article 3 raises fundamental questions around the concept of family, and the presumption of consensus within 'functional' family units already discussed above demanding consideration of the respective roles and responsibilities of children, parents and statutory and non-governmental bodies. This provision implicitly acknowledges that it is no longer acceptable to presume that parental rights and the interests of their children are coterminous.

---

[9] Authors' addition.

[10] This issue is considered in detail in chapter seven.

[11] At least in terms of EUROSTAT and Commission funding priorities, a point returned to in chapter two.

The recent introduction of the Charter of Fundamental Rights in the European Union arguably goes some way towards addressing some of the concerns as to the children's rights lacuna in European legal, policy and citizenship formulations. This instrument, adopted at the Nice Summit in December 2000, expresses a commitment to consider and promote the rights of the child in the drafting, implementation and enforcement of EC legislation and serves to amalgamate, to some degree, the provisions of the UNCRC (specifically, Articles 3 and 12), and the provisions of the European Convention on Human Rights. In particular, it includes a right to education (Article 14(3)); a right to non-discrimination on grounds of age (Article 21(1)); the right to be protected and cared for, to express their views freely and be listened to (Article 24(1)); the best interests principle (Article 24(2)); the right to maintain a relationship with both parents unless contrary to child's interests (Article 24(3)); and the prohibition of child labour and protection of young people at work (Article 32). Although as yet only of declaratory effect, these provisions represent a clear albeit tentative acknowledgement of children's rights as distinct from those of adults and reveal a clearer commitment to render children more visible at Union level. What is perhaps more significant is the fact that the Charter provisions are not actually linked to, nor are they contingent upon, the operation of the free movement provisions. Instead, they articulate a human-rights based approach and, in the process, consolidate the correlation between children's rights discourse and the social or civil aspirations of European citizenship.[12]

The methodology adopted for the research presented in this book has sought to mirror the citizenship aspiration of promoting inclusivity. By developing and applying an innovative qualitative approach to cross-national research, our aim is to involve children more meaningfully, not only as policy recipients but also as policy evaluators. This raises issues of more general applicability within the context of citizenship. Lister, (1997, p.7) citing Turner, for instance, has described citizenship as, 'a platform for interdisciplinary research on the problems of social membership in advanced societies'. This book is concerned precisely with the evolution of social membership at EU level and seeks to evaluate the scope and quality of that membership within the context of children's citizenship status and experiences under EU law.

---

[12] The extent to which the European institutions have taken such developments on board to advance children's stake in European citizenship will be considered in particular in chapters four, seven and eight.

The Research Project

The research project on which this book is based focused on the specific situation of children in families in which at least one of the parents has at some point moved from one Member State to another. The three-year study adopted a specifically socio-legal approach and was concerned to examine both the legal framework shaping the formal rights of this group of migrants and the experiences of the children concerned.

The first phase of the research included an evaluation of the supra-national legal and policy context. This necessitated an analysis of the free movement of persons provisions, the material rights available to migrant workers and their families, and the criteria governing eligibility under the provisions. In particular, the first phase of the research considered the ECJ's interpretation of the concepts of 'family' and 'child' and the extent to which these definitions restrict entitlement, exclude certain families and children from Community protection and promote relationships of dependency.

Existing Community rights for migrant workers and their families are based on an ethic of non-discrimination and are not, as such, directly concerned to promote harmonisation. The geography of migration and the domestic social policy context (particularly in the receiving states) determine social status. Project partners in the four countries involved in our study thus played a crucial role in representing the social context within which the study was located and enabled us to compare systems of support for children in Greece, Sweden, Portugal and the UK.[13]

The empirical focus of the research has been on children as social actors and on their understanding and experiences of migration. For the second phase of the study, the project team identified and interviewed parents and young people (aged between 11 and 18) in 180 families.[14] The sample also included children in families in which one or both parents was an EU migrant (not necessarily from the same Member State) and children in families in which one or both parents had returned 'home' following a period of residence in another Member State (the 'returnees').

In order to understand the significance of regional context to the availability of and access to social benefits, the sample included families

---

[13] Successful collaboration lies at the heart of effective operationalisation in such large-scale qualitative projects and this is discussed in more detail in chapter two.

[14] These included 50 in Portugal (extracts from the Portuguese interviews included in subsequent chapters of this book are prefixed with a 3); 50 in Greece (pre-fixed with a 4); 30 in Sweden (pre-fixed with a 2); and 50 in the UK, including 11 in Northern Ireland (pre-fixed with a 0).

resident in cosmopolitan regions (typically the capital cities), which usually provide stronger networks of formal and informal support for migrant families, as well as more peripheral areas where families and children may be more isolated from such networks. Efforts were made to ensure a broad coverage of nationalities and to avoid over-sampling specific populations whose experience may be particularly distinctive, such as the children of academics or language teachers.

In most cases, parents were interviewed separately from their children to provide us with some impression of the background to the situation and to identify any 'sensitive' issues (around bereavement or family breakdown for instance). Many children were very young when they first moved or were born after the initial migration and had limited recall of such events. In a few cases, parents and children were interviewed together or only one party was interviewed (for example, in cases where the child has a profound disability or where the parent was not available for interview).

The interviews were of a qualitative, largely unstructured nature and followed a list of topic areas designed to assess migration and family histories and the impact of these on children's integration and quality of life.

The Structure of the Book

The following chapters seek to combine a more theoretical discussion of the legal, policy and methodological framework underpinning our study with extensive reference to the interviewees' personal accounts of their migration experiences.

Chapter two sets the scene by considering some of the methodological issues raised in the operationalisation of our research, focusing on two issues in particular. Firstly, it discusses the relevance of current debates around contextualisation and culture-boundedness for comparative research on migration. Secondly, it considers the development and virtues of a child-centred approach to social research and assesses the validity and transferability of these investigative methods to work at a cross-national, comparative level.

Having outlined the importance of contextualisation to comparative research, *chapter three* endeavours to develop our understanding of the circumstances in which these forms of intra-EU migration are taking place through an evaluation of the factors shaping the migration decisions of families. The findings emphasise the importance of understanding migration as an ongoing process closely related to the evolution of the life-course of both parents and children. Whilst parental employment, and particularly that of the father, plays a key role in the initial decision to move, other family-related considerations often emerge as important factors necessitating a review of location.

Another important dimension of context concerns the legal framework within which families are moving and the impact of moving upon their citizenship status and access to social benefits in the host state. *Chapter four* thus describes and analyses the concept of 'family' under the free movement of persons provisions and critiques the status of the 'child' within this concept. The chapter moves on to draw out disparities between the formal definition of 'family' under Community law and the reality of demographic structures and family practices across the EU by reference to European and national statistics and, more specifically, the characteristics of our own interview sample.

Chapters five to nine report in more detail on the findings of the interviews with migrant parents and children. *Chapter five* focuses on the migration decision-making process itself. It begins by setting the context for a discussion of children's engagement in migration decision-making within the emerging framework of children's rights and moves on to discuss respondents' perceptions of the involvement of children in family migration decisions.

Chapter six considers the impact of moving on families and how respondents subsequently managed kin relationships transnationally. The discussion in this section considers both the relationship with the wider extended family but, also, the impact of migration on the immediate nuclear family itself and the incidence of separation of children and parents. Whilst such separation was often a consequence of balancing respective interests at any point in time – with education emerging as an important variable – in many cases, it was triggered by forms of family breakdown. Divorce and separation have a key impact on the legal status of parents and children in migrant families, particularly transnational or 'international' migrant families. *Chapter seven* is devoted to a consideration of these issues and documents developments in European law within this area, as well as reporting on the experiences of family breakdown amongst our sample population.

Concerns around children's education performance, integration and progression figure prominently in family migration decisions. Chapters eight and nine, therefore, focus exclusively on this important issue. *Chapter eight* charts and evaluates the development of EU education law and policy and the educational rights of the children of EU migrant workers. It then considers the problems arising out of divergence in domestic provision, for example, in terms of academic progression and integration in the host state. *Chapter nine* moves on to consider the issue of language and the implications of adapting to a new linguistic environment on children's formal learning experiences and social integration. It reports on the challenges faced by migrant children in attempting to cope with these processes and the role of teachers, parents, public authorities and other migrant organisations in supporting their transition.

Chapter ten, the concluding chapter, draws together all of the material presented in the nine preceding chapters to consider whether European law has developed children's citizenship significantly beyond the parasitic rights derived under the free movement provisions towards a more engaging, universal concept which is of relevance to children and young people more generally within the EU.

2 The Challenges of Working with Children in a Cross-National Context

Introduction

This chapter considers some of the methodological issues raised in the operationalisation of our research. The project objectives included not only an analysis of the status and experiences of children who have moved within the EU: it was also concerned to develop and evaluate a model for comparative research involving children. The project presented a number of challenges, reflected in the research strategy. Firstly, it attempted to counter what has become a dominant tradition in comparative research to 'follow the primrose path of doing what was easiest to do on the basis of information gathered by others' (Cochrane and Clarke, 1993, p.8) through a combination of secondary analysis, legal and policy evaluation and in-depth qualitative work. Secondly, it complemented information about children (obtained from parents and agencies) with children's own perceptions of their experiences and opportunities using a variety of techniques. Finally, it sought to achieve these objectives through collaboration involving an inter-disciplinary team of academics and practitioners and a range of organisations representing migrant families. As such, it provides important insights into the problems of conducting cross-national research on childhood and, more specifically, working with children. The project thus sought to go some way in filling an identified research vacuum and to demonstrate the feasibility and effectiveness of in-depth, child-centred comparative research that is often dismissed as too difficult, methodologically inadequate or prohibitively expensive.

The chapter focuses on two aspects of the project's operationalisation that pose important and interesting challenges to comparative inquiry (*cf.* Ackers, 1999). First of all, it discusses the relevance of current debates (around contextualisation and culture-boundedness) for comparative research on migration. As a piece of evaluative research with a focus on EU law and policy, the study represents something rather different to more traditional cross-country comparisons. The focus on migration also raises serious challenges to traditional comparative approaches which often focus on one area of policy or social phenomenon in two or more locations. In migration research, it is not only the policies themselves that operate transnationally but also the recipients of policy. Many migrants move, over their life-course, not only once but on a number of occasions and often to disparate destinations. In addition, the children of EU migrants frequently live in 'international' families with relatives and affective ties across a number of countries. Context, as a source of values and reference points, thus becomes a highly complex matter.

The second challenge concerns the limited attention, within existing comparative research, to the situation of children. At national level, increasing interest in childhood and in working with children in research has precipitated a concern with issues of method and approach. Little attempt has been made to assess the viability and transferability of such methodological developments to comparative work. Through this discussion the chapter also introduces the reader to the research strategy adopted.

Context and Culture in Comparative Social Policy Analysis: Following the 'Primrose Path'?

International migration is, by definition, a transnational phenomenon demanding a cross-national approach. The domination of migration research by the discipline of geography has, however, tended to result in an over-emphasis upon econometric and quantitative methods (Ackers, 1998; Boyle, Halfacree and Robinson, 1998; Kelson and DeLaet, 1999). Singleton, a prominent EUROSTAT statistician on asylum and migration, refers to the 'positivist imperative' that continues to 'drive a thirst for statistical data in migration related research' (1999, p.156-7). Arguing for the exercise of caution in the interpretation of international migration statistics, she suggests that existing aggregate data present only a limited and partial view of a complex and dynamic set of social phenomena. Hantrais and Mangen (1999, p.91) make similar reference to the 'over-reliance on highly aggregated data' in comparative research.

Increasing interest in comparative work has coincided with an explosion in the availability of on-line data facilitated by the growth in, and widespread access to, computing facilities and the Internet. Levitas and Guy (1996, p.63) argue that the relative ease and limited cost of using these data, 'carries the danger of forgetting that the concepts used in any research derive from the questions and interests of its original intentions'. This point has particular resonance in the case of work on childhood and children's rights. The lack of attention to children in comparative policy analysis to some degree reflects the relatively low political priority attached to children's issues and the consequences in terms of data availability. Certainly, in the context of EU, tightly drawn boundaries of legal competency have lead to an emphasis on 'economic' over 'social' matters. The consequences of low political visibility can be seen, not only in the context of children's derived legal entitlement, but also in terms of the availability and quality of secondary data which generally reflects prevailing political priorities and the emphasis on the Single Market (Levitas and Guy, 1996). As Pringle (1998, p.134) suggests, '[p]ut simply, children are not workers and are themselves not a primary focus for European Union attention'. Ruxton (1996, p.16) develops this point to show the implications of this in terms of data availability:

> [T]here is no mention of children in the Treaties of the European Union; and Union statistics on children and childhood are often inadequate compared to data gathering on other issues.

To the extent that the availability of secondary data has largely driven comparative inquiry, it is not surprising that so little attention has been paid to children. The lack of suitable and reliable aggregate data on children and childhood has undoubtedly proved a deterrent to comparative research. The limited reliability of migration data should not, however, lead us to dismiss entirely the value of secondary analysis. In order to place both Community law and the qualitative work with children in the wider geographical context of intra-Community migration, the children and migration project has included cautious analysis of available data on the presence of children in migration stocks and flows, drawn from the European Labour Force Survey (see chapter six). These statistics provide a useful, if inadequate, framework within which to discuss both policy and qualitative findings.

However, concerns about the validity of large-scale statistical analyses in comparative research reflect more than the 'practical' problems of inaccuracies in the data. Recent work in the field of comparative social policy research has emphasised the importance of recognising the influence of context and, more specifically, the impact of socio-political, economic and cultural traditions on domestic social policy (*cf.* Hantrais and Mangen, 1999). This concern is, in part, a reaction to the inadequacy of previous comparative approaches that attempted to isolate and compare discrete dimensions of policy effectively extricating policy indicators from the wider social context. Consequently, research failed to acknowledge the inter-relationship between different aspects of policy in Member States – such as education and employment policy[1] – and the embeddedness of policy within a complex mesh of national variables. Policy outputs and in particular those represented in 'sanitised' aggregate statistics often proved misleading and partial. Castles and Mitchell (1992), for example, pointed to the lack of any simply linear relationship between welfare expenditure (the basis on which many comparative models are constructed) and redistributive impact. Mabbett and Bolderson (1999, p.40) refer to the 'very strong cash income orientation' of much comparative social policy analyses reflecting the reliance on available aggregate data. Hantrais (1999, p.92) traces the evolution of approaches to cross-national comparison from these, 'universalistic culture-free' approaches to 'culture-boundedness'. The latter approach she suggests places 'the theory and practice of contextualisation at the nexus of cross-national comparative studies'. Whilst rejecting on the one hand the notion that social reality can be context-free, neither is it so entirely context-bound that comparison has no potential. The 'case-study' approach to comparative method is perhaps a reaction to these concerns (Ackers, 1998). Mabbett and Bolderson (1999, p.55) outline the potential benefits and disadvantages of this method:

> In the context of comparative social policy, the characteristic feature of a case study approach is that the research examines the specific institutional, historical and political features of each country covered ... it allows the researcher to tell a country-specific story, and thereby escapes the problem of operationalising concepts in a uniform way across countries.

On the other hand, 'years of immersion are needed to write a good case study' (1999, p.36). The dissemination of case study research often takes the form of an edited collection with individual chapters devoted to a description of the countries concerned (such as in Alcock and Craig, 2001 for example). Whilst interesting and useful arguably such approaches are not genuinely comparative.

Hantrais (1999) goes on to advocate a 'compromise' position (the 'societal' approach) that locates social phenomenon in their socio-cultural, economic and political contexts. To that extent, context becomes an explanatory variable, 'an enabling tool' rather than a barrier to comparison.

---

[1] For discussion, see Ackers and Abbott, 1996. A call for research proposals by the European Commission (VP/2002/011) specifically acknowledges the relationship between social policy and economic objectives inviting submissions under the heading 'the costs of non-social policy'.

Further, Hantrais also suggests that the choice of contextual factors is determined by the nature of the research topic, the disciplinary mix of the project team and the resources available. Overall, she identifies a number of 'possible contexts' in cross-national comparative research including (amongst others) legal frameworks, political systems and cultural environments. On the basis of this approach, Hantrais (1996, p.2) had previously defined the essential features of cross-national and comparative research as being:

> ... when individuals or teams set out to examine particular issues or phenomena in two or more countries with the express intention of comparing their manifestations *in different socio-cultural settings* (institutions, customs, traditions, value systems, lifestyles, language, thought patterns), using the same research instruments either to carry out secondary analysis of national data or to conduct new empirical work. The aim may be to seek explanations for similarities and differences, to generalise from them or to gain a deeper understanding of social reality in different national contexts.

Clearly, context is highly important. The discussion in the following section considers the problems of operationalising the 'societal approach' and in particular, identifying and defining relevant 'contexts', in research concerned with population mobility in the EU.

Achieving Effective Contextualisation in Supra-National Policy Evaluation

Our research has demanded a sensitive and careful approach to the identification of context. If we take as an example one of the areas in which we were interested (the impact of migration on the educational rights and experiences of migrant children) we can immediately see the complexity of the challenge.

In the first instance, it is clear that the policy context operates at a number of levels encompassing the role of the EU and its engagement with provision in the Member States. As education policy falls into one of the areas of 'shared competence' permitting diversity in approach, it is also important to understand the relevant domestic situations which form part of the context within which migration decisions are made and children experience education.

Charting and evaluating available educational services in the countries in question is only part of the story, however. Just as formal legal rights are often not exercised and therefore do not translate into citizenship experience, the existence of an 'objectively' appropriate and accessible service may not imply use. The issue of context is thus further complicated if we are interested to understand the user interface: here the influence of cultural factors on decision-making processes and policy uptake or use becomes highly complicated when dealing with a population which has experienced multiple migrations, inter-marriage and often international schooling. In these circumstances a wide variety of cultural influences guide and shape family decision-making.

The purpose in this section is thus to consider the application of recent debates, within the field of comparative social policy, around contextualisation and culture-boundedness for research on children and intra-Community migration. In particular, it focuses on two dimensions of particular relevance to migration research. The first concerns the problems of identifying the relevant policy-context in situations where supra-national and domestic policy[ies] are inextricably linked. The second considers the importance of extending the scope of the 'societal approach' beyond the explanation of policy development and delivery to the citizen/user interface in order to advance our understanding of policy-impact and citizenship experience.

Traditionally, comparative social policy analysis has sought to compare discrete aspects of social policy or social phenomenon in two or more national contexts. In that sense, the nation state constitutes an important frame of reference. Hantrais (1999, p.98) suggests that nation states are often preferred, as a convenient frame of reference, 'since they possess clearly defined territorial borders, and their own characteristic administrative and legal structures'. Alcock (2001) refers to the increasing influence of global and international forces on national policy agendas including 'supra-national agencies' such as the World Bank, the International Monetary Fund and the EU. European integration poses new challenges to traditional cross-country comparisons particularly for those studies, such as ours, that explicitly focus on EU law and policy. It may be increasingly difficult to identify areas of policy untainted by supra-national policy, however, either directly or through the effects of policy externalities. Hantrais (1999) raises a number of considerations in this regard that include:

- the impact of enlargement and the changing social map of Europe;
- the impact of multi-level governance;
- the tendency of studies focused on the nation state to obscure internal (regional and local) diversity and;

- the development of pan-European NGOs as policy actors under the civil dialogue strategy;[2]

The following section examines the latter two points in more detail before raising some additional problems specific to migration research.

Context and Multi-level Governance: 'Nested Citizenship' in the EU

The children and migration study was essentially a piece of evaluation research designed to describe and critique the concept of 'Citizenship of the Union' and understand its impact on the lives of those people who exercise their free movement rights. Understanding the citizenship status of a migrant child within the EU demands consideration of the interaction of several layers of context. In the first instance, we need to chart the framework of legal rights at EU level (under the free movement provisions) and consider the extent to which these generate rights in the host state. The EU does not directly provide material welfare, however. It is responsible for the framing of social rights that must then be delivered through its Member States. Faist (2001, p.39 and p.46) uses the language of 'nesting' to describe this situation:

> European citizenship is nested in various sites ... [it is] a multi-tiered membership system consisting of a mixture of rights guaranteed by regional, state, inter-state and genuinely European institutions [although] the web of governance networks allows for enshrining a few new rights at the supra-national level these interconnect with and re-adapt social rights and institutions in existing welfare states.

This complex vesting of citizenship rights at various levels of governance raises serious challenges to effective contextualisation in comparative inquiry. Firstly, we need to be clear about our approach to policy in order to ensure that all key policy actors are embraced within the evaluation. Secondly, if we wish to understand the context within which EU policy is formulated and implemented then we need to understand something about the policy-making process at that level and the cultural and political influences responsible for the shaping of its laws and policies. Having described and evaluated EU policy at this level, attention should be paid to its interface with domestic policy. This raises concerns around the

---

[2] We have pointed to the role of NGOs such as EURONET, for example, in promoting a children's rights agenda in the EU.

enforcement and implementation of European law by Member States. There is little point in celebrating or critiquing newly minted laws or policies if their implementation fails or is uneven or inadequately communicated. When dealing with a situation of shared competence and the consequences of subsidiarity in the social field, we must consider the engagement of those rights and resources deriving from the EU with national law and policy. Finally, having charted the legal and resource framework the research must consider the citizen/user interface and, in the context of our work, the ways in which migration shapes the exercise of these formal rights.

The Policy Concept and the Role of the European Court of Justice (ECJ)

Hantrais' (1999) definition of 'possible contexts' in cross-national comparative research identifies the importance of legal contexts. We have referred elsewhere to the limitations of much traditional discipline-bound research that failed to take a broad and holistic approach to the concept of policy (Ackers, 1998). In particular, we made reference to the reluctance of many lawyers to consider the social context within which the law is implemented and exercised and the failure of those social policy analysts who do embrace the legislative framework to consider the role of the courts as policy actors. We will move on in a moment to consider the implementation of European law and policy by Member States. It is important, to also consider the implementation of free movement rights at European level. Although the Treaty sets out the broad commitments, policy frameworks and competencies, it is for secondary legislation to add 'flesh to the bones' and, ultimately, for the ECJ to translate these into rights through its interpretative role (*cf.* Ackers and Dwyer, 2002; Brown and Kennedy, 2000; de Búrca, 1998). Policy evaluation must thus extend beyond a simple description or enumeration of statutory rights to consider the impact of the ECJ on citizenship rights. de Búrca (1998, p. 231) urges a more holistic approach which takes account of the courts as policy actors:

> It seems fair to say that many non-lawyers working in the field of European integration have been unaware of or unwilling to accept the role that law can play in the policy-making process ... Ultimately, it cannot be denied that the Court of Justice is an institutional actor with a considerable degree of autonomy and normative influence, which plays a significant role in the Community's policy-making process.

In our endeavour to understand the European legal framework shaping the rights of migrant families and children our research has involved detailed analysis of Community legislation and its interpretation by the ECJ.

The Interface with Domestic Law and Policy: Implementation, Enforcement and Welfare Diversity

In addition to the challenges of evaluating the EU policy context, the 'nesting' of citizenship demands attention to the supra-national European/domestic policy interface. This raises a number of concerns of importance to our study including the implementation of European law and the effects of that implementation in the context of welfare diversity.

Whilst it is important to detail and critique legal developments at the EU level, it is also important to remember that many laws are not fully or effectively implemented either at national or regional level and that methods of implementation may vary. To that extent the European context may have a variable impact on the rights and experiences of individuals. The EU can influence Member States in a number of ways. Where its competency is undisputed (such as in the case of the right to free movement itself), it can legislate quite confidently and proactively creating rights that are immediately actionable in the Courts of Member States (usually through the implementation of secondary legislation in the form of regulations). The political sensitivity surrounding EU involvement in the social sphere has, however, often meant that more gentle and persuasive methods have been preferred. This raises important questions around enforceability, uniformity of implementation and territorial justice. If a child moves to a country such as Sweden, for example, that has effectively implemented the Council Directive 77/486[3] on the education of children of migrant workers, it will benefit from the right to extra language support both in Swedish and its mother tongue and also from the more progressive domestic policy on children's rights (see discussion in chapter nine and Pringle, 1998). If it moves to another country, such as the UK, where many education authorities do not appear to know about the Directive let alone implement it, then a migrant child has limited opportunity to benefit from Community law.

On top of the problems of unevenness in enforcement, it is also important to consider the impact of subsidiarity and the persistence of

---

[3] Of July 1977 on the education of the children of migrant workers, OJ 1977, L199/32. Discussed further in chapters eight and nine.

welfare diversity on the resource frameworks available to migrant families. To the extent that the free movement provisions generate genuine and actionable social rights it is important to remember that these are based firmly on the principle of non-discrimination (Article 12 EC).[4] European law, at least in terms of its ability to extend forms of social entitlement accorded to host nationals to Community migrants, does not explicitly promote social harmonisation. What this means in practice is that the child of a Community migrant worker has an equivalent social status to the child of a resident national. An evaluation of EU policy, in this research context, therefore demands an awareness of the interface of free movement rights with domestic social policy. Whereas the right to move freely derives from Community law, the implications of the migration decision (in terms of location in the host state) depends on the level of implementation at national level and on the social policy infrastructure of the receiving state. The effect of exercising European educational rights thus depends on the character of the education system in the respective locations. The right to receive education on an equal basis to national children may mean that a child in one country can enter state education at 3 years old whilst in another they have to wait until they are 7. Their right to learn a second European language in school will also depend on the curriculum of the host Member State (or region).

Understanding migration decision-making processes and post-migration experience thus demands evaluation of the package of rights and benefits available in the sending and receiving country (assuming that the persons concerned are aware of their rights). Attention to the sending country is important not only in terms of what they are leaving behind but also in the sense of what might accompany them, on the basis of national citizenship. In some circumstances a family may be able to transport various occupational benefits and continue to claim them in the host state. We found a number of German migrants, for example, living in Portugal who were financially dependent upon German child benefit payments and health insurance that they continued to claim. In addition to European rights, various bi-lateral agreements exist between Member States extending important additional benefits to the persons concerned. These may include very tangible rights to healthcare or more complex arrangements between two Member States designed to deal with family breakdown, child custody and abduction (see chapter seven). Indeed, Warnes (2002, p.149) suggests that rights based upon bi-lateral agreements may have more impact than European citizenship itself:

[4] Much more detail on the legal framework is provided in the substantive chapters.

> [G]iven the failure of social Europe to deliver inclusive citizenship, the best course is to continue the half-century-long process of elaborating bilateral agreement and administrative arrangements between the national social security agencies.

To add to these transportable rights, some Member States actively provide services specifically designed for their own nationals in the territory of another Member State. The best example of this, which is discussed in more detail in chapter eight, concerns the establishment of designated schools, staffed by nationals of the sending country, adhering to the national curricula of those countries and either partially or wholly funded by the sending Member State. In the UK and Portugal, for example, we visited a number of Spanish, Swedish and German schools organised for the benefit of expatriates and designed to facilitate continuity and progression of mobile children. These kinds of institutions represent another 'nesting' site in the complex resource framework shaping migration decision-making.

So far, we have considered the relationship between European law and domestic social policy and the extent to which free movement rights translate into claims against the domestic welfare state (and statutory education systems in particular). In our recent work we have emphasised the importance of taking a broad view of the mixed economy of welfare and the relationship between the different forms of social provision to a holistic understanding of migration and citizenship (Ackers and Dwyer, 2002). Alcock (2001) refers to the preference of many commentators to use the language of 'welfare mix' rather than 'welfare state' in order to encompass the contribution of the whole range of actors involved in social policy provision. Social rights and resources are not only vested at different governance levels within the 'public' sector but also across different welfare sectors. Some rights are not only more generous but also more transportable than others (such as contributory benefits or private welfare) whereas other rights are extinguished by migration (through various means-tested benefits and, in particular, carers' benefits). We have also emphasised the importance of embracing fiscal welfare (tax differentials) and occupational benefits such as contributory insurance schemes and the kinds of 'fringe benefits' or perks attached to some forms of employment. These additional dimensions need to be taken into account when defining the relevant contextual boundaries shaping migration decision-making and experiences. The current project adds considerable weight to these arguments when we consider the kinds of enhancements made available to highly skilled and professional Community migrants as part of some company re-location and mobility schemes. These typically include not only the provision of or subsidy towards housing costs but private healthcare, subsidised travel and assistance in the payment of international or boarding school fees.

Consequently, evaluating migration decision-making and the impact of moving on citizenship demands an understanding of the interface of EU law with the welfare diversity that persists at domestic level and the wider resource pools that comprise the decision-making context of migrant workers and their families.

The Tendency to Obscure Internal Diversity

Hantrais' (1996, 1999) reference to the limitations of adopting the nation-state as the frame of reference in cross-national research includes the tendency of such studies to obscure internal diversity and promulgate the impression of cultural and social homogeneity within nation states. The principle of subsidiarity not only shapes the distribution of responsibilities and powers between the EU and its Member States, but also determines spatial access to social goods *within* domestic jurisdictions resulting in problems of territorial injustice and uneven provision (Ackers and Abbott, 1996; Spicker, 1991). This is of particular significance in the case of services and benefits for families and children (including educational services) that are often partially financed and provided at a local level. Accordingly, access to material and social support for migrant children is, to a significant extent, influenced by regional location. In Athens, for example, services for children and migrant families are far better developed than in more remote areas of Greece. In the UK, service provision in policy areas in which local authorities retain a degree of autonomy (such as childcare or services for young people) results in considerable variations in service provision over space. Support services for migrant families both at the level of statutory provision but also in terms of community networks are much better developed in the larger, more cosmopolitan cities. London, for instance, hosts a large number of migrant organisations many of which provide services (including language tuition, for example) and social support for their members.

Our previous experience of this kind of research (Ackers, 1998) identified some key differences in policy implementation and resource frameworks within Member States. London, in common with other more cosmopolitan capital cities, had a more highly developed NGO sector representing the interest of migrant communities and providing social and educational activities. More peripheral and rural areas generally lacked the ability to support the kind of responsive statutory and voluntary institutions identified in large urban areas effectively restricting the choices available to migrant families and their children.

In order to deal with these complex spatial dynamics, the children and migration project allowed for an element of policy analysis (including key informant interviews) at each of these levels to effectively contextualise our interpretations of the qualitative interviews with parents and children. The influence of location on citizenship entitlement was taken into consideration, in this study, in designing the sample so as to cover a range of different localities and experiences. Working within our resource constraints, we therefore undertook to sample families in the capital cities of the partner countries *and* in the more peripheral and rural areas (in the UK this included locations in London, Devon, Cambridge, Yorkshire and Northern Ireland).

The importance of understanding the national and regional context within which migrant children were living resulted in the preparation of country reports for each Member State that summarised both the national legislative and policy context and evidenced examples of unevenness in provision.

Culture, Values and Citizenship: The 'User' Interface

The arguments for effective contextualisation in comparative research reflect to a large extent the limitations of approaches that attempted to extricate social institutions or a 'narrowly defined set of interventions' (Mabbett and Bolderson, 1999, p.37) from their social context. The driver in many respects was the commitment to developing evaluation strategies in comparative research capable of informing more effective and culturally-sensitive policy borrowing and exchange. Mabbett and Bolderson's (1999, p.54) definition of cross national research exemplifies this approach:

> Cross-national social policy-oriented studies describe, analyse and map different countries' welfare configurations, their specific policies, or their response to common issues. They are used to test or develop theories or hypotheses, to construct models, to conduct evaluations, to show more clearly the contours of one country's arrangements, to promote 'peripatetic learning' or the borrowing of policies or practices.

It is not possible to understand the function of healthcare institutions or labour markets and family-friendly policies without knowing something about the economic, cultural and political context within which they have developed and continue to operate. Welfare institutions and policies evolve over a period of history under the influence of many factors and, on that basis, it is far too simplistic to attempt to identify the parameters of any particular institution or policy, generate a template and transpose it in another context and then expect it to have a similar effect. In sum, context shapes the evolution and effect of social policy. In the same way, social policy shapes context. Hantrais (1999, p.97) gives the example of comparative research in the field of industrial relations which, 'has recognised the value of analysing nationally-specific institutional frameworks as generators of norms, practices and mutual expectations'. So, just as norms, practices and expectations have informed the development of social institutions or rights so the institutions themselves shape cultural practices and values.

Concerns to ensure that such 'policy borrowing' is both effective and culturally sensitive have emphasised the identification of key socio-cultural, economic and political variables, shaping the evolution of social policy infrastructures. While the importance of placing these infrastructures 'in context' is fundamental to our understanding of the dynamics of policy development, there is a danger that the lessons of contextualisation will be restricted to an understanding of policy inputs or 'formal policy' (for more discussion see Ackers, 1998; O'Connor, 1993; Schunk, 1996). The more limited attention given to the dynamics of change at the 'recipient end' in comparative research and to the interaction of context with human agency and values restricts the ability of researchers to predict the effectiveness of policy exchange and the impact of policies on citizenship experience. Comparativists have paid less attention to the influence of 'culture' and values on the response of users to these institutions and the social rights and resources that emanate from them. An interesting example of this concerns the right of Community migrant workers to be accompanied by ascendant relatives. Our research on a linked project on retirement migration considered the effect of this right of dependant elderly relatives to move with or 'move to join' the citizen-worker (Ackers and Dwyer, 2002). In practice, this right, although generous in itself, did little to obviate the pressures of 'caring at a distance' as many of the dependant persons did not wish to or were unable to exercise it. Although ostensibly a convenient policy response to the 'problem' of family dislocation, these measures were evidently not informed by the experiences of migrant families and failed to take account of the diversity of domestic provision in the care of dependant elderly people.

The importance of these structure-agency issues to outcome is well established in single-country studies and has informed numerous reviews of the mediation of policy by variables of ethnicity and culture within multicultural societies. To the extent that research and policy has begun to recognise the relationship between cultural pluralism and social institutions, the focus has been on diasporic communities and the challenges these present for the nation state and for service delivery and domestic social institutions. There is a tendency, however, to assume that populations are relatively static, that migrants 'settle', and that culture is less of an issue within the population of EU migrants. In contrast, Ruxton (1996, p.15) underlines the importance of developing comparative approaches capable of exploring, for example, children's responses to laws and services. He refers to the lack of research on:

> ... legal and policy frameworks, or on the effects of these on children. Neither is there much transnational research comparing outcomes of particular types of service. And children's perceptions of the variety of the circumstances they face have as yet been almost completely ignored.

Context and Culture in Migration Research

So far we have discussed the importance of defining the appropriate parameters of context and trying to locate our understanding of social processes and policy in that context. In the main comparative social policy involves the research (or researchers themselves) moving across national boundaries with the social phenomenon and institutions under study, although under the influence of supra-national policy, remaining firmly within those contextual (typically nation-state) boundaries.

The impact of context (and culture-boundedness) on the comparative researcher, as the mobile worker, has been acknowledged to some degree. Hantrais, for example, refers to the potential influence of the 'researcher's own cultural value system and thought pattern' (1996, p.17) and the risk that researchers might, 'seek to analyse practices in different cultural settings through their own (inappropriate) conceptual lens' (Hantrais, 1999, p103).

When migration law and policy becomes the focus of comparative enquiry it is not only the researchers who are mobile, however; the subject matter and policy-recipients or users also have transnational experiences. Neither the context nor the recipients are spatially fixed and contained within defined boundaries. On the one hand, the rights and resources (or 'basket of goods') under consideration only exist in the context of mobility (to that extent that mobility is the 'trigger' to European citizenship entitlement). On the other, the recipients of the rights as users or citizens are, by definition mobile. How, in this situation, can we begin to define the parameters of context? The resource framework and number of potential 'scenarios' is vast as are the potential sources of cultural influence on the decision-making processes and experiences of migrant families and children.

Multiple Movers and Dispersal

Migration researchers have, in the past, tended to characterise migration decision-making in terms of a limited and chronologically sequenced number of discrete moves. So, the migrant worker might be expected to move in the first instance for work. 'He' may then be joined by his partner and or children and eventually they may return ' home' on retirement (we have referred to this in our previous work as the male breadwinning model). In reality migration within the EU rarely takes this form and is rather characterised by repeated moves over the life-course often to a number of destinations (for more discussion see Ackers, 1998; 2001; Ackers and Dwyer, 2002). The European Commission report (CEC, 2001) referred to the normalisation of a 'peripatetic lifestyle' as mobility is increasingly expected of European employees. Many people move in the first instance as single people, often but not exclusively for work or educational purposes and form partnerships and families in the post-migration context (Ackers, 1998). Members of these people's families (siblings, children and parents) often also move, perhaps to other locations. One consequence of this 'flux' is inter-marriage or international partnerships. Many of the children we interviewed in the course of this research lived in international families with parents originating from different Member States (*cf.* chapter five). Migration decision-making processes often resulted in temporary or long-term separation of family members (including separation from parents, grandparents and siblings) perhaps as a result of educational decisions or family breakdown and re-constitution.

EU migrant children typically have family in a number of locations across Europe and beyond and have experienced living in, visiting, making friends and going to school in at least one country. As a consequence, cultural reference points and experiences are highly diffuse.

Our previous work has shown how cultural and moral values shape the ways in which migrant women (Ackers, 1998; 2001) and retired migrants (Ackers and Dwyer, 2002) responded to and exercised rights. The provision of high quality institutionally-provided childcare in a cultural context in which use of such services is encouraged (such as Sweden or France, for example) did not necessarily translate into a high rate of usage on the part of migrant women. Although some clearly embraced the opportunities presented, others did not do so and interpreted such provision as either work-forcing (a denial of opportunity) or bad mothering. The context within which they were relating to the resource framework reflected their own experiences of living in and having contacts with another country and the cultural values deriving from that (amongst other things).

We have already referred to the problems of territorial justice and unevenness in terms of access to statutory and voluntary sector institutions and the more beneficial resource frameworks available to migrants living in London, Lisbon or Athens. When talking to migrant families, on the other hand, we found many whose location decisions were influenced by the desire to be away from these kinds of 'resources'. This may reflect a desire to integrate more effectively with host nationals and eschew expatriate organisations and networks or a love of isolation itself or 'alternative lifestyles' (as was evident amongst the 'eco-migrants' of the Alentejo region and Ireland).

Capturing the influence of culture on migrant children is more complex still. It is not only their migration history and the memories and values that are shape values and experiences but the on-going transnational contact they continue to have with a range of family members, friends and institutions. Accounting effectively for the impact of context and culture-boundedness on children's experiences of moving to and living in another country and exercising citizenship thus demands consideration of the relative strength or influence of numerous 'reference points'. These reference points are dispersed across geographical space and mediated by factors such as age, gender, kinship relationship, location and length of residence (*cf.* chapter ten). They are also constantly in flux. To that extent, their experiences are refracted through a complex multi-dimensional prism. Understanding this context demands an approach that is both capable of encompassing this vast diversity of experience while achieving an adequate level of comparability. Penn (1998, p.14) sums it up nicely:

> Comparative research cannot be a straightforward matching of experiences, just as translation from one language to another is not a straightforward exchange of words ... It becomes important to use methodologies of investigation which do not obscure diversities of experience, but seek instead to highlight them.

In practice, the research, reported in chapter four, has identified complex patterns of migration and a close relationship between mobility and life-course, with many people making multiple moves, often precipitated by changing family circumstances. An evaluation of the citizenship status and experience of this population 'in flux', characterised by a high degree of inter-marriage and on-going mobility, raises difficult questions around the meaning and appropriate basis of culture-boundedness. Country of residence remains an important variable in predicting migrant children's attitudes towards European integration. Indeed, analysis of the interview findings on children's identity, reported in chapter nine, suggests that the children of EU workers in Sweden and the United Kingdom (by definition not Swedish or British children) articulate the kind of Euro-sceptic attitudes commonly associated with nationals in the host state. Host country is, however, only one dimension of context. The country of emigration, the national background of their parents and grandparents, migration experiences and length of residence are all important variables in an understanding of attitudes and experiences.

The response of children and parents to domestic education policy also needs to be understood in the context, not only of host country policy frameworks and cultural values, but also of their pre-migration experiences. This may reflect attitudes towards discipline, the value of different pedagogic approaches, school hours, the relative merits of private or comprehensive education or of international education and denominational schooling (see chapters eight and nine). As a result, the research process takes on a 'chromatographic' character, effectively crystallising out the various dimensions of context and sources of values that shape migration and family decisions and citizenship experience. Different national contexts will prove important variables both in terms of 'sending' and 'receiving' states (bearing in mind also that many families were returnees) and so too will the relevant supra-national structures, which not only react to cultural traditions in Member States but also generate and transmit values. These examples illustrate the problems of adhering to principles of culture-boundedness, as a key aspect of contextualisation, in research concerned with children and migration.

Whilst we fully endorse the emphasis on context and the influence of culture not only on the evolution of social institutions but on the perceptions and attitudes of users, we have to conclude that, in a migration context, achieving full and effective contextualisation represents a significant operational challenge. The following section moves on to identify some other methodological challenges for the comparativist interested in researching childhood.

Engaging Children in Comparative Research

We have already referred to the lack of interest in comparative work on children and childhood and the extent to which this can be explained by the lack of available secondary data. While issues of data availability and political priority (which directly influence research funding opportunities) may partially explain comparativists' relative disinterest in children, there may be other, epistemology-driven, explanations for the failure of national research agendas to adopt a comparative approach.

In the context of a project concerned with 'cultures of care', Chamberlayne and King (1996, p.103) refer to the reorientation of social policy within the EU to promote the 'strengthening of informal social infrastructures'. This policy shift, they contend, requires both a great expansion of research and a change in approach in order to 'restore the study of human agency to social policy' in cross-national work:

> Understanding 'the subject' and relations between the personal and the social in welfare requires a turn to qualitative methods, and their development for comparative purposes (1996, p.96).

Recent years have witnessed a mushrooming of specialist centres, based in UK universities, drawing together and catalysing research interest in childhood and child-focused work.[5] The growth in this research area has spawned an interest, not only in aspects of policy evaluation and outcomes (or what has become known as 'child-proofing' policies) but also on questions of epistemology and technique. The UN Convention on the Rights of the Child (UNCRC), with its emphasis, in Article 12, on the 'best interests principle' and the 'views of the child' has provided an important impetus both in substantive policy areas (such as child law, for example) and in the context of research practice. Brannen and O'Brien (1996, p.1) allude to the relationship between the growing political interest in children's rights and questions of method and approach:

> In the emergent sociology of childhood, children are being conceptually liberated from passive dependency on adults and elevated to the status of social actor. In common with childhood researchers, we have become conscious of the invisibility of children's perspectives and voices and the fact that children's worlds have typically become known through adult accounts.

---

[5] This also reflects the commitment of funding bodies such as the Nuffield Foundation to supporting this type of research.

The notion of 'listening to children' and of actively encouraging the participation of children in research processes has led to a critique of quantitative and other approaches which imply, 'an over-reliance on indirect measures of children's well-being and/or adult reports of their adjustment' (Neale and Smart, 1998, p.10). Concerns about the validity and ethics of using 'proxy' measures (such as parents' or teachers' accounts, for example) and the effect of power differentials on the research process (and the relationship between researchers and child respondents) have encouraged the development of new sources of 'evidence' and a shift in favour of more intensive, qualitative, approaches. A report by Save the Children UK (1995, p.37) advocates the development of co-researching, or working alongside children in research, 'in order to ensure the outcomes are relevant'. This reflects a commitment to the active participation of children in research processes as a means of generating more sensitive and effective evaluation. Ruxton (1996) suggests that the failure to consider children's perceptions in transnational research may reflect the difficulty and expense implied in attempting to operationalise such approaches at comparative level. There may be wider epistemological issues at stake here also. Hantrais (1999, p.94) refers to the tendency of 'culturalist approaches' to prefer the kind of in-depth ethnographic work which:

> ... placed such great emphasis on social contexts and their specificity, distinctiveness or uniqueness [so] that meaningful comparisons and generalisations were made very difficult.

No doubt concerns over the viability and appropriateness of developing qualitative, child-centred, methods in a cross-national context (with serious concerns about language and ethnocentrism compounded by the 'problem' of diversity in research traditions) has proved a further deterrent to comparative inquiry.

The following section discusses recent debates around issues of method and research approaches when working with children and young people. As such it raises questions about rights and ethics that are as important to an evaluation of substantive law and policy as they are to research policy.

Working with Children

Oakley (1993) suggests that traditionally research has tended to focus upon children as 'objects' rather than 'subjects'. Concerns around the objectification of children are central to any debate about research with children and young people. Mayall (1999, p.10) argues that traditional approaches to research with children were dominated by 'certain psychological theories' about children and child development, at the center of which lies an:

> ... adult proposition that [children] lack essential characteristics of adulthood ... [and] that adults may successfully steer them through dangerous waters towards adulthood.

This research tradition reflects upon, and is informed by the 'caretaker thesis' a process whereby adults act on behalf of, albeit in the 'best interests' of children. In explaining the thesis within the context of decision-making, Archard (1993, p.53) suggests that the proposition rests upon the fact that what a child decides to do has the potential for affecting not only the immediate future, but also its future adult self. Thus decisions and their implications are too important for children and, correspondingly, need to be taken outside of their control. As such, the adult acting in the capacity as a caretaker is left having to, 'choose what the child would choose if competent to make choices, and choose with regard to the interests of the adult that the child will become' (Archard, 1993, p.53).

Archard argues that a fundamental tenet of the caretaker thesis rests upon the notion that children and young people are immature or, as Brown and de Loache (1978) suggest, 'universal novices'. This notion of children and young people has impacted directly upon the ethical considerations involved in undertaking research with children.

Within such definitions, children remain subordinate to adults, with little say in how they live their lives or in decision-making structures both within the family and wider community. Mayall (1999, p.11) outlines the implications of this approach to research practice and suggests that:

> ... understandings of what children are and of what knowledge about them is needed are assumed ... and these understandings have been allied to certain methods to produce a strong research tradition.

Put simply, research within most academic disciplines does 'not have a culture of listening to children' (Lansdown, 1994, p.38). As a consequence children, reflecting upon their status within wider society, have rarely been seen in the research equation other than as objects that require attention and control, where they may be either the cause of social problems, or perceived as passive victims of policy.

In recent years new approaches, influenced in part by feminist research methods, have developed a concern to give a voice to children (see, for example Edwards and Alldred, 1999; James and Prout, 1990). Accordingly, the emergence of research with children as 'actors' and 'subjects' has coincided with the emergence of a new sociology of childhood and children. As a result, the use of proxies to relay what children want, think and like has been increasingly discredited as researchers have become aware that 'adult' accounts are 'not necessarily coterminous with the values of the home or the school' (Hood et al, 1996, p.128).

At the same time, supranational and national instruments have increasingly recognised children's rights to consultation, access to information, and freedom of speech and opinion.[6] There has been a growing recognition within social science research that children's opinions can and should be elicited on issues that affect them (Morrow and Richards, 1996). As a consequence, children have become legitimate research *subjects*.

At national level, then, impetus has developed towards more inclusive and democratic approaches to work with children based on the principle that 'in the end the justification for the research…is to make children heard' (Hood *et al*, 1996 p.119).

Arguably, there is more to research than simply giving a voice to respondents, however. The theoretical ideas shaping the research in the first instance and the legal and policy analysis work involved are of importance as was the work with parents. Putting children and childhood on the agenda and promoting a mentality of child-audit throughout EU and national policy-making is in itself a valuable goal. Indeed, in some situations research that falls short of engaging directly with children is also extremely important (such as some of the work we are doing on the legal framework in relation to cross-border family breakdown, for example). On the other hand, it is important that we exercise a little modesty and honesty when claiming to give voice to children. Criticising the tendency 'even of naturalism' to present research as orderly, coherent and logically organised (or 'hygienic') concealing the 'messiness' of empirical work Stanley and Wise (1993, p.166) refer to the 'dishonesty' of much feminist interactive methodology which claims to have broken down research hierarchies and to be undertaking research, not on but 'with' women. Rejecting what they call the 'fictitious sympathy' approach as similar, in many respects, to positivism in its failure to acknowledge the importance of the 'situated nature of the researcher', Stanley and Wise (1993, p.166) suggest that:

---

[6] These issues are picked up again in the context of migration decision-making in chapter five.

> The best alternative is that researchers should present analytic accounts of how and why we think we know what we do about research situations and people in them. The only way we can avoid overriding other people's understandings as 'deficient' in some way is not to attempt to present these within research. Instead we should be much more concerned with presenting *ourselves* and *our* understandings of what is going on.

Working at comparative level in cross-national teams raises particular challenges in this respect making it more difficult to represent the voices of children directly. According to Hantrais and Mangen (1996, p.10), 'cross-national research by its very nature demands greater compromises in methods'. The challenges of delegation involved in team-working coupled with the demands of transcription and translation mean that, by the time the findings are disseminated, children's voices have passed through a series of human 'filters'. Hopefully this does not mean that, in the process, the main perspectives and views of children are lost.

In seeking to give a voice to children, we are confronted by a fundamental need to ensure that research methodology is informed by an appropriate and relevant ethical base.

Ethical Issues in Research with Children

Edwards and Alldred (1999) note that the debate concerning ethics in research with children has tended to be dominated by those involved in medical research. Here researchers have focused upon the differing *risks* that children may be exposed to as a result of their continuing involvement in clinical research. Consequently, a medical perspective has dominated many of the ethical debates concerning research with children. As such, it can be difficult to identify or establish a debate that considers ethics in research with children from a socio-legal perspective. This view is supported by Morrow and Richards (1996) who cite the absence of any specific mention of children in general guidelines on research ethics from academic disciplinary organisations such as the British Sociological Association (BSA). As a consequence, it has only been in more recent years that guidelines concerning ethical social science research practice with children has evolved, with Alderson (1995) establishing perhaps the clearest and most commonly adhered to set of guidelines for the researcher. Ethics, Alderson proposes, encompass matters including the designation of research objectives; the costs and benefits of the research for children; issues of privacy and confidentiality; selection, inclusion and exclusion;

funding; information for children and their parents and carers; and, finally, matters of consent and concerns around the impact of research on children.

The involvement of an adult in consenting to a child participating in research, as noted above, is explained through the caretaker thesis that refers to children's perceived competence in making decisions. Alderson suggests that this is perhaps a 'smoke screen' as competence is not a concrete term or a variable that can be independently measured or assessed. Instead, rejecting Piagetian notions of cognitive development, Alderson (1995, p.173) argues that competence is a variable that:

> ... develops unevenly, depending on children's ability, experiences, confidence, and relationship with their parents who reward or punish growing independence from babyhood.

Alderson goes on to suggest that competence is subjective and 'often seems to be as much in the eye of the beholder as in the ability of the child' (p.175). Morrow and Richards (1996, p.95) agree with such sentiments, suggesting that it is futile to rely upon judicial definitions of competence such as those focusing upon chronological age:

> [C]hildren's competence to consent to participate in research depends upon the context and partly on precisely what they are consenting to undertake.

This is perhaps only part of an explanation concerning the position of children within decision-making processes. Tymchuk (1992) contends that the issue of parental consent relates not so much to children's abilities, but rather to notions of parents' rights and the ability of parents to have a say in what happens to their children. Edwards and Alldred (1999) expand upon such arguments and propose that the debate concerning consent demonstrates and reflects issues of power, silence, and respect, which in recent years have been the impetus behind the desire to undertake research with and for children. Such a situation however leaves researchers in a quandary. Do they go along with the status quo and ask permission of parents, or do they address issues of power and disrespect directly and ask permission of the child themselves and, in so doing, risk allegations of unethical practice? Morrow and Richards (1996) suggest that in practice a researcher acting ethically must have regard for the wider interests of children and respect the need for informed consent. Thus, researchers should consult with parents or others acting as guardians, but they note that it should not end here. Once permission has been sought from a parent, Morrow and Richards advise that the *assent* of the child or young person to be involved in the research also needs to be sought (Assent is taken as meaning affirmation, based on an understanding by the young person of the research purpose and, the child's role and expectations in the research process (Mitchell, 1984)). Moreover, such consultation needs to be undertaken in language that children and young people can understand (Porter, 1985). Edwards and Alldred (1999) extend this and state that if researchers are concerned with empowering children, then they need to recognise that children and young people have the right of 'informed dissent' which ensures that children are able to refuse to participate in research. This must be irrespective of an adult's consent for the child to participate in the research. Children's sense of power in research needs to be real to them and something that they can exercise. Therefore, a child's consent to participate should be constantly checked throughout any research exercise in order to allow the young person to decide whether or not they want to continue. In practice this should be taken as meaning the decision to opt for continuation as opposed to a decision to finish or cease involvement.

The issue of informed consent directly relates to concerns for the protection of young respondents' interests. The protection of young people's interests, within the context of research, relates to a number of themes, the principle one being protection from the risk of harm, both during and as a consequence of the research process. This reflects upon the emphasis placed upon ethics by medical practitioners where issues of risk in research can have fatal consequences. Within social science research, risk has implications on the nature of the research methodology, which is discussed below, but it also impacts upon the respondent's right to privacy and to confidentiality. By implication this leads to questions about what should researchers do when young people disclose information that suggests a young person has been or remains vulnerable to harm, and how can this be balanced with issues concerning confidentiality? Morrow and Richards (1996) argue that irrespective of their role within research, researchers as adults, have a moral obligation to protect children, even if the implication is that it means losing access to material or damaging a relationship of trust by disclosing information to appropriate authorities. In explaining this Morrow and Richards refer to Grodin and Glantz (1994, p.97) who note that research with children:

> ... presents a powerful tension between two sometimes conflicting social goals: protecting individual children from harm and exploitation, while at the same time increasing our body of knowledge about children.

At all times the protection of children from harm must remain paramount. In walking this tightrope researchers are responsible for designing appropriate methods that involve children and young people in research to discover their views, opinions and experiences, in ways that respond to, and have regard for, the ethical dilemmas that can occur.

The children and migration project was designed and implemented with these considerations in mind and is presented here, not as a template, but as a means of beginning to identify and discuss approaches to policy evaluation, at comparative level, which are child-centred and relevant to an understanding of migration. It is worth repeating Stanley and Wise's (1993) concerns, at this juncture, about the importance of contextualising research findings within an open and honest discussion of the 'messiness' of research processes, identifying compromises and 'failures' in order to produce, as far as it is possible, 'unalienated knowledge' and resist the further mystification of research. The dangers of a chapter of this nature lie precisely in the risk of mystification and of conflating wider epistemological concerns with questions of technique, implying that there is something particularly distinctive and specialist about comparative or child-centred methods. Some researchers have questioned the inference that childhood research 'presupposes a special knowledge about children and competence in some particular child-centred techniques...[with] the assumption that some techniques are better suited to studying children than others' (Solberg, 1996 p.58). It is not so much technique that is at issue here but rather broader concerns about the production and interpretation of knowledge. Hantrais and Mangen (1996, p.12) make a very similar point in the context of comparative inquiry when they suggest that, 'there is nothing particularly distinctive about the methodology of cross-national research'.[7]

What distinguishes the approach adopted in cross-national research to that of much national work with children is the nature and demands of team-working. The next section discusses some of the specific challenges of working in cross-national teams and describes the approach adopted in the children and migration study.

Promoting Contextualisation through Research Collaboration

The importance of 'situating' research, and in particular, recognising the influence researchers have, as human agents, on the generation and interpretation of knowledge is common to all research. These broader considerations affect all forms of social research, irrespective of substantive or spatial scope. Recognition of researchers' cultural backgrounds as key

---

[7] Mabbett and Bolderson (1999, p.34) similarly argue that 'there is no distinct social science cross-national method'.

components of contextualisation is, however, of particular significance to comparative inquiry. The requirement of partners in EU-funded projects has encouraged a move away from 'safari' approaches (Hantrais and Mangen, 1996, p.4) in favour of more collaborative working. The level and quality of research collaboration, at the different phases in the life of comparative projects, nevertheless varies considerably. Arguably pressures to develop very large research teams may actually militate against effective collaboration as such teams become unwieldy, imply hierarchy and administrative over-load. The sheer costs of team meetings in these projects typically results in one or more partners assuming responsibility for initial project definition (and submission), research design, analysis and report-writing whilst the majority of partners perform a 'data gathering' function. To that extent there is very little scope for contextualisation. Effective contextualisation, in terms of recognition of the influence of culture throughout the research process, demands more genuine and participatory involvement of partners from project design and identification of issues and approaches (perhaps the most crucial stage) through implementation and interpretation of findings. The extent to which this is achievable depends on the financial resources available and the commitments of partners.

The children and migration project involved on-going collaboration between the partners and participants in the UK and abroad. This commenced at the project design and proposal phase and was facilitated via team meetings (which alternate between Member States) and visits during the course of the research. The alternation of meeting locations between partner countries, together with the visits, underline the importance of spending time in partner countries, in order to build up insight and experience of the research contexts. In this respect also, the issue of context is quite different to other forms of research, as concerns to 'match' researchers with interviewees (in terms of national background) becomes problematic. By definition the respondents are not nationals. The importance of partners derives from their awareness of domestic policy frameworks, of the values that underpin these and of the migration histories and the spatial location of different groups.

The meetings involved the presentation of papers building on partners' specific expertise. In a multi-disciplinary team of this nature, for example, the British group provided material on Community law, the Greek partner on inter-cultural social work and the Portuguese team on comparative work with children. The meetings were used to 'thrash out' issues of method and approach. This often proved difficult given the diversity of disciplinary and cultural backgrounds but was stimulating and effective in achieving 'compromises'.

In the context of working collaboratively with a team of partners from a range of cultural and disciplinary backgrounds, however, compromise does not necessarily imply sloppiness or a lack of rigour but rather the benefits of negotiation and shared experience that researchers are able to avoid in single country studies. Materials and transcripts of interviews and reports were circulated on an on-going basis and the project director distributed regular 'project up-dates' by e-mail summarising decisions and debates with individual partners. Partners produced both interim and final reports on aspects of sampling, domestic policy and national migration traditions in order to promote the effective contextualisation of the interview material.

Constraints on project finance and partners' time made it difficult to involve all participants in data analysis. Where possible, partners were invited to come to England to receive training in the use of the qualitative software package, NUD*IST, and to collaborate in this part of the project. Where this was not possible partners were invited to identify areas of interest to them and contribute sections to the final report (and publications based on the research). They were provided with partially analysed data (or on other aspects of the research not dependent upon the interview findings). Drafts of papers were circulated to partners for comments prior to their inclusion in any reports. In practice much of the final report (and the current publication) was drafted in England by the co-ordinating team. Effective collaboration in final report writing is both time-consuming and difficult, for partners in particular, given the fact that they are working in a second language. Moreover, it is rarely possible to achieve a level of funding which allows for salary recovery for this phase of the work.

Conclusion

This chapter has discussed the relevance and applicability of concepts of context and culture-boundedness and the challenges faced by researchers embarking on cross-national studies of childhood. The discussion around contextualisation emphasises the importance of context, not only to our understanding of policy evolution but also to outcome (and the interface of structures with users). As such, research involving 'mobile' citizens presents particular problems concerning the choice of relevant contexts. A particular concern of the project has been the development of an approach capable of 'listening to children'. Without doubt the complexities of language (involving not only transcription but also translation) and team-working introduce a wider range of 'filters' than smaller, single person, single country projects. In that sense we are hearing, not children's voices as such, but rather their interpretation and re-interpretation in the course of the research process. This represents a good example of 'compromise in method' involving the sacrifice of 'quality' to some extent. The benefits of the quantity and diversity of this sample, however, and our ability to address a wider range of experiences arguably outweigh the disadvantages. Moreover our ability to evaluate, from user's perspectives, aspects of supra national policy is clearly a distinctive feature of this approach. The current project has attempted to develop an approach capable of 'understanding the subject and the relations between the personal and the social' (Chamberlayne and King, 1996, p.96) in the context of comparative research on children and migration.

3 Family, Work and Mobility in the European Union

Introduction

Academic studies of international migration have been slow to explore the relationship between family and mobility and rarely, if ever, consider the involvement of children in migration processes or the impact of migration on children. This is largely explained by the dominance of economically deterministic, human capital approaches which typically subsume women and children within families as the passive appendages of male breadwinning husbands and fathers.[1] Where families are considered within the body of migration literature, they tend to be analysed under the category of 'family re-union' or through an examination of remittances perhaps reflecting the prioritisation, historically, with mass flows of migrants, from economically deprived to economically prosperous countries or regions. Baldassar and Baldock (2000, p.62) for their part describe the relationship between family and migration within the context of their sample of early Italian migrants in Perth who were 'performing their duty of care to their kin through migration'. Migration at that time (1920's) was the only method of maintaining the extended family in Italy. Orsi (1985, p.18), in his analysis of Italian migration to America, notes that:

> the decision to migrate was a family decision, taken as part of a broader strategy for survival ... The goal of emigration was usually to strengthen and preserve the family, and the decision to emigrate was taken on its behalf.

One of Baldassar and Baldock's respondents explained how 'the migrants gave oxygen to the family' (2000, p.68). This phenomenon was also noted in recent work on retirement migration which included a sample of returning Southern European workers many of whom had moved in the first instance to find work and provide financial support to their families

---

[1] For more discussion see Ackers (1998) and Boyle et al (1998). There is a developing legal literature on children and migration which focuses, in the main, on the rights of refugee children and issues surrounding international abduction and adoption policies (Rosenblatt & Lewis, 1997, and Doek et al, 1998) These are not empirical studies.

back home through remittances (Ackers and Dwyer, 2002). Phizacklea's (2000) and Anderson's (2001) research on the transnational household strategies of migrant domestic workers, similarly identify the strong relationship between family and migration. In particular, their research highlights two key factors – the importance of remittances in supporting the extended family and their children's education – in the migration decision-making of Filipino domestic workers.[2]

We talked, in chapter two, about the importance of contextualisation in comparative research. Understanding the migration processes taking place within the EU at the present time forms a key dimension of context shaping the experiences of migrant children in our sample. For the majority of families the factors shaping family migration decision-making can be distinguished from the work outlined above. Baldassar and Baldock's (2000) research encompassed a contrasting sample of mobile academics who had very different motivations for migration. For the majority of these respondents the move to Australia was:

> clearly part of an individual career move, not the outcome of a tradition of migration based on family and community strategies of survival. They were not performing a duty of care to their kin through migration (2000, p.73).

It is perhaps this latter picture of contemporary migration flows of more highly skilled 'individuals' that best fits with our sample of EU migrants. Indeed, our research–the current project and in our previous work with migrant women and scientists[3] – would support this characterisation in general terms with evidence of a highly mobile population of young single persons.[4] On the other hand, as we have indicated in our previous work, migration is not a one-off event; for the majority, it is an on-going process closely engaged with the life-course. During this process many people form partnerships, have children and reconsider location in response to changes in family circumstances. Boyle et al's (1998) review of recent research on family and migration also identifies the importance of life-course and the

---

[2] This formed the topic of a recently completed ESRC-funded project. The research itself involved interviews with Filipino women working in the UK. Although it included questions about the impact of having children on decision-making processes, it did not involve work directly with children. Some of the findings are reported in Phizacklea (2000) and Anderson (2001).

[3] The findings are reported in Ackers 1998 and Ackers 2001 respectively. Where reference is made to this work, please consult these sources.

[4] This was by no means always the case. Some of the people interviewed in our sample, and particularly the older returnees to Southern Europe had moved initially under pressure to find work. Their experiences will be considered later in this chapter.

impact of factors such as partnering, parenting and children's schooling on migration behaviour. With reference to inter-regional as opposed to international migration, they draw attention to the development of 'age-migration schedules' that identify a 'striking similarity' in patterns with:

> relatively high rates of mobility shortly after birth, a trough of mobility between ages 3 and 13 followed by a steadily rising trend towards a peak between 17 and 30. Thereafter mobility falls steadily with age (1998, p.111).

This third chapter focuses on the relationship between work, family and migration in the decision-making processes of our sample. It opens with a presentation of some of the available statistics on intra-Community mobility that provide a framework within which to locate the migration trajectories of their children. Migration decision-making is rarely based upon one isolated factor. In practice, interviews with migrants reveal a whole cluster of factors and rationale shaping migration decisions, some of which might take precedence at a particular point in the life-course. Employment features strongly in the migration decision-making process of this sample at least in terms of supporting the initial out-migration and we discuss in some detail the impact of career on mobility. The importance of career trajectories and progression at an early stage of the life-course often and increasingly coincides with partnering and the commencement of family formation.[5] This is reflected in the interviews with some parents who identified the tensions of dual career situations as factors shaping family migration decisions.

Although we use the notion of 'family' migration decision-making, we would not intend to gloss over the existence of competing and often conflictual interests and the bargaining processes that take place within families. Indeed, the involvement of children in these processes forms the focus of discussion in chapter five. The impact of partnering and parenting on mobility is clearly more pronounced for women who are far more likely to be the 'joiners' or 'tied movers' and this dimension is discussed below.[6]

We have already emphasised the importance of understanding migration as a process and migration decision-making as constantly under evaluation and review. Our sample included a proportion of returning

---

[5] Although there is evidence of delays in family formation, particularly amongst professional women, the lengthy period of qualification in many careers often means that permanent contracts and stable positions are established much later on. In science careers, for example, people were often in their late thirties before they secured a permanent position (Ackers, 2001).

[6] The gender dynamics of parental decisions are discussed in Ackers, 1998.

families and, for many of these, subsequent return moves were motivated by the emergence of factors related to the life-course. Figuring high amongst these was the issue of children's needs and children's educational progression. To that extent, it is not only the life-course and career progression of the parents that demands attention but the relationship between that and the increasingly influential effect of children's life-courses and, in particular, their educational trajectories (linked to their future career paths).

Another factor of increasing importance is the impact of post-migration family breakdown and divorce. We have noted the prevalence of single people (many of whom are women) amongst intra-Community migration flows (Ackers, 1998) and the tendency of family formation to take place post-migration and often involve unions with host nationals.[7] Within this specific context, divorce and separation often triggers a return move, usually instigated by the mother accompanied by the children. This represents another dimension to the relationship between family and mobility in an EU-context. Its impact on migration decision-making is considered in this chapter and its consequences in terms of legal rights and citizenship experience are discussed more fully in chapter seven. Many of the mothers who return home following divorce do so in order to access informal care networks back home. Moreover, the emergence of care needs within the wider family (particularly amongst ageing parents) impacts on return moves. Finally, the respondents (mainly but not exclusively the adults) talked extensively about issues connected with integration (with family and society) and homesickness as factors which play an increasing role in migration decision-making at later stages of the life course, perhaps when economic needs have been satisfied and careers firmly established. Many women reported missing home around the time of childbirth and some children also referred to the desire to return home.

The following section looks at the profile of the sample of interviews in the present study in terms of their length of residence in the host state and also the number of moves they reported having made. The discussion then moves on to examine the migration decision-making processes of the sample, the factors triggering moves and also the involvement of the children themselves in family decision-making.

---

[7] Some 53 per cent of the sample of children interviewed lived in 'international families'. See chapters four and six for further discussion.

'Peripatetic Lives': Mobility amongst the Interview Sample

Table 3.1 below indicates the degree of mobility experienced by the children in our study. About a quarter of children had moved only once and a further 35 per cent were born in the host state following the migration of one or both of their parents. The remaining children (about 42 per cent) had made a series of moves at international level in some cases simply returning 'home' after a single move or, in others, making successive moves. The prevalence and impact of repeated moves, with many children moving up to six or more times, is evident in the cases reported below:

Table 3.1 Mobility amongst the children in the study

Migration History	% of Respondents
Born in the Host State	35%
Single International Move	23%
Multiple International Moves	23%
Returnees	19%

In terms of length of residence, some 60 per cent of children had lived in the host state for at least 11 years and many of these were actually born in the host state (see above). A further 15 per cent reported having lived in the host state for between six and ten years and 25 per cent had lived in the host state for five years or less.

Family and Mobility: Reasons for Moving

The parents and children we interviewed were asked to describe their migration histories and to explain the reasons behind the moves they had made. It is at this point during the interview that speaking to parents proved so important since many of the younger children were either not fully aware or did not recall the reasons for their parent's move. This was particularly the case, of course, for those children who were born in the host state. While some factors proved quite prevalent, the diversity of motivations is notable. In many cases respondents cite not one variable but rather a series of events or considerations which, taken together, tipped the balance in favour of a move.

Their reasoning often included economic factors, both in the immediate sense of securing employment but also reflecting wider concerns about the relative economic prosperity of the home or host state. For others, it was family matters that precipitated a move (or often a return) to the home state. A group of EU migrants of particular interest, identified in the course of the research in Portugal, had moved in pursuit of wider 'quality of life' factors. The families interviewed in the Alentejo region of Portugal form part of a movement of what have become known as 'eco-migrants' motivated by environmental concerns and the desire to promote a self-sufficient mode of life.

Respondents' answers can be 'grouped' into separate categories to give some impression of the factors involved: Paid work or economic factors; family, which included partner-related issues, concerns about children, care issues and family breakdown; homesickness and the desire to 'return' home; and other factors, such as the environment, for example.

European Employment Trends: Assessing the Implications for Children of 'Career-Long Peripatetic Lifestyles'

Whilst the political agenda and, to a large extent, migration theory has been slow to consider the mobility of highly skilled persons, recent work has drawn attention to the increasing prevalence of professional and highly skilled migration in patterns of intra-Community migration (Koser and Salt, 1997; OECD, 2002). Salt and Ford (1993, p.292) refer to the 'international immigration market among the highly skilled [driven by] the development of a global economy and characterised by the internationalisation of companies and human resources'. Policy developments at EU level also pay particular attention to the mobility of highly skilled people. In January 2000, the European Commission published its strategy in relation to the development of the European Research Area (CEC, 2000) which referred to the importance of mobility to scientific development and excellence in the EU:

> Greater mobility of researchers, promoting a European dimension into scientific career and making Europe attractive to researchers from the rest of the world are among the key elements for achieving the human resources to meet the future needs of European research (CEC, 2000, p.19).

The Commission's Action Plan for Skills and Mobility similarly notes the relatively low level of mobility within the EU and identifies mobility as a potential solution to labour market bottlenecks and skills shortages (CEC, 2002). On a similar theme, the European Commission's High Level Task Force on Skills and Mobility (2002, p.12) notes how:

> At any one time, imbalances in the location of jobs and labour available to fill those jobs, gives rise to the coexistence of regions with skill shortages at the same time as others with high unemployment. [Whilst] geographic mobility may not in itself solve the underlying imbalance [it may] allow time for the skills of the local labour force to adapt.[8]

The European Commission has acknowledged that the realisation of the requisite level of labour mobility is likely to lead to the normalisation of what it has termed a 'career-long peripatetic lifestyle' in many areas of employment and especially in highly skilled industries and services (CEC, 2001, p.5). Similar forces are evidently active at national level. A recent paper by the Confederation of British Industry (CBI), for example, suggests that employee mobility represents, 'one of the five key pillars of a flexible labour market' (Hadley, 1998, p.4).[9]

Whilst the advantages to European economies and the Single Market are often emphasised, it is also important to ensure that the persons concerned and their families do not take the burden of this form of mobility and that more holistic measures are in place to facilitate it. A recent report prepared by the Council of European Professional and Managerial Staff (EUROCADRES) (2001, p.2) identifies the benefits of professional mobility to European labour markets and the individuals concerned but also raises some of the remaining legal and political obstacles:[10]

> The free circulation of Professional and Managerial Staff allows them to enhance their employability and to strengthen their competence. It develops the capacity to ease the bottlenecks existing for some kinds of jobs and thus

---

8 Reported in the UK House of Lords Select Committee on the European Union report (15th Report: 'Working in Europe: Access for All', 26 February 2002).

9 The CBI Employee Relocation Council has recently set up a European Mobility Forum (EMFO) funded by the European Commission to highlight the importance of mobility issues within the overall business context and establish a network of interested companies and European Employer's federations. The EMFO produces a regular newsletter (Employee Mobility Update) and organises meetings to discuss mobility issues ranging from the legal implications of international employee relocation, social security and pensions, international recruitment and career development to the availability of housing.

10 Evidence to the UK House of Lords Select Committee on the European Union, November 2001 to be found at http://www.tuc.org.uk/international.

> contributes to improve European competitiveness and growth. However, periods of working abroad should not have detrimental effects on people's working and living conditions or on their families.[11]

Progression in European labour markets is thus increasingly conditional upon mobility. Indeed, other research with mobile scientists (Ackers, 2001) identified an expectation of repeated mobility with many respondents having spent consecutive periods on contracts involving moves between three or four countries.

The consequences of these developments in European labour markets can be seen in the interviews with our sample of parents and children. Overall, 67 per cent of the families (117 cases) had moved primarily for a work-related reason. In a couple of cases, it was not so much for a specific job but for broader concerns about the economy and cost of living. For example, one respondent commented that 'things were better in Sweden' (210), whilst another, conversely, remarked, 'We were young and poor then and we figured it was better to stay in a poor country ... With two children, it was much easier economically for us to live in a poor country' (324).

In the overwhelming majority of cases, however, moves were motivated by the demands of parents' and mainly fathers' employment. The importance of work as the principle motivation behind the movement of families can be contrasted with the findings of the previous gender and migration project (Ackers, 1998) where women identified a far wider range of factors (including the desire to travel and learn languages or to study). This difference can be partly explained with reference to the demographic profile of the current sample: the focus on children (and the requirement that there were children present in the household at the time of interview) meant that we were sampling people at a later phase in the life-course with different priorities and responsibilities.

It is perhaps worth clarifying at this point what we mean when we refer to 'skilled migration'. Kofman (2000) points to the heterogeneous nature of this population and cites Salts' work on skilled migration that distinguishes twelve categories. These include corporate transferees, professionals, consultants, entertainers, business people, academics, researchers and students, and finally the spouses and children of these categories.[12]

---

[11] Key concerns raised include problems in the recognition of qualifications and diplomas, supplementary pensions and access to information.

[12] Kofman (2000, p.46) refers to OECD figures which suggest that the proportion of highly skilled migrants amongst long-term permit holders in the UK had risen to over 80 per cent.

In many cases the fathers in our study were employed by multi-national companies and were either 'posted' abroad or had fixed-term contracts for periods of one to three years. It is in these situations that children experienced the highest frequency of moves, often moving just before or after their father's new posting. Some examples are given below:

> All these moves took place due to my father's work. He was working for a big international company and he was transferred to the country and town that the company decided needed him. When he returned to Athens he started his own business and this way we have been able to settle down. [431].

The following mother recounted a long history of family moves expressing the situation as a 'career in migration – a way of life':

> We have a career in migration due to my husband's job. He works for an international company that takes projects all over the world. I have lived in Mexico, in Israel, in Libya ... then we went to New Zealand for one year only. We have been residing for three years in Colombia and in London. Afterwards we had a 'migration break' residing in France [home] for two years. It was strange for us! Finally we spent three years in Peru and five years ago we came to Athens. Moving from one country to another was nobody's choice. It became a way of life [434].

The cohort of respondents interviewed in the course of this project presented very much this model of male-breadwinning migration behaviour with initial mobility moves motivated primarily by the employment situation of the fathers.[13]

Dual Careers, 'Trailing Wives' and Fertility

Although in the majority of cases the father's employment proved the critical element in the migration decision, the impact of the mothers employment also emerged as a factor in family decision-making, particularly in dual career situations. In the overwhelming majority of cases our research confirms other work conducted on the phenomenon of the 'trailing wife' or 'tied mover'. Marriage, suggest Bonney and Love (1999, p.347), 'transforms women from independent persons to ancillary

[13] Chapter five focuses on the migration decision-making process itself and discusses in some detail the influence of father's employment.

supporters of male partners in their primary occupational roles'.[14] It is, nevertheless, worth considering for a moment the tenacity of this 'model' in the context of highly skilled mobility within the EU. To what extent, for example, are the partners of highly skilled men also likely to be skilled and, in that sense, less prepared to be 'footloose' and sacrifice their own career progression? Although there is little research in this area, Kofman (2000, p.52) argues that existing data points to a much lower proportion of women amongst inter-company transfers and suggests that women 'still face difficulties in being sent on overseas assignments'.

Raghuram (2003) also refers to the lack of research on family in the specific context of highly skilled migration, noting that there are 'very few studies exploring international tied migration amongst the skilled [and] little analysis of the ways in which the shift in the skills of the primary migrant reconfigures family migration' (p.1 and p.9). Raghuram also draws attention to the importance of understanding the market dynamics of the specific employment sector within which migrants are employed on the basis that:

> ... differentiating between the conditions of these different categories of skilled migrants is necessary for understanding the nature of the family migration that occurs alongside...Crucial differences [exist] between those whose migration is tied to that of men who move for a fixed period of time, through mechanisms such as inter-company transfers and thus have secure jobs to go to. Where migration has not been facilitated by the employers, through for instance relocation packages and career pathways, the migration is more 'risky' and both men and women may be called upon to work at different times in order to allay some of those risks. Hence, the nature of migration, how it is arranged and secured, is also critical in influencing women's labour force participation (p.10).

Boyle et al's review of research on family and migration (1998) identifies the lack of research on the relationship between mobility and fertility.[15] They conclude with the suggestion that women who make international moves may be more likely than their non-migrant peers to postpone family formation. Certainly, the impact of the 'expectation of mobility' on the respondents in our work on science mobility was felt particularly keenly once researchers began to establish partnerships and have children. Whereas women were equally mobile when young and single, their attitudes towards the prospect of repeated mobility once they

[14] For further material on 'tied movers' see Ackers (1998, p.164-170) and Boyle et al (1998).

[15] These issues are revisited in chapter four.

had partners and children differed markedly to their male counterparts. The following example is typical of women scientists' responses:

> I think it's a bit frustrating for both young men and women, the fact that, if you want to stay in the scientific community you have to go abroad to another institute, to get more experience. So you have to go to another country and then after a while you want to come back and find a permanent position in your country. This is what I want. I don't want to go to US, for instance, I want to come back to Scandinavia. So, this is very difficult and frustrating. But I think it's worst for women, I suppose, because this is the age at which most people have children as well, and in most families it is still the woman who takes care for their children. Therefore she hasn't only her career to think about but also the children. So I think it's even harder for women (reported in Ackers, 2001, p.68).

At this point women often considered leaving research careers and moving into careers more conducive to a 'follower' strategy, enabling them to either remain or move with their partners. Indeed, it was evident from this study of highly qualified women scientists that the 'trailing wife' scenario applied irrespective of skill level and was perhaps even more prominent in careers that demanded mobility. This finding is corroborated by Raghuram's work (2003, p.11-12) on medical mobility:

> What is clear is that men remain the primary migrants and most women in skilled migration households usually follow men … Women in such households are often themselves skilled as suggested by the dual career model.

The women scientists in the 2001 study (Ackers, 2001) also talked about the prospects of delaying or foregoing motherhood in order to progress in mobility-dependent careers. Indeed, women were significantly less likely than their male peers to have children. As one key informant put it, 'the main reason why people who have children don't go [abroad] is because they don't want to go and disturb the routine of the children'. One respondent refers to the impact of having children on her own career-related mobility:

> I have my family here ... So, I don't have the goal of going somewhere abroad for a postdoc. But I have my family here, and I have to take care of them. And I somehow think that ... it's not so possible to ... be abroad and

> be a good mother and a good wife ... but if I was a person without a family, yes, I would go abroad again.[16]

Interestingly, echoing these findings, Kofman (2000) refers to Reynolds and Bennett's work (1991) which found that where women were sent abroad by companies, they were 'generally unaccompanied by their families' (Koffman, 2000, p.52). According to Reynold's and Bennet's research, only 25 per cent of American female expatriates were accompanied by their partners, compared to 80 per cent of American men who are accompanied. Combining paid work with family responsibilities in a migration context thus appears far more challenging for women than men.

In many cases then, women put their careers on hold in order to support their partner's career progression and facilitate his mobility. This was not always the case, however, and our research in both the science study and the current project did find examples of dual career situations and the tension these caused both between couples (particularly in the science sample), and the impact of this tension on children. The CBI paper referred to earlier identifies dual career situations as a 'major obstacle to mobility' (Hadley, 1998, p.9) since the demands for geographical flexibility conflicts with wider concerns around employee retention, the development of flexible working and the promotion of family-friendly employment policies.[17] In terms of the prevalence of these kinds of situations, it is interesting to note here that some 47 per cent of the women researchers interviewed in the science project had partners who were also working in science. It may well be that, in view of their comments about the management of these situations following the birth of children, this figure drops considerably as women withdraw from these careers and either leave the labour market altogether or move to other more secure or less demanding jobs.

Given these findings, it is not surprising that for the cohort of respondents in the current project, the majority of initial migrations (as opposed to return moves) were motivated by the demands of fathers' careers. There were some cases in which the mother primarily motivated the initial move although this was by no means as prevalent as father-determined moves. A child in the following example describes briefly how she and her mother had moved with her mother's work to Italy for a year leaving the father behind:

---

[16] For further discussion on the relationship between care and mobility see chapter six.

[17] In response they propose measures such as spouse/partner assistance policies (to enable partners to gain employment in the host state) and additional support in integrating children into host educational systems.

> My father was left in Sweden, and of course he expected us to come back [219].

The interviews also found examples where mothers took periods of unpaid leave or secondments from their employment in order to accompany their partners and children for the duration of the move. In this situation, women tended to return home in advance of partners in order to preserve their right to resume employment. The following case illustrates the complex manoeuvres some families make in order to safeguard their mutual employment prospects and cope with bringing up children in situations when parents are themselves geographically separated. The respondent, a mother originally from Finland, moved to Sweden in 1978 when she got a temporary job in a Swedish company. Since she was a student at a Finnish University, she had no intentions to move permanently to Sweden. She met her partner and they fell in love. Later on she was offered a job in Finland and the couple had a long-distance relationship for several years. In 1983, they had their first child, a daughter. The respondent spent her parental leave in Sweden before returning to Finland. During the period between her daughter's first and second birthday they stayed with the child's grandmother in Finland. Then, since the mother had difficulties finding suitable childcare, the daughter moved to be with her father in Sweden when she was two years old. In 1987, they had their second child, a son, and since then the mother has lived in Sweden. However, she kept her job in Finland for four more years, until she finally gave in her notice in 1991. Talking about her decision to delay the move to Sweden the mother comments:

> I don't know … It was difficult to travel between [Sweden and Finland], and difficult to move … I haven't regretted that I decided to move here. But it was very difficult in the beginning. I was very negative against everything in Sweden. I really don't know why … Maybe it was because I didn't know the language well enough. Since I use language all the time in my work, I felt that I had to do everything twice. I also liked my job in Finland, and I didn't want to give it up until I had got another job in Sweden [201].

Two other respondents' experiences highlight similar tensions:

> When we had been there for three years my leave of absence was about to end. Then I had to go back, because otherwise I would lose my job. And my husband could only prolong his contract for a shorter period and ... we didn't want to risk it. Therefore I returned to Sweden together with our children [228b].

Another father described how he chose not to leave Sweden to accompany his wife and two sons to Amsterdam since he did not want to give up his job. The boys lived in Holland with their mother for two and a half years before moving to an English boarding school. During this time, their mother was still living in Amsterdam and their father in Stockholm. The two boys later moved back to Sweden and then subsequently moved to France with both parents for the purposes of their father's work.

The father in the following case moved to Greece a year before his wife and child because his wife wanted to wait until her application to work in Greece as a part-time secretary was approved:

> My husband could not refuse the job in Greece but on the other hand I didn't want to leave my job. The first year of living separately was difficult but fortunately the next year I was able to join him [413b].

These cases illustrate the very complex nature of family mobility, often necessitating the temporary dislocation of family relationships as pressures to move are re-negotiated and family arrangements re-configured. Although in the overwhelming majority of cases it was the father's employment that precipitated the initial outward move (and many of these are reported in chapter five), the research did uncover evidence of the impact of dual careers and the attempts by migrants to balance these with the needs of the family as a whole.

Partnering, Parenting and Mobility

Previous research involving female migrants identified a significant proportion of women whose moves were primarily motivated by their desire to join partners they had met either in the partner's country, perhaps whilst on holiday, or after meeting him elsewhere (as a student, for example). That research indicated that, where such international partnerships demanded the mobility of at least one of the partners to enable them to live together, it was, in the main, the women who moved (Ackers, 1998, p.164-172). Similarly, 37 per cent of our sample in the current project reported making moves that were primarily motivated by the need or desire to join partners. In most cases, one partner (typically the woman) had met their partner during a short visit or holiday or whilst studying and had subsequently moved over to join them in their home country, as the examples below testify:

> I had never planned to leave my country. I just happened to meet my husband in Majorca on holiday [001].

> It was not really my decision to come to Portugal. I met my husband and … [348].

Around 50 per cent of the parents had, in fact, met their partners following migration and in many, but by no means all cases, they married a national of the host state. We referred in the introduction to the importance of seeing migration as a process often under constant review and the extent to which this encompasses return. We have noted in particular the extent to which having children impacts upon migration decisions and specifically on the situation of mothers. Family formation and the point at which children begin to reach secondary school age (but typically before then) often precipitates a review of family migration decisions and, in some cases, a return to the home state by some or all of the family.

When asked to explain the reasons for moving (or returning), many parents gave reasons linked to their role as parents and their children's well-being. In 23 cases, reference was made to the needs of children as a factor shaping migration decisions. Some parents referred to the dislocation brought about by migration and the importance of ensuring that their children were 'settled in':

> We need to see if the children settle here, but that was the intention when we came back this time [085].

> And because of our daughter, I think we really needed to go back. She didn't have a lot of friends and ... It seemed like a good time to go back [220].

In the following case the move was precipitated by family breakdown (with the child's father moving to Italy). The mother's description of the situation, however, suggests that she considered the return to her home country as beneficial to her son, enabling him to avoid the tensions she experienced as a migrant child in the UK:

> I always wanted to return to Greece. I was unhappy in England. I didn't like it and I couldn't identify with British people. I wanted to go back as soon while my son was still small because I didn't want him to go through the difficulties I experienced from my own migration when I was a child. [406]

Some parents suggested that whereas a temporary stay and the experience of living in another country may be beneficial for their children, longer periods could prove more problematic, both in terms of their educational progression and their sense of cultural and social identity:

> They offered us to stay for another five years, but we thought that it would be too long. If they had offered my husband a job for another two years, we would have considered staying. But you never know what will happen with your children, and how they'll react [222].

In the following example, the mother said that their previous move from Greece to Austria was motivated by a wider concern to broaden their children's horizons. She emphasized the fact that the move would not disrupt their children's education as they could attend the Greek school at which their father worked and, in any event, they could return after a short period (which they did):

> We wanted to move to Austria for the children. It would be beneficial for them to live in another country apart from Greece. My husband mentioned that as a teacher, he could apply to teach in a Greek school abroad. I thought that it was a great opportunity [437].

Another group of respondents who lived in Portugal and Greece were motivated by the desire to find a 'positive' environment within which to bring up their children:

> We decided to come to Portugal because we thought that this was still a peaceful country and every parent's fear is crime, isn't it? And people are generally friendly and we liked the environment [301].

> I would like them to grow up in a warmer environment, not only physically but also socially. So we decided to come to Portugal [320].

> … to give the children a really nice childhood, free of fear and danger and weird people and violence and all the rubbish you get in the UK [334].

By far the most commonly cited factor precipitating return moves were concerns around children's education. In some cases, parents became anxious about the impact of the migration on children when it came to their first admission to school. Some of the concerns expressed below reflect worries about the educational system of the host country, but in most cases it was the longer term consequences of allowing their children to become integrated within those systems and the impact this might have on their own ability to move again in future. This reflected also long term concerns about educational progression to secondary school and higher education raising issues around the recognition of qualifications (issues discussed in more detail in chapters eight and nine):

> We moved to Greece in 1984. My first son was six years old and the second was four. They had to start schooling and we didn't want them to suffer school changes [417].

> We decided to return to Greece for the children's schooling. If they continued to attend German school, then we would have stayed until they completed their education [420].

> We did think about living in Greece [but] there were several obstacles: the children were too small, we couldn't afford it financially etc. Finally we made our decision [to move] when my older daughter was going to go to school [424].

> The factors that we took into our consideration in order to make our decision to move in Greece were my husband's job and the children's schooling. We didn't want them to change educational system. These factors determined the time and the place of our residence [432].

In the last case reported here the mother (who is French) cites the children's schooling as the principal factor determining their move from France. She moved back to Greece in advance of her (Greek) husband so that her children could commence studying at the French school. In that sense it was more of a concern about continuity in one school rather than a desire to embed her children in the education system of the host state.

In many cases the timing of the move, which often implied separation of the family,[18] was dictated by concerns about progression in education systems:

> My husband has been always trying to find the opportunity to return to Greece. He was looking for a job but despite the good offers they were not good enough to cover the expenses of a big family. Therefore we postponed our departure. When our daughter was going to start school, we considered that it was the time to take the big decision. The child should start school in the country where she would reside during her school years [403].

---

[18] Chapter six discusses this in greater depth.

The following woman said that she returned to the UK from Australia for a number of reasons connected her daughter's educational needs and her daughter's relationship with her grandparents. However, whilst these concerns were important, they also need to be seen alongside the breakdown of her relationship with the child's father and his subsequent return to Italy:

> Well, I just thought when she was getting older, just to be nearer her grandparents here and I suppose [for] the education here which I knew. And then [my daughter's] father decided to go back to Sicily so we came here [059].

The impact of relationship breakdown referred to in this case was not unusual and very often triggered a review of location decisions. Once again there is no research specifically on this issue. Boyle et al (1998 p.118), however, do consider the impact of divorce on inter-regional mobility and suggest that, 'inter-county mobility rates for divorcees are still higher than for those who remain married'. The findings of our current project suggest a relatively high level of family breakdown amongst EU migrant families and a strong relationship between this and mobility. Analysis of the experiences of family breakdown and its legal implications form the focus of discussion in chapter seven. The purpose of the following section, therefore, is to consider the impact of divorce, separation or bereavement on mobility and the extent to which this may precipitate migration typically a return 'home'.

In fifteen families, some form of family breakdown was cited as a key factor determining migration. In most cases this amounted to the return of the mother with her children to her home state following a divorce or separation. There were also two cases of bereavement resulting in the mother's return and in one family it was the father who returned home with his children. The following case describes a situation involving an international family and the impact of pressures upon the mother to return home with her children in the aftermath of family breakdown. After meeting her Dutch partner on holiday, the respondent moved to Holland to live with him. She worked full-time as a qualified nurse until they had two daughters. After that, she worked part-time in order to spend more time with her children. When the girls were aged 2 and 6 the husband 'walked out' and moved in with someone else. In Holland the family lived together in a rented house but on he paid her no maintenance and she could not afford to keep the house. He divorced her immediately (within 6 weeks she said). Unable to support the children and home on her part-time salary, she moved back to the UK into a small privately-rented flat near her parents, who now support her financially. As a single parent in the UK she has found it impossible to return to work given the poor salaries in nursing compared to Holland and the inflexible working hours. The respondent said that she would have been better off financially had she remained in Holland where payments to single parents were far more generous and nursery provision more developed but she lacked any family support there.

This example provides a poignant illustration of the complex interaction of variables, including migration status, the geographical dislocation of informal support networks, the articulation of motherhood and paid work and the relationship, at national level, between family law and social policy provision. In practice, this respondent could have been financially autonomous had she remained in Holland where the State has more effectively socialised the costs of bringing up children in single parent families. Returning to the UK system, which places increasing emphasis upon absent partners to financially support single mothers and provides relatively little in the way of affordable childcare to enable mothers to return to paid employment, left her with little room for manoeuvre. Moreover, the fact that her ex-husband had remained in Holland made it extremely difficult for her to enforce child-maintenance payments without resorting to complex, lengthy and costly legal proceedings. The apparently 'irrational' decision to return home, however, reflected her need for family support and to remove herself from what she felt at the time was a threatening and stressful situation, given the proximity of her ex-partner.

In many cases, the migration histories of the children's parents, often resulting in international partnerships combined with subsequent migrations as a result of family breakdown, exposed children to a complex fusion of cultural experiences. In one case, for instance, a female respondent met her Italian husband when they were both at university in the UK. But, 'together with my son, marital problems were born' [406]. When the couple eventually separated, the father went to live in Italy and she decided to return to Athens. Their son had been travelling back and forward to Italy for periods of contact with the father ever since.

Similarly, another female respondent first moved to Australia from Portugal with her Portuguese parents at the age of six. Her father remained in Australia after he and her mother divorced. At the age of 12, she moved back to Greece with her mother and her mother's new partner. Her step-father describes their reasons for moving:

> When we both obtained our divorces, we were living together and our lives had been back to normal after the tremendous changes. We realised then

> both that we had missed the European, the Mediterranean way of life. We decided to leave Australia [407].

For many of the parents, as in the previous case, the move represented a desire to start anew, perhaps leaving 'failed' relationships and memories behind. This was also the case where parents had lost a partner. One woman, for example, came to the Alentejo region of Portugal five years previously following the death of her first husband in an accident. At the time she had three young children. She described how she 'cried for a year' before meeting her new partner. She eventually re-married and they moved to Portugal to escape the memories of her previous relationship. She said she could never go back because the memories were too painful.

In the following case, on the other hand, the children moved from Sweden to Greece because their Swedish mother could no longer cope and she had asked their Greek father to take them. The children, in this case, were strongly opposed to moving over to Greece to live with their father. The father explains:

> In 1996, the children's mother, we were already separated, asked me to take the children to Greece because she couldn't cope any more. She had financial difficulties. My situation was still difficult but I couldn't say "no". Actually I was totally unprepared and the children too. They didn't want to come [410].

In all but the final example discussed above, it is the children's mother who moves following family breakdown. This was by far the most common consequence of family breakdown in the interview sample. The following story presents a particularly complex scenario involving family breakdown and re-constitution and a series of moves. The family moved to Bermuda in 1987 following the father's work demands where they stayed until 1992. Before returning to settle down in London, the family spent a year on the island of Guernsey. The parents subsequently divorced. The mother describes how a further opportunity to move to Greece effectively divided the family in two:

> I got married again in 1995 and both children were living with me and my new husband. When a new opportunity to leave England and to go to Greece for work-related reasons again came up in 1997, the children had two alternatives: either to stay in London with their father or to come with me to Athens. My daughter decided to stay as she was in a critical point at school, but my son – who is younger and more attached to me – decided to come to Greece [409].

The children in the following case also made a series of moves, all of which were determined by family separation. In common with the previous example, the children were very much passive 'victims' of earlier migration decisions but latterly, the daughter at least, exercised some degree of 'choice' in making her own decisions about where to live. The children's moves in this family came about as a result of disputes between the parents following their separation. In 1986 the mother, who was then pregnant with their third child, deserted her husband and returned to Germany with the two children. The father then brought the case to the Greek Courts which awarded him temporary custody of the two children. He went to Germany in 1988 and brought back only his son:

> My son had great difficulties in his adjustment in Germany. Therefore as soon as the Court Decision was issued, I brought him back to Greece. He had already forgotten the Greek language and he started all over again. My daughter did not want to come back and she stayed in Germany with her mother and sister who, in the meantime, had been born. Ever since, a long-lasting fight between my wife and myself started. Contact between the children lapsed for approximately five years as my wife wanted to take revenge on me for taking my son to Greece. In 1995, we spent the summer vacation all together in Germany. This re-established the contact between me and the children and improved our relationship. The following summer my daughter came to Greece on vacation. During the Christmas vacation of the same year, my daughter told me that she wanted to stay here and live with us. She had relationship problems with her mother and also she wanted to get to know me. Her mother didn't refuse and I didn't either [412].

The daughter presented the following perspective on the moves:

> I was very small when I left Greece and went to Germany the first time. I was just three-and-a-half and my brother was five. I don't remember many things. We went to my mother's home-town ... I don't remember the time that my brother came to Greece with my father. I didn't know Greece until I came here on summer vacation some years ago. It was nice then. The following year I came again, and having some problems in Germany, I decided on the spur of the moment to stay here with my father. I'm happy that I had a free will and my parents didn't try to prevent me or force me to stay somewhere [412].

The cases reported above illustrate some of the problems arising as a consequence of family breakdown in this population of EU migrant families. The level of inter-marriage and repeated mobility in our sample have increased the likelihood of a second phase of migration following the divorce or separation of parents and the geographical dispersal of family members across the EU and beyond. An important factor triggering the return moves of mothers to their home state was the need to access informal support networks there and, in particular, their own mothers. To that extent they were moving in order to access care.

In other situations care-related moves were made in order to provide care to elderly parents or to support sibling carers. In ten of the families interviewed, respondents referred to the care needs of an elderly relative as a key factor bringing about a move. The relationship between mobility and care is picked up again in chapter six when we consider how families manage kinship across several countries.

Missing Home

In the introduction to this chapter we referred to Baldassar and Baldock's (2000) sample of academic migrants which they described as motivated by highly individualistic concerns around career progression. Moving, often as single people without responsibility for partners and children and perhaps not facing the implications of increasing levels of dependency amongst parents, they were able to make fairly straightforward decisions motivated primarily by career and life-style considerations. Many of the scientists interviewed in other research (Ackers, 2001) also made reference to the migration as an exciting individual project – an adventure – and although some expressed concerns about integration in the workplace, many neither expected nor invested heavily in wider social integration. In any case, the majority considered their move as temporary. At that point in their lives they saw themselves primarily as individuals and not as members of a wider family or community. As the life-course evolved, however, many of our adult respondents began to talk more forcefully about their need for integration either socially in the host country or personally within their extended family networks and the influence of this on their decision to return 'home'.

The following group of cases included families who made a return migration because they simply wanted to go back home. In all but the last example, it was parents who expressed this sense of wanting to return. Many of the children had never lived in the 'home' country before and the very concept of home raised complex tensions that are discussed in more detail in chapter five. Indeed, in the first two examples, the parents' decision of when to return was motivated by a concern that if they delayed the move any further their children may not wish to accompany them, fracturing the family:

> The primary reason for us moving back was because we were homesick. The problem is that we were getting older – 47 – and if we'd have waited another couple of years and then come back, well where am I going to get a job? Okay, I was guaranteed a job there until I was 65 and guaranteed a pension but we would have been in a foreign country with foreign people and all our family is here. And we could have said that we would stay there for the children but there was no guarantee that when they were old enough they wouldn't have moved away. They might have even wanted to come here or wherever and we would have been left over there by ourselves [055].

The following parents suggested that the timing of their return was influenced by concerns about their daughter's willingness to consent to accompanying them:

> We'd been there long enough and if we had have waited any longer, well we might not have got the girls back and so we just decided to come back. [052b].

Return migration, at this point, was thus seen by the parents as a means by which to preserve the family unit. It was clear that repatriation was inevitable at some point and the timing of it was designed to minimise the risk of leaving children behind.

In a small number of cases respondents referred to concerns about their treatment in the host country. Some parents specifically referred to experiences of discrimination in the host state which prompted their return:

> I'm Dutch and I met my Portuguese husband in Holland – he was working there and he wanted to go back to Portugal. The discrimination against foreign people was getting worse every year so it was difficult [315].

> I was aware of my husband's wish to have his family in Greece. He has told me, "Here I am nothing. In my home-town, I will be a respected doctor and my family would be a prominent family" [417].

The mother in the following case was also Dutch and moved back to Portugal with her husband for a better quality of life. In this example, it was not so much overt discrimination but a reaction to the kind of unskilled labouring work that prompted the initial emigration on the part of her husband. The thought of enduring this kind of heavy manual work into retirement was evidently a factor encouraging their return:

> We came to live in Portugal because my husband was missing [home] and he had the chance to change to another job. He tried and tried, doing shift-work in a factory, it was very tiring. And to work like that until the age of 65 he thought, 'no, this is not my life', and tried to change. But it's very hard [316].

The following cases describe dreams of returning 'home' and its influence upon migration decisions. It is interesting to note that the majority of these experiences are recounted by returning Greek migrants, most of whom would have moved initially for work and who do not fall into the category of highly skilled migrants discussed earlier. For them, the idea of return was not simply a thought or dream – they had, in fact, remitted finances to support the building of a house in Greece in preparation for their return. The woman in the first example recounts a story of her own migration history going back to her own childhood and to a previous, failed, attempt at repatriation:

> I migrated to Stockholm in 1958, when I was eleven years old. I come from a big poor family. I was the youngest child. My parents sent me to a maternal aunt in Sweden in order to have a better life. I met my [Greek] husband when I was eighteen and we got married. We always wanted to return to Greece as soon as we could secure a decent living there. We first returned in 1985 to my husband's home-village. The conditions were not very favourable and we didn't succeed in making a living. Therefore we went back to Sweden in 1990. The dream of repatriation was always there. We knew that sooner or later, we would go back home. Finally, we returned for good three years ago [419].
>
> The dream of every Greek migrant is to return 'home'. We started building this house soon after our daughter's birth. We wanted her to be brought up in Greece. When it was completed we repatriated [421].

> We had been thinking about living in Greece for a long time [but] there were several obstacles: the children were too small, we couldn't afford it financially etc. Finally we made our decision [to return] when my older daughter was going to go to school [424].

> We settled down in [Holland] where we both worked, but my husband insisted on moving to Athens where his family was. He used to say that we would have better living conditions in Greece. He owned the house where we are living today. This way, our income would be enough and it wouldn't

> be necessary for me to work out of the house. I could stay at home raising my son [443].

> There were many reasons why we decided to settle down in Greece and not in Sweden. Homesickness and my parental family's pressure to repatriate were some of them [444].

> My husband started building a country home in [a small town], for the summer vacation and he was travelling very often to Greece. At that time, he asked me if I would live in Greece. It took me a year to make my decision. He wanted to go back so much [411].

It is interesting to see how the reasoning around return often involved a range of factors including the existence of property but also the lower cost of living which, in one of the examples, meant that the wife could contemplate withdrawal from paid work to spend more time with her son. For another respondent, the desire to return to Greece was coupled with pressure from her parents to move back. Return moves were not necessarily planned towards the end of working life but instead coincided with concerns around parenting and children's education.[19]

Return moves can also be initiated by children. In the following illustration, the child expressed a desire to move back 'home' to Sweden even though her family remained in Belgium. Her decision reflected concerns about her education but also about her connection and knowledge of life in her home country:

> [I want] … to get back to my roots, I suppose ... I had graduated from the Scandinavian school, and I had a feeling that I wanted to go back home again. One reason for this was that I didn't want to stay in Belgium. I don't know, I'd been living in Belgium for such a long time, and I knew what it was like. It would probably have been different if I had chosen to study at a Belgian university or something, but I still had a feeling that I wanted to do something else. And then I realised that I hadn't really been living in Stockholm. When we moved to Belgium, I was only a child, and we were also living outside the city … I think I wanted to go home, to discover what Sweden was really like. But I suppose the main reason was that I just wanted to go home [225].

[19] Research on retirement migration, on the other hand found that many respondents waited until they qualified for a pension before they returned to their country of origin (Ackers and Dwyer, 2002).

Conclusion

This chapter has begun to contextualise the experiences of parents and children discussed in the rest of the book. It started by considering the nature of intra-EU migration flows and the increasing prevalence of highly skilled migrants within these. The 'expectation of mobility' in many areas of work in the EU and beyond is generating a pattern of mobility quite distinct from traditional forms of labour migration which typically involved an initial move and then settlement in the host state or, in some cases, eventual return. We have witnessed the persistence of this model, to some extent, in the responses of some of our Southern European returnees. For the majority of our sample, however, mobility reflects the normalisation of 'career long peripatetic life-styles' not only in academic research and science but also in work with many large multi-national companies and businesses. Increasing levels of student mobility and travel in general are also likely to result in a more positive attitude to mobility and, together with the processes discussed above, an increase in international partnerships. International partnerships themselves both reflect and facilitate mobility as families and career opportunities are geographically dispersed.

Divorce rates amongst migrant families are likely to at least mirror the increases in divorce within the European populations as a whole. Experienced in a transnational context, family breakdown has a serious impact on the location decisions of family members typically precipitating another phase of mobility for mothers and their children. Children in both 'intact' and divorced families will have affective ties in more than one country and increasingly experience kinship in a transnational way.

EU migrant children also face the challenges of educational progression in European education systems that remain quite disparate in very many ways. These concerns around educational progression have emerged as a major factor in the migration decision-making process for both parents and children.

Finally, it is perhaps no surprise given the peripatetic nature of intra-EU mobility that many migrant parents have no intention of 'settling' in the host state. For them return is not simply a 'myth' or dream shaping their experiences of living in another homeland.[20] It is a planned event and the

[20] The concept of the 'myth of return' was used widely in the 1970s and 80s in the UK in the context of post-colonial migration (*cf.* Anwar, 1979). It drew attention to the impact of ties, both financial (through remittances and property ownership in the countries of emigration) and affective and the impact of these upon the integration of migrants. Many, of course, would not return home although there is increasing evidence of return moves to the

continued contact with the home country facilitates their re-insertion. Parents often spoke about homesickness and their desire to return to their families and countries of origin at least at a later phase in their lives. Whilst some older children also expressed this concern, for many children the concept of 'home' is less clear-cut following a series of moves and the dispersal of family and friendships across countries. Within this context, for children at least, return moves present serious challenges often with greater social implications than the initial out-migration which might have taken place when they were very young or even before they were born.

The material presented in this chapter emphasises the importance of understanding migration as an on-going process shaped by the changing circumstances as families form, reform and evolve. Whereas the father's employment plays a large part in the initial migration, subsequent moves often reflect more complex attempts to balance a wider range of interests including the employment situation of mothers but also, importantly, the needs of children.

All of the issues raised here are developed further in the subsequent chapters. The next chapter focuses on another important dimension of context – the legal framework shaping the mobility rights of EU migrant families.

Caribbean. For a discussion of return migration in the Portuguese context, (see Cavaco, 1993).

4 Concepts of 'Family' and 'Child' in Community Law

Introduction

An important dimension of our study was to examine the impact of migration on families, an area to have undergone dramatic legal developments since the latter part of the 1990s. Chapters one and three have noted how family entitlement under Community law arose initially out of a need to facilitate the mobility of workers. From the 1960s onwards, therefore, the EU institutions, and particularly the ECJ, extended important residence, employment and social rights to family members who moved with migrant workers. A number of soft-law measures introduced as early as the 1980s acknowledged a growing awareness of the impact of Community law on the family and, indeed, the impact of the family on the success of Community law.[1] Today, European family-related rights have come to be associated more broadly with the pursuit of gender equality and with the reconciliation of work and family life (McGlynn 2000, 2001a, 2001b), as well as with concerns to ensure the recognition and enforceability across Member States' jurisdictions of decisions relating to parental responsibility and marriage dissolution.[2]

The gradual shift in emphasis from the so-called 'parasitic' rights, extrapolated from sporadic ECJ interpretations, towards a more genuine endeavour by the EU to engage with the 'family agenda', is attributable to a

[1] See for example Recommendation Nº R (90) 2 of the Committee of Ministers concerning violence within the family and Recommendation no. R (84) 4 Social Cohesion and Quality of Life. Later measures include European Parliament Resolutions of 9.05.93 on family policy in the European Community, OJ C-184 (1983) 116; of 14.12.1994 on protection of families and family units, OJ C-18 (1995) 96; of 12.12.1996 on measures to protect minors in the European Union, OJ C-20 (1997) 170; of 18.08.1996 on abduction of children of bi-national marriages in the Member States, OJ C-261 (1996) 157; and of 20.01.1997 on improving law and co-operation between the Member States on the adoption of minors, OJ C-20 (1997) 176. Also, see Recommendation Nº R (90) 2 of the Committee of Ministers concerning violence within the family and Recommendation no. R (84) 4 Social Cohesion and Quality of Life.

[2] These will be considered in detail in chapter seven.

number of important factors. First, family rights are much more integral now to the functioning of the internal market, largely because of the continuing propensity to move, not only for work-related reasons, but also for education, health, retirement or to fulfil caring obligations (Ackers and Dwyer, 2002). This has contributed to a growing incidence of cross-national family formation and migration and to the development of more accessible and receptive social welfare and education regimes within Member States to accommodate EU nationals and their families.

A second and perhaps more subtle factor which has served to promote family rights at EU level relates to the growing prominence of fundamental human rights as a direct concern in the development, articulation and interpretation of EU law (Neuwahl and Rosas, 1995; Betten and MacDevitt, 1996; Alston, 1999; Lenaerts, 2000; Stalford, 2002). Although the European institutions have, since the very inception of the European (Economic) Community, acknowledged an implicit commitment to respecting and protecting fundamental human rights,[3] this has generally been conditioned by and very much subject to the economic rationale underlying the Community polity.[4] The EU has manifested a more concrete and visible declaration of its human rights commitments more recently, however, first of all by virtue of Article 6(2) of the Treaty of Maastricht (formerly F(2)), and latterly through the introduction of the Charter of Fundamental Rights in the European Union, on 7th December 2000.[5] This instrument contains explicit reference to the rights of the family in all its forms, in addition to a number of provisions targeting the needs and interests of the child, consistent with the UNCRC 1989.[6]

These developments are highly significant in terms of the ongoing Community endeavour to develop the concept of Union citizenship in a more universal and holistic way. Clearly, the gradual extension of the range of social rights available under the free movement provisions provides one important and tangible aspect of this. The introduction of a more explicit human rights component as well as enhanced opportunities for direct

[3] See for example, Case 29/69 *Stauder v. City of Ulm* [1969] ECR 419.
[4] For examples, see Case 36/75 *Rutilli v. Minister for the Interior* [1975] ECR 1219. See further Case 130/75 *Prais v. Council of the European Communities* [1976] ECR 1589 referring to Article 9 ECHR; Case 44/79 *Hauer v. Land Rheinland Pfalz* [1979] ECR 3727; and Case C-65/98 *Safet Eyup v. Landesgeschaftsstelle des Arbeitsmarktservice Vorarlberg* [2000] 3 CMLR 1049 referring to Article 8 ECHR.
[5] [2000] OJ C364/1.
[6] Particularly the 'best interests' and 'agency' principles enshrined in Articles 3 and 12 of the UNCRC respectively.

participation, however, represent more prominently the civil and political dimensions of citizenship in favour of children and other family members.[7]

Moreover, although they are relatively recent, these measures have arguably provided a more positive framework within which to address not only the rights of family members, but also, in a more direct way, the rights of children. As the discussion in chapter one has highlighted, children's rights at EU level have, in the past, largely been incidental to those of the wider migrant family, evolving only as a by-product of their worker-parents' rights under the free movement of persons provisions. In more recent years, however, there has been a growing emphasis placed on the rights of children as autonomous actors and on the need to promote a European Community which engages with children and young people more directly (this itself raises certain dilemmas relating to the pragmatic and ideological need, on the one hand, to locate children's rights within a family framework and, on the other, to recognise and promote children as independent agents). The targeted provisions of the Charter of Fundamental Rights in the European Union clearly acknowledge this tension and, although they are only of declaratory force, represent a more decisive commitment to advancing the status of children at EU level beyond the dependency model of the free movement formula.

Building on the material presented in chapters one and three the first section of this chapter provides a detailed overview of the evolving concept of 'family' and 'child' under the free movement provisions and the role of the ECJ in interpreting and advancing individual and family rights in this context. It will also consider some of the most recent constitutional and legislative developments that have taken place in favour of the child and family and make some tentative assertions as to whether this promises a more secure (citizenship) status for them in the future. The chapter then moves on to present some background statistics on the structure of EU migrant families and, more specifically, on the demographic characteristics of the interview sample. Juxtaposing this data with the formal concepts of 'family' and 'spouse' in Community law enables one to draw out the extent to which the latter is out of step with the empirical reality across European societies. It also reveals the potential impact of this disjunction on those families and family members falling outside 'traditional' models.

---

[7] That is, presuming that we are applying a traditional Marshellian interpretation of citizenship in an EU context (see Stalford, 2000).

The Concept of 'Family' in Community Law

For the most part, any mention of children and the family remained conspicuously absent from European Treaty provisions bearing testimony to the diminutive value traditionally attached to them as a policy priority at Community level. Entitlement accruing to family members has instead developed incrementally out of vague and ill-defined secondary measures aimed principally at supplementing migrant workers' rights. Regulation 1612/68[8] and Regulation 1408/71[9] in particular provide the bulk of entitlement for migrant workers and their families.

Regulation 1408/71 aims principally to co-ordinate Member States' social security systems to secure workers and their families' access to state assistance following migration to another EU Member State. Regulation 1612/68, on the other hand, governs access to and conditions of employment for migrant workers. Both of these Regulations explicitly extend entitlement to children and other family members. For example, Article 11 Regulation 1612/68 entitles family members to undertake paid employment in the host state (even if they are non-EC nationals), Article 12 grants the children of EU migrant workers access to the education system of the host state under the same conditions as nationals, and Article 7(2), which entitles the migrant worker to 'the same social and tax advantages' as nationals of the host Member State, has been construed by the ECJ to include social and tax rights enjoyed by family members.[10]

Article 10 of Regulation 1612/68 defines the 'family' to include a worker's, 'spouse and their descendants who are under the age of 21 or who are dependants as well as dependent relatives in the ascending line of the worker and his spouse'. Regulation 1408/71, on the other hand, defines 'family member' more indirectly by reference to the national legislation regulating the allocation of the specific benefits claimed. This is generally determined by the extent to which a family member is deemed 'dependent' (Stalford, 2000). Thus, Regulation 1408/71 provides that:

---

8 Implements Articles 39-43 EC. OJ Sp. Ed. 1968, No. L257/2, p.475, amended by Regulation 312/76, OJ Special Edition 1968 L 257/2.

9 OJ 1971 I 149/2.

10 For examples see: Case 65/81 *Francesco Reina and Letizia Reina v. Landeskreditbank Baden-Wurttemberg* [1982]ECR 33; Case 41/84 *Pietro Pinna v. Caisse d'Allocations Familiales de la Savoie* [1986] ECR 1; Case 94/84 *Office National de l'Emploi v. Deak* [1985] ECR 1773; Case 32/75 *Anita Cristini v. Société nationale des chemins de fer français* ECR 1085; Case 76/72 *Michel S. v. Fonds national de reclassement social des handicappés* [1973] ECR 437; Case 63/76 *Vito Inzirillo v. Caisse d'Allocations Familiales de l'Arrondissement de Lyon* [1976] ECR 2057.

> Where the said legislations regard as a member of the family or the member of the household only a person living under the same roof as the worker, this condition shall be satisfied if the person in question is mainly dependent on that worker (Article 1(f)).[11]

Judicial interpretations of these provisions confirm that the threshold of family life, for the purpose of free movement-related rights, is firmly set at legal, heterosexual marriage or, in the case of children and other family members, a biological link or relationship of (financial) dependency with the migrant worker. Indeed, there is now an impressive body of academic literature critiquing the exclusive nature of European family rights and of the ECJ's reluctance to advance the concept in line with changes in family practices and family forms across the Member States (Lundström, 1996; Moebius and Szyszczak, 1998; Ackers and Stalford, 1999; Woods, 1999; McGlynn, 2001b). Even in the wake of important constitutional and legislative developments at EU level, the ECJ has reminded us that 'Community notions of marriage and partnership exclusively address a relationship founded on civil marriage in the traditional sense of the term',[12] thus renewing concerns (with implications for children) about the derived entitlement[13] of non-working partners who are not married and cohabiting, including those living in same-sex relationships.

The Concept of 'Spouse' in Community Law and the Rights of Cohabitants

Article 10 of Regulation 1612/68 and relevant ECJ rulings suggest that a legal marital relationship is required for a non-working or third country national parent to qualify for free movement privileges. Unmarried partners of EU nationality may qualify in their own right if they undertake paid work. This opportunity to achieve independent status is more restricted, however, for unmarried partners or divorced spouses of third country nationality who may not be able to claim a right to work.[14]

---

[11] For examples see Case 44/65 *Hessische Knappschaft v. Maison Singer et Fils* [1965] ECR 965 where the ECJ confirmed that Article 51 EC (now Article 42) allows extension of certain social security rights contained in Regulation 1408/71 to migrant workers' *dependent* family members.

[12] Case T-246/97, *D and Sweden v. Council,* [1999] ECR II-1 para.26.

[13] These benefits extend to families as an indirect benefit to the worker; as such they are derived rights, dependent upon the continued entitlement of the worker and the claimant's status as part of his or her family.

[14] The status of divorced spouses of third country nationality is considered in detail in chapter seven.

Most notoriously, in *Netherlands State v Reed*,[15] the ECJ declined to extend the concept of 'spouse' under Article 10 Regulation 1612/68 to cohabitants. Ms Reed, a British national, accompanied her partner of five years when he took up employment for the subsidiary of a British company based in The Netherlands. After a period spent looking for employment, Ms Reed applied for a residence permit on the basis of her relationship with her partner (claiming her derived entitlement). Her application was dismissed on the grounds that she was not the spouse of a Community national. The case was then referred to the ECJ. In its judgment the Court emphasised the importance of a Community-wide definition drawing parallels with its case law on the concept of worker:

> The term 'spouse' has a specific meaning in Community law ... [therefore] divergence in the application of the law on an issue important for freedom of movement, would be just as unacceptable as divergence with regard to the term 'worker'. (p.1285)

Ms Reed argued for a more liberal interpretation of the provisions in light of the legal and social developments that had taken place in the two decades subsequent to the drafting of Regulation 1612/68. The ECJ, however, rejected this argument, contending that:

> When, in support of a dynamic interpretation, reference is made to developments in social and legal conceptions, those developments must be visible in the whole of the Community; such an argument cannot be based on social and legal developments in only one or two Member States. (p.1286)

The Court concluded that the term 'spouse' in Article 10 'applies to marriage partners only and does not include cohabitation'.

It is difficult to assess whether, in practice, this decision relates to the empirical difficulty of establishing evidence of a 'general social development' across the Member States or, indeed, whether the Court actually considered any empirical evidence of this kind. The wording of the judgment, however, suggests that if the Court was presented with sound factual evidence to this effect, it would support a broader construction in the future:

> In the absence of any indication of a general social development which would justify a broad construction and in the absence of any indication to the contrary in the Regulation, it must be held that the term 'spouse' in

---

[15] Case C-59/85 *Reed v. The Netherlands* [1986] ECR 1283.

> Article 10 of Regulation 1612/68 refers to a marital relationship only. There is no reason, therefore, to give the term 'spouse' an interpretation which goes beyond the legal implications of that term, which embrace rights and obligations which do not exist between unmarried companions. (p.1289)

D'Oliveira (1993, p.45) argues that when sufficient evidence is available to demonstrate the increased incidence of cohabitation across all Member States, the Court's approach will change. This optimism presumes an underlying 'rationality' in the Court's jurisprudence in this area suggesting that sound evidence of a European trend in cohabitation could bring about a change in the law (Ackers and Dwyer, 2002).[16] Clearly, despite abundant evidence in this regard, little has changed to significantly advance the concept of spouse or family under the free movement provisions as the following discussion will illustrate.

Demographic Changes in Partnering and Parenting across Member States

Most recent European statistics report that the marriage rate has declined since 1960 from an annual average of 8 to 5.1 per thousand by 1995 (EUROSTAT, 2000). Kiernan (1999, p.14) observes that the traditional marital model upon which EC law is predicated accounts for 60 per cent of women in Greece and Portugal (between the ages of 25 and 29 years). In the Nordic countries of Denmark, Sweden and Finland, as well as in France, around a third in this age group is married. Marriage is seemingly most popular in Western Europe, although they too have shown a downward trend overall. Ireland, for example, saw the number of marriages decline from a peak of 21,800 in 1980 to 16,200 in 1996.[17]

Kiernan (1999, p.5) notes that 'one of the most important engines behind the decline in marriage rates is the rise in cohabitation, particularly since the beginning of the 1980s in many European countries'.[18] The most common form of cohabitation that emerged during the 1960s and 1970s was identified amongst young people in their 20s and 30s living together as either a prelude to, or as an alternative to marriage. There is also a growing prevalence today of couples living together following the breakdown of a

---

[16] The extent to which EU institutions are beginning to respond to changes in rates of divorce will be considered in detail in chapter seven.

[17] Although recent years have witnessed a slight upward movement to 19,200 in 2000 (Council of Europe, 2001).

[18] See also the research findings of Lewis, Datta, & Sarre, 1999 commissioned by the then Lord Chancellors' Department (LCD), UK.

previous marriage. According to Kiernan (1999a, 2001), cohabitation would appear to be most common in Denmark where people aged 16 to 29 are more likely to be cohabiting than married and where more than one-fifth of all 30 to 44 year olds cohabit. A similar pattern emerges in all the other EC countries in that cohabitation is more common among younger age groups. After Denmark, it appears to be most prevalent in France and the UK, whilst in the Southern European countries and Ireland, although on the increase, cohabitation remains relatively uncommon.

Clearly current EC law relating to the family reflects the situation in some countries to a greater extent than others, reinforcing the correlation between patterns of married life and cultural, legal and religious environments. An example of this is provided by the Republic of Ireland where the comparatively low rate of cohabitation and divorce can be attributed to both the influence of the Catholic Church and the fact that divorce was only legalised following the 1995 referendum.[19] There is undoubtedly, however, a gradual convergence of practices in this regard. These changes necessarily impact upon the number of children born and reared within non-marital relationships.

Fertility Rates Across the EU

Figures from the European Labour Force Survey (EUROSTAT, 1996) show a concentration of men and women in the 25-49 age group with a lower representation of elderly and young persons within the EU migrant population. The majority of EU migrants are, therefore, at the stage of their lives associated with establishing long-term partners, childbearing and child-rearing.[20]

As could be expected, younger men and women aged 20-24 and older men and women aged 40-44 are less likely to have children present in the household. The Council of Europe (2001) noted in its report on recent demographic developments in Europe that the decline in the fertility rate – that is, the average number of children per woman – is perhaps the most salient phenomena in European demography. It attributes this to a number of factors including the low rates of mortality, especially infant mortality; the delay of marriage and maternity reducing the reproductive period; the diffusion of modern methods of contraception; women's increased

[19] Family Law (Divorce) Act 1996. It is noteworthy that Ireland records the fastest increase in single parent families and in marital separation.

[20] Clearly the growing incidence of retirement migration in more recent years has increased the prominence of elderly people within this population (see Ackers and Dwyer, 2002).

participation in the labour market; and the difficulties associated with reconciling work and family life in addition to trends in migration. In 2000, none of the EU Member States recorded a fertility rate high enough to ensure the replacement of generations (that is, of at least 2.1 children per woman). The Council of Europe (2001) report announced that France, Ireland, Luxembourg, Denmark, Finland and the Netherlands all registered the highest fertility rates at between 1.7 and 1.8 children per woman, while the EU average is 1.5 children. Italy and Spain recorded some of the lowest fertility rates of 1.23 and 1.24 respectively (Council of Europe, 2001).

This is clearly affected by a widespread increase in the average age of childbearing across the EU. The Council of Europe (2001) report state that the UK (29.1) and the Netherlands (28.6) occupy the top of the hierarchy in relation to mean age at the birth of the first child. The peak years of parental responsibility are between 29 and 39 during which time over 80 per cent of both national and EU migrant women have children present in their household (Council of Europe, 2001).

Kiernan (1999, p.6) draws a correlation between the 'dramatic' rise in non-marital childbearing across European states in recent decades and developments in cohabitation. She reports that:

> At one extreme are most of the Nordic countries where well over 40 per cent of births in the 1990s were outside marriage and at the other extreme lie countries such as Italy and Greece with 10 per cent or less of children born out of wedlock. In countries such as Ireland the rise has been particularly dramatic, the proportions having increased from 8 per cent in 1985 to 15 per cent in 1990 and to 26 per cent in 1997. Furthermore, cohabiting couples in the 25-34 age group with at least one dependant child ranged from 31-61 per cent across the EC Member States.

Kiernan observes also that over 1 in 2 of Nordic women, as well as French and British women in cohabiting unions, had a dependant child compared to one in three in other countries, such as Austria and the Netherlands.

More general data recording births outside marriage (including lone-parenthood) report that in Ireland, over 30 per cent of births were outside marriage in 2000 compared with 5 per cent in 1980, a figure which has been steadily increasing in recent years (Council of Europe, 2001). This rate is surpassed by the UK where the proportion of births outside marriage rose to 39.4 per cent in 2000, compared with 38.8 per cent in 1999, 12.5 per cent in 1981 and 8.2 per cent in 1971. A similar increase is recorded in Portugal where the proportion of children born outside marriage increased sharply, from 9.5 per cent in 1981 to 22.2 per cent in 2000 (20.8 per cent in

1999). Italy continues to record one of the lowest rates of extra-marital childbearing. The number increased from 48,118 in 1999 to 54,770 in 2000, constituting 10.2 per cent of the total number of live births. This data is largely consistent with the comparative study carried out by Bradshaw and colleagues (1996) which reported that Italy had the lowest rate of children living in lone-parent families (6 per cent), and the UK had the highest (21 per cent), followed closely by Denmark and Germany (19 per cent) and Sweden (18 per cent). See also Ditch, et al (1998) for aggregate data from a variety of sources on lone parents. Again, these figures demonstrate that while in some countries (predominantly those of Southern Europe and the Republic of Ireland) marriage remains the dominant context for having children, the rate at which children are being born and reared by cohabiting parents is on the increase.

It is important to consider whether similar trends occur within the EU migrant family in order to assess the impact of (limited) Community definitions of spouse and dependency on this group. The next section, therefore, examines the marital status and demographic structure of the EU migrant population and the number of children within this.

Marriage, Partnering and Childbearing in the EU Migrant Family

The data presented in the table below indicates the relatively high proportion of EU migrants who are married in comparison with the population in general.

Table 4.1 Marital status of nationals and EU migrants compared by gender (%)

Marital Status	Male National	Male EU	Female National	Female EU
Single	45%	38%	38%	34%
Married	50%	56%	47%	54%
Divorced	3%	3%	4%	4%
Widowed	3%	2%	12%	8%

Source: European Labour Force Survey (EUROSTAT, 1994).

The impression created by these figures of a migration of married, same-national, couples is, however, misleading since they probably reflect more the demographic structure of this population and the high concentration of young adults and workers who migrate rather than any greater propensity to marry as such. Furthermore, detailed empirical work with EU migrant women in a project preceding the current research, showed that many women moved as single women and not, as often assumed, as the passive partners of make breadwinning families (Ackers, 1998). However, this research did suggest that marriage and subsequent family formation in the host state acted as barriers to future mobility in many cases:

Table 4.2 Marital status of migrant women at the point of migration and at the time of interview

Marital Status	On Migration	At Interview
Single	222	61
Married	90	206
Cohabiting	18	38
Separated	2	10
Divorced	8	17
Widowed	1	9

Source: Ackers (1998)

The pattern identified in the current project is quite similar, although we did not ask for detailed information about parents' marital status prior to their move:

Table 4.3 Current marital status of the sample of parents interviewed

Marital Status	% of Respondents
Married	78.7
Divorced	8.2
Separated	6
Cohabiting	4.4
Widowed	2.7

Amongst the sample, there were eight cases in which parents were unmarried and cohabiting. The lower rate of cohabitation probably reflects the tendency of many cohabiting couples to marry when they have children. Moreover, since the statistic reflects the parents' marital status at the time of the interview, it does not reveal periods of cohabitation prior to the birth of their children.

The decision in the current project to target families in which there was a child aged between 10 and 18 was referred to in chapter two. The majority of children interviewed fell into the categories of 10-14 year olds (41 per cent) or 15-18 year olds (48 per cent). In that sense, these families may not be representative of other EU migrant families which may contain a greater proportion of children in the younger or older age brackets (who fell outside our sample). We did, however, collect some general data from the respondents on the numbers of siblings within the household and/or family.[21] The majority of children interviewed had at least one brother or sister with relatively few living as single children:

Table 4.4 Number of children in respondents' families*

Number of Children	% of Respondents
1	16%
2	48%
3+	36%

* This figure includes step-children

'International Families'

The majority of women interviewed in the previous gender and migration project (Ackers, 1998) discussed above, met their partners and subsequently married in the host state resulting in high levels of intermarriage or what are conveniently referred to in this book as 'international families'.[22] Similarly, 96 of the 180 children (53 per cent) interviewed for the current project lived in such families.

[21] This was not always the same as in some cases step-children lived with a different parent or children had remained in a different country to complete their education. These issues are discussed in chapter six.

[22] By this we mean families in which the parents and/or children currently, or in the past, have held a different nationality to that of their partner (many women, in particular, take their partner's nationality or assume dual status upon marriage).

The fact that the majority of children lived in these types of families reflects the migratory patterns of their parents. Around 50 per cent of the parents had, in fact, met their partner following their move and in many, but by no means all cases, married a national of the host state. The remainder came to the host state together, often from a common home state, but also quite commonly from another Member State (in other words, it was not their first international move).

The prevalence of 'international families' is also reflected in the nationality status of the children of whom 79 had dual nationality. Of these, 69 were dual EU nationals and the remaining 10 held *both* Community nationality and the nationality of a non-Member State. The international nature of the majority of families has important consequences in situations of family breakdown, typically implying the geographical separation of parents and children.[23] Restrictions are also placed on a third country national partner who may have legal residence under domestic immigration law in one Member State but who will not be able to migrate to another Member State unless she/he is married to an EU national, even if the couple are cohabiting and have children.[24]

The data presented above provides some important contextual background about EU migrant families and assists us in assessing the potential impact of Community law. Of course, there are difficulties inherent in making reliable comparisons on the basis of national demographic statistics that vary significantly in accordance with divergent methods of data collation. The above data does serve, however, to illustrate widespread changes in family life and family formation that manifest themselves in the migrant as much as the non-migrant family. Furthermore, although domestic and comparative data does not reveal the rate of migration amongst less conventional family forms, the fact that national figures indicate a widespread increase in cohabitation, it would seem reasonable to suggest that similar partnering and parenting patterns characterise the EU migrant family. The prevalence of children within the EU migrant family, in spite of a widespread decline in the fertility rate across the EU, highlights the extent to which restrictive concepts of 'spouse' can impact upon children.

---

[23] Reported in chapters six and seven.

[24] The proposed Directive on the right to family reunification will clearly impact upon the status of these individuals if it is implemented. This is discussed in the next section.

Legal and Policy Responses at Member State Level to the Developing Nature of the Family

Member States have responded in varying degrees to the dramatic changes that have taken place in how individuals negotiate their personal relationships and family life through the implementation of legal and policy measures. The Netherlands, for instance, instituted the formal registration of partnerships for both heterosexual and homosexual couples in 1998, making legally registered cohabitation functionally equivalent to marriage.[25] Family law in Sweden, Finland and Denmark has been adapted to endow cohabiting couples with comparable rights to married couples, whilst the French government has instituted Civil Solidarity Pacts (PACS) allowing heterosexual and homosexual couples (co-residing for a minimum of three years) broadly equivalent inheritance, tax, health and tenancy rights as those held by married couples.

While developments at national level are to be welcomed, empirical reality has yet to trigger a redefinition of 'family' at the European level under free movement provisions. As such, EU law continues to cater for the neat and increasingly uncommon scenario of the nuclear male breadwinning family, where both parents hold Community nationality and are legally married. This entrenched and highly exclusive status of 'family' raises a number of practical and ideological concerns with potentially serious consequences for children. Firstly, it may constitute a barrier to mobility for the whole family. Hantrais (1997) suggests that the way in which the family is conceptualised (under Regulation 1612/68) may be an important factor in encouraging or deterring intra-European family migration. Where the Community worker is required or decides to move, the non-qualifying partner (typically the woman) may be forced, in view of the situation, to remain in the home state with consequences for themselves and their children in terms of, for example, residence, contact and parental support. Lundström (1996, p.271) clarifies this situation:

> If we consider the situation of cohabitees who are contemplating moving to one of the [EU Member States] where a job offer has been made to one of them, we are concerned ... with an 'illegitimate' family which is facing certain choices and risks which do not confront 'legitimate' families. In the light of the risks the couple may feel obliged to cease cohabiting and live in separate countries. The choice of declining the job offer and staying in the country of abode is another risk-avoiding option, which in addition allows

[25] The Netherlands in this respect went one step further than Denmark which implemented this measure in the context of homosexual relationships in the early 1990s. This will be further discussed later in the context of same-sex couples.

> the couple to remain together. It also represents a failure for the notion of the freedom of movement. Only marriage would put an end to the dilemma of choices. [26]

While the child has a right to reside in the Member State in which the migrant parent is working and, in this respect, is in a privileged position compared to the worker's unemployed partner, the law may be essentially depriving the child of its ability to exercise choice in terms of residency by limiting the rights of the unmarried partner (Schiewe, 1994, p.250-1).

Secondly, the free movement family formula conflicts with more recent Community measures in the domain of family rights. A recently adopted directive on family reunification, for instance (adopted on the basis of Article 63 EC), seeks to introduce a right to family reunification for third country nationals who are legally resident in the territory of a Member State.[27] Family members eligible under this proposed directive include the applicant's spouse or cohabitant, their children, the children of just one of the partners or spouses, any ascendant relatives and dependent children (Article 5) (Brinkmann, 2000; Kostakopolou, 2002).[28]

A third concern arising out of the application of the traditional free movement formula is its patent inconsistency with established human rights practice and, notably, with parallel interpretations of family rights under Article 8 of the European Convention on Human Rights 1950 (ECHR). More specifically, the Strasbourg institutions have gone some way towards acknowledging modern patterns of family life by applying what is commonly referred to as the 'reality test', whereby *de facto* family relationships are taken into account when considering whether or not 'family life' exists. In other words the European Court and Commission of Human Rights draws a distinction between family *relationships* and family *life*, acknowledging that one is not necessarily synonymous with the other to trigger the protection of Article 8. Instead, they assess the reality of the ties between the family members as well as evidence of close personal links such as a relationship of emotional (as opposed to merely economic)

---

[26] Indeed, the previous project on women and migration provides evidence of individuals marrying strategically in order bring themselves within Community protection (Ackers, 1998, pp.260-269).

[27] COM (1999) 638 final 1999/0258 (CNS). See also proposed amendments, COM (2000) 624), 10 October 2000. Finally approved by the Council of Ministers on 22 September 2003, this directive will not apply to Denmark, the UK and Ireland.

[28] A similar extension to the concept of family is also apparent in EU provisions relating to divorce and parental responsibility and will be considered in more detail in chapter seven.

dependency between the parties (O'Donnell, 1995; Liddy, 1998; Kilkelly, 1999; Stalford, 2002).[29]

The disparate approaches of the EU and ECHR systems is increasingly difficult to justify as the EU articulates ever more formally its commitments to fundamental human rights and adherence to the minimum standards set out in the ECHR. This has manifested itself in the adoption of the Charter of Fundamental Rights in the European Union.[30] Its non-binding, porous provisions clearly articulate the principles enshrined in the ECHR, reproducing Article 8 within its Article 7.[31] Such a move supports calls for a shift in approach by the ECJ in its interpretation of 'family' from one based exclusively on a legal or blood tie towards the 'reality', *de facto* approach of the European Court of Human Rights.

There is evidence, however, to suggest that the ECJ may be on the brink of addressing some of these anomalies. The joined cases of *Baumbast and 'R' v. Secretary of State for the Home Department*[32] involve claims by third country national spouses to remain in the host state with their children following the departure of the EU migrant worker husband either because of divorce or to take up work elsewhere.[33] Recommending an ongoing right of the family members to remain in the UK, Advocate General Geelhoed, in delivering his Opinion, referred to the limitations of the concept of spouse and family under Regulation 1612/68:

> Regulation 1612/68 dates back to a time when family relationships were relatively stable. The social legislation of the 1950s and 1960s – like the regulation – makes provision for the traditional family in which the husband is the breadwinner and the wife takes care of the household and the children. The traditional family of course continues to exist but has become much less dominant amongst the forms of cohabitation in the Western world. Family relationships and forms of cohabitation have become less stable and more varied ... An additional factor is that families in which spouses are of different nationalities or where children of other nationalities are present are occurring more and more frequently, precisely as a result of

[29] For examples see *Boughanemi v. France*, judgment of 24 April 1996, Reports 1996-II, no.8, p.593, 22 EHRR 228; *Kroon*, ECHR, Judgement 27 October 1994, § 30; *Marckx* (1979) 2 EHRR 330; *Keegan v. Ireland*, Judgment of 26 May 1994, Series A no.290.

[30] Adopted at the Nice Summit on 7th December 2000, Official Journal of the European Communities, 2000/C-364/01, 18.12.2000.

[31] Article 7 provides that "Everyone has the right to respect his or her private and family life, home and communications".

[32] Case C-413/99, Opinion of Advocate General Geelhoed, delivered on 5 July 2001, and Judgment of the Court of 17th September 2002, Case C-413/99.

[33] The legal issues raised by these cases are considered also in chapters seven and eight in the context of divorce and the educational rights of EU migrant children respectively.

> the increasing mobility of persons. These families may include nationals of non-Member States. For those reasons those persons have on their own account no right under Community law to reside in the United Kingdom (paragraph 23).

The Advocate General referred also to the need to adhere to fundamental human rights principles in the interpretation of Community law, noting that 'Regulation 1612/68 must … be interpreted in the light of the requirement for respect for private and family life set out in Article 8 of the Convention for the Protection of Human Rights and Fundamental Freedoms' (Paragraph 58). Acknowledging also the relevance (although of a non-binding nature) of Article 7 of the Charter of Fundamental rights, he went on to note that:

> As a general principle, there is family life where there is a lawful and genuine marriage. Other relationships of sufficient permanence stand on the same footing as such as marriage. Moreover the family link may only be broken in exceptional circumstances by subsequent events (paragraph 59).

Despite these tentative steps by the Advocate General towards a more rights-based conceptualisation of the family, the ECJ considered the issue in the light of the potential impact deportation would have on their children. The ECJ did not, therefore, grasp the opportunity to clarify and update the status of divorced or separated third country national migrants, but instead based the women's ongoing right to remain in the host state on the caring and educational needs of their children.

The Status of Same-Sex Couples under Community Law

Similar definitional restrictions inherent in Regulation 1612/68 and other aspects of Community law arise in relation to same-sex partners whose status has come under more recent ECJ scrutiny thus throwing traditional notions of the family into further disarray. In *Grant v South West Trains*,[34] for instance, the ECJ declined to extend the scope of Article 141 of the Equal Pay Directive[35] to entitle the homosexual partner of an employee with the same pension rights as those available to heterosexual employees' cohabitees (McGlynn, 2000: 225; Stychin, 2000; Wintemute and Andenæs, 2001). Equally, in *D and Sweden v. Council*,[36] the Court rejected

[34] Case C-249/96 *Grant v. South West Trains* [1998] IRLR.

[35] Council Directive 75/117 of 10 February 1975, OJ 1975, No. L45/19.

[36] Above note 12.

homosexual registered partnership as the basis for a claim to a household allowance which was otherwise granted to married, divorced, or separated partners and dependent children. Failure by the ECJ to adopt a more progressive stance in this regard is based on a perceived 'lack of consensus' among Member States about the value and sustainability of non-marital relationships.[37] It is this alleged 'lack of consensus', however, that has seen an increasing number of Member States (the Netherlands, Denmark, Sweden, Luxembourg, and even the UK) instituting registered partnerships to endow same-sex couples with similar legal rights as married couples. The same alleged 'lack of consensus' has seen the legalisation of gay *marriage* in the Netherlands[38] with similar moves underway in Germany, Belgium and Finland to relax laws to allow same-sex weddings (Shelley, 2001; Stalford, 2002; Sumner, 2002).

Other EU developments have not been entirely consistent in their exclusion of same-sex couples from the ambit of Community protection. In *P v. S and Cornwall City Council*, for instance, the ECJ extended the Equal Treatment Directive to cover discrimination on grounds of trans-sexuality.[39] This case law has been supported by additional legal and policy developments within the EU institutions. For example, the European Parliament, in its Resolution on Equal Rights for homosexuals and lesbians in the European Community called for 'full rights and benefits of marriage [to] be made available to same-sex couples.'[40] More significantly, the Treaty of Amsterdam 1997 introduced Article 13 into the EC Treaty providing a legal basis allowing the Council to 'take appropriate action to combat discrimination based on sex, racial or ethnic origin, religion, or belief, disability, age or *sexual orientation*.' This has been substantiated by a range of funding and policy initiatives aimed at promoting equal treatment of lesbians and gays across the Member States. For instance, the European Parliament, as part of its adopted report and resolution on the respect for human rights in the European Union, denounced the continuing social and legal discrimination of gays and lesbians across the Member

---

[37] It is interesting to note that in *D and Sweden v. Council*, the ECJ referred to but declined to rely on Article 8 ECHR (paras 58-62). It also declined the opportunity to consider the case in the context of Article 7 of the new Charter of Fundamental Rights in the European Union.

[38] On April 1st 2001, the Netherlands became the first Member State to legalise adoption by same-sex couples of children whose ordinary place of residence is in the Netherlands.

[39] Case C-13/94 [1996] ECR I-2143.

[40] Resolution adopted 8 February [1994] OJ C61/40.

States and issued a series of recommendations to address their specific human rights concerns.[41] These included calling upon Member States:

> to guarantee one-parent families, unmarried couples and same-sex couples rights equal to those enjoyed by traditional couples and families, particularly as regards tax law, pecuniary rights and social rights ... if they have not already done so, to amend their legislation recognising registered partnerships of persons of the same-sex and assigning them the same rights and obligations as exist for registered partnerships between men and women ... and calls on those States which have not yet granted legal recognition to amend their legislation to grant legal recognition of extramarital cohabitation, irrespective of gender; [and] that rapid progress should be made with mutual recognition of the different legally recognised non-marital modes of cohabitation and legal marriages between persons of the same-sex in the EU (paragraph 56 and 57).

The Parliament accompanies this with a cautionary warning: 'the European Union will reject the accession of any applicant country which, either in its legislation or in its practice, fails to guarantee respect for human rights' (paragraph 77).

Consistent with these developments, in November 2000 the Council of Ministers of the EU adopted a directive 'establishing a general framework for equal treatment in employment and occupation' (The Framework Directive).[42] This obliges the Member States to introduce by 2nd December 2003 comprehensive legislation prohibiting discrimination at the workplace on the grounds of religion or belief, disability, age or sexual orientation (Article 1).[43]

It is important to note the extent to which the language of non-discrimination can provide a powerful rhetorical tool to advance the status of same-sex and other cohabiting couples. In the case of *Reed* mentioned above, for instance, the defendant, having failed to qualify as a 'spouse' under Article 10 Regulation 1612/68, succeeded on the basis of the equal treatment principle in Article 7(2), arguing that the worker's right to be joined by his partner facilitated his integration in the society of the host

---

[41] European Parliament resolution on respect for human rights in the European Union (1998-1999) (11350/1999 – C5-0265/1999 – 1999/2001(INI)) under the heading of: 'Lifestyles and types of relationship'. See also, the European Parliament resolution on the situation as regards fundamental rights in the EU (2002) – 2002/2013 (INI); the European Parliament resolution on human rights in the world in 2002; and the EU's human rights policy 2002/2011 (INI).

[42] COM (1999) 565 final 1999/0225 (CNS) For a detailed overview of the provisions of this directive, see ILGA Euro-letter n° 92, October 2001, Copenhagen.

[43] In accordance with Article 13 EC.

state and therefore constituted a 'social benefit'. The same principle could theoretically be invoked by Community nationals (and their partners in registered partnerships) who migrate to those countries (such as the Netherlands) in which national law recognises such partnerships as the legal equivalent of marriage. On this basis, a refusal to allow a homosexual third country national to reside with their employed partner in another Member State would amount to discrimination under Article 7(2) if such a right is granted to its nationals. Indeed, the *Reed* judgement has provided the incentive for European Parliament and Council proposals for a new directive on the right of citizens of the Union and their family members to move and reside freely within the territory of the Member States.[44] The proposed directive states that 'family member' should include 'spouse, as well as the unmarried partner, if the legislation of the host Member States treats unmarried couples as equivalent to married couples and in accordance with the conditions laid down in any such legislation' (Article 2). Whilst these developments essentially represent a welcome codification of the *Reed* decision, they do little to significantly enhance the status of cohabitants moving to less permissive Member States (such as Ireland and Greece) where there is still no parallel provision for same-sex national couples.[45]

The discussion so far has detailed how substantial social rights have been extended to spouses and the children of Community workers. The case law, however, demonstrates that while children obtain enhanced status by virtue of their relationship with their migrant parents, the Court's primary concern remains an economic one: that is, to facilitate the mobility of the worker. Its perception of the family and children as a secondary, less pressing and certainly less economically valuable consideration is reflected in the ECJ's persistently restrictive definition of 'spouse'. Whilst avoiding the tendency to imply that the interests of families and children are necessarily coterminous, the definition and status of the family in Community law will have important consequences for children, particularly those who fall outside Community protection. The next section, therefore, shifts the focus onto children in families who *do* fall within Community definitions in order to examine the quality of children's status as autonomous agents under EU law.

---

[44] COM (2001) 257, final. For the latest developments, see COM (2003) 199 final.

[45] Again, it is interesting to speculate on the potential impact of the Charter of Fundamental Rights in the European Union in this context and particularly of Article 21 which explicitly prohibits discrimination on grounds of sexual orientation in line with Article 13 EC. For a useful analysis see Sumner, 2002.

Proposals for a General Free Movement Directive

The widely-critiqued definition of 'family' described above has provided the object of recent proposals for reform. The proposed general directive on free movement for citizens of the Union and their family members[46] mentioned above represents arguably the most significant overhaul of the free movement legislation since the 1960s.

The proposal represents an attempt to set out citizenship and free movement rights more comprehensively within a single document and to bring the rights of migrant family members in line with nationals who move internally within a given Member State. As already stated, the definition of 'family member' is broader than that of Regulation 1612/68 in that it covers not only the spouse, but unmarried partners, provided that the host state treats unmarried couples as equivalent to married couples (Article 2(2)). In that sense, unmarried partners capacity to qualify as a family member remains contingent on the individual Member State's approach to these partnerships and will differ, therefore, depending on the Member State in which the family wish to reside. Article 4 of the Directive strengthens the non-discrimination ethic underlying the application of free movement by extending the number of prohibited grounds for discrimination in line with Article 13 EC.[47] Chapter II (Article 6) of the proposed directive grants family members a general right to move and reside for up to six months provided they have a valid passport or identity card. Those that wish to stay more than six months are governed by Chapter III (Article 7) which relates to the employed, self-employed, the economically independent, students and any family members of these individuals. Furthermore, a new right of permanent residence is granted to EU migrants and their families who have legally and continuously resided in the host state for four consecutive years (Article 14) and, in some circumstances, even earlier (Article 15). Significantly, a new Article 13 sets out the applicable rules in cases of divorce or relationship breakdown to ensure that this does not automatically imply the loss of free movement status, even where the ex-spouse of partner is of third country nationality.[48] Finally, Articles 20-21 confirm the right of family members to equal

---

[46] Proposal for a European Parliament and Council Directive on the Right of Citizens of the Union and their Family Members to Move and Reside Freely within the Territory of the Member States, COM (2001) 257 final, OJ C 270 E, 25.09.2001.

[47] To cover sex, race, colour, ethnic or social origin, genetic characteristics, language, religion or beliefs, political or other opinion, membership of a minority, property, birth, disability, age of sexual orientation.

[48] For further suggested refinement of these provisions, see the European Parliament Report, 23rd January 2003, Final A5-00009/2003.

treatment in the allocation of benefits, and access to and conditions of employment and education.

If implemented, these will consolidate the status of family members as independent rights-bearers under Community law. The institution of a right to remain afforded to third country nationals following family breakdown is particularly welcomed and will no doubt impact positively on the experiences of any children involved.

The Concept of 'Child' in Community Law

The substance of Regulation 1612/68 and its accompanying case law prompts a discussion of the nature of a migrant child's status and the extent to which Community law presumes and reinforces paternalistic relationships of dependency on breadwinning parents. As already noted, the categories of individuals entitled to benefit from the provisions of the Regulation are defined by reference to their relationship with the EU migrant worker. This suggests that, unless the children qualify as workers in their own right, their status as EU migrants is incomplete and certainly not an independent one. To the extent that children under employable age are unable to qualify as workers, they have less ability to 'jump up a tier' and claim independent status as Community workers. In that sense they have less scope to exercise agency than spouses.

Article 12, for instance, which refers specifically and exclusively to children, is conditional upon an ongoing relationship of dependency with the parent worker. Thus, in *Brown*[49] it was decided that Article 12 would not create rights in the host state for a child born after the migrant worker parent ceased to work and reside there. The definition of dependency was discussed in some detail in *Echternach and Moritz.*[50] *Moritz* involved a German national who had moved with his family when his father secured employment in the Netherlands. The child then spent most of his primary and secondary education in the Netherlands, returned with his parents to Germany and subsequently went back on his own to the Netherlands where he claimed financial support to continue his studies. The Netherlands initially refused this support on the grounds that he was no longer dependent on the migrant worker-parent:

---

[49] Case 197/86 *Steven Brown v. Secretary of State for Scotland* [1988]CMLR 403.

[50] Joined Cases 389 and 390/87 *Echternach & Moritz v. Netherlands Minister for Education* [1989]1 CMLR 393, discussed also in chapters eight and nine.

> The rights and duties of the son are solely determined by his father's employment ... he has his own accommodation ... is over the age of majority ... lives with his partner ... and is no longer supported by his parents and thus no longer forms part of the family for the purposes of Article 12 of Regulation 1612/68 (paragraph 42).

More specifically the Netherlands' government suggested that children's rights were both derived from and coterminous with those of the qualifying parent:

> The rights concerned are rights derived from those of the worker himself. The Treaty does not confer any independent right on children' (paragraph 43).

Advocate General Darmon took the Commission's view, however, that the decisive criterion was not the parent's departure or dependency as such, but whether or not the proposed studies were related to the child's previous residence. He concluded that 'the fact that the parent moves does not deprive a child of his rights' (paragraph 43).

The decision of the Court in this case undoubtedly extends the autonomy of the migrant child. Indeed, the Advocate General acknowledged the vulnerability that might arise should a child's rights be made conditional upon the continued residence of the parent-worker which would 'place the family in a highly precarious situation, quite often dependent on the father's behaviour' (paragraph 48). Rather than confronting the whole issue of derived entitlement, however, the Advocate General reaffirmed the derived basis of children's rights whilst suggesting the need for a broad interpretation in order to comply with the facilitating mobility test:

> An interpretation of the regulation making the derivative rights of members of migrant worker's families in a host state strictly conditional on those workers' maintaining their residence in the host state would be likely to affect the freedom of movement of workers (paragraph 49).

The effect of this ruling would seem to be that the child must be able to demonstrate that, at some point in time, he or she was living in a relationship of dependency with the qualifying worker-parent in the state in which the child is making the claim. Once this qualifying condition is met, the child may retain their status following the departure of their parent. In that sense, the Court stops short of granting the child an independent entitlement maintaining the albeit tenuous link with the facilitating mobility principle.

Lubor Gaal[51] marks a more radical departure from a literal interpretation of the dependency criteria and discussed in some detail the concept of 'child' in Community law. The case involved a Belgian national who was dependent on the German state in *loco parentis* following the death of his father. Gaal's claim for financial assistance to enable him to pursue his university studies in the UK was rejected by the German authorities on the grounds that he no longer fell within the eligibility criteria under Regulation 1612/68 (i.e. he was neither under 21 nor 'dependent' on his father). In his Opinion, Advocate General Tesauro referred to the lack of any judicial interpretation of the concept of child in Regulation 1612/68: 'The fact is that not one article and still less the preamble contains a definition of child which must be applied to each of the provisions' (paragraph 7).

In the absence of any specific definition of 'child' in Article 12, the German authorities implied the dependency criteria in Article 10 (see above), thereby restricting Gaal's entitlement. The Court, however, found that Article 12 is not subject to the same conditions of age or dependency as are the rights governed by Article 10(1) and Article 11 of that Regulation. The effect of this ruling would seem to be that the concept of child under Article 12 is not subject to any requirement of age or dependency. The biological child of a migrant worker is thus endowed with the same educational rights as those available to national children. This ruling significantly enhances the independent status of migrant workers' children on the basis of their status as the biological children of migrant workers. In the process, however, it reaffirms the dependency requirement for claims made on any basis other than Article 12. Indeed, Advocate General Tesauro refers to the difficulties of operationalising dependency as a mechanism for the interpretation of Community law:

> Even persons under 21 years of age may have dependants, it is equally true that the idea of a person being dependent on someone who is, in turn, dependent on another makes no sense at all (paragraph 13).

Referring here to *Echternach and Moritz,* Advocate General Tesauro specifically recognised the complexity of intergenerational (life-course) dependencies (which are by no means unusual in practice). The case of

---

[51] Case C-7/94 *Landesamt fur Ausbildungsforderung Nordrhein-Westfalen v. Lubor Gaal* [1996]ECR 1-1031.

Lebon[52] provides an example of intergenerational dependency in that the claimant, as well as being the child of a migrant worker, had a child herself. The claimant was a French national who had lived in Belgium since her birth with her parents. Lebon claimed a subsistence allowance from the Belgian welfare authorities having returned from a two-year period working in France. The allowance was withdrawn some months later on the basis that there was no evidence of her intention to find employment. On appeal to the ECJ (on the basis of the 'social advantages' clause in Article 7(2) Regulation 1612/68), it was held that the applicant was no longer entitled to receive the benefits since her previous allocation was based on her status as the child of a migrant worker and that in the circumstances, 'that benefit does not constitute for the worker a social advantage...in as much as he is no longer supporting his descendant'.[53]

This decision raises two main issues. Firstly, the case illuminates the inconsistencies inherent in Regulation 1612/68 as regards its personal scope, particularly in the light of the *Lubor Gaal* decision in which the age and dependency criteria of Article 10 were not applicable to claims under Article 12 of the Regulation. On this basis, it would seem that had *Lebon* applied for a maintenance grant to study under Article 12 as opposed to social security provision under Article 7(2), she would not have been excluded in spite of her failure to satisfy the dependency criteria. The law, therefore, treats some migrant children more favourably than others, according to whether they decide to pursue full-time studies or not and according to whether their parents are alive or not thus reinforcing functionalist and consensus-driven conceptions of family relations.

Secondly, *Lubor Gaal* raises wider questions about the rationale underpinning the Court's more expansive approach. Whilst it evidently advances the status of migrant workers' children as independent citizens, the reasoning behind this interpretation suggests an adherence to the 'facilitating mobility' idea and the 'importance of eliminating all obstacles to the mobility of workers' (paragraph 8). We have already noted the lack of research evidence to substantiate this claim. In practice, the research findings suggests that prospective migrants have very little detailed awareness of their Community rights and are often moving at a point in their life-course when such concerns are of tangential interest to them.[54] In

---

52 Case 316/85 *Centre public d'aide social de Courcelles v. Marie-Christine Lebon* [1987]ECR 2811.

53 Above note at p. 2836.

54 We are referring specifically here to the Gaal case and the impact it has on the dependency requirement under Article 12 as, in most cases, children would qualify under the age/dependency criteria This is not to understate the importance of other decisions affecting the personal scope of entitlement (on the concept of spouse, for example).

that sense, 'facilitating mobility' becomes a somewhat theoretical and empirically unfounded rationale for the extension of material rights.

In very recent years, however, some highly significant legal and judicial developments have occurred adding considerable substance to children's potential as rights-bearers, both as independent Community citizens and as part of the family unit.

Firstly, the decision in *Baumbast* (referred to above) sought to develop even further the ECJ interpretation of Article 12 Regulation 1612/68 in *Lubor Gaal* and *Echtnernach and Moritz*. While the facts of Baumbast ostensibly address the rights of the non-EU parent to remain with her children in the host state as primary-carer following the father's departure, the ECJ's rationale for allowing her to remain rests primarily on the children's status under Community law. It conceded that there would be little sense in enabling the children to pursue their schooling in the host state independently of their worker parent without also accommodating their need to be cared for by the other parent. Interestingly, therefore, this case creates a situation whereby the children, who initially derived their Community entitlement under the free movement provisions from the migrant worker parent, subsequently become the key source of entitlement for their non-qualifying parents. Cullen (2002) argues that this decision represents not so much an attempt to significantly enhance children's independent Community status, but rather, reflects the common tendency to develop their rights within the family unit. The fact that the spouse and children's ongoing claim to Community entitlement was considered in isolation from that of the migrant worker, however, represents a positive departure from the ubiquitous 'facilitating mobility' model.

Humer[55] is another case in point. It concerned the claim of a child to receive an advance on her child maintenance contributions from the Austrian authorities after her father had defaulted on his payments. The ECJ concluded that her status as the child of a migrant worker entitled her to claim benefits directly from the Austrian authorities since such support was available to Austrian nationals. It was deemed irrelevant that the child had always lived in France with her divorced Austrian mother and had never herself migrated. Whilst the child's status under Community law is developed within the confines of her family life, there is much to suggest a move towards broader considerations as to the child's general welfare as the basis for extending entitlement (Cullen, 2002).

The Charter of Fundamental Rights in the European Union is, again, significant in this respect not least because it seeks to address the exclusively family-based approach to children's rights by recognising the

---

[55] Case C-255/99, judgment of 5 February 2002. This is discussed in detail in chapter seven.

independent interests of the child.[56] While a number of the Charter provisions are applicable to children (in much the same way as the general provisions of the ECHR),[57] Article 24 of the Charter contains a set of tailored provisions, echoing in particular the spirit and content of the 1989 UNCRC:

1. Children shall have the right to such protection and care as is necessary for their well-being. They may express their views freely. Such views shall be taken into consideration on matters which concern them in accordance with their age and maturity.
2. In all actions relating to children, whether taken by public authorities or private institutions, the child's best interests must be a primary consideration.
3. Every child shall have the right to maintain on a regular basis a personal relationship and direct contact with both his or her parents, unless that is contrary to his or her interests.

Although the emphasis here is much more on child protection than agency (Cullen, 2002), the Charter represents a significant and direct expression of children's rights at EU level where virtually none had existed before. Indeed, while the Charter is currently of non-binding force – and, in that sense, is more aspirational than revolutionary – it has placed children much more firmly and visibly on the Community agenda. Certainly, the increasing regularity with which the EU institutions are already referring to the provisions of the Charter demonstrates its potential as a 'child proofing' mechanism for future law and policy-making.[58]

---

[56] Of course, we are not suggesting that the family unit is not a crucial arena for developing and nurturing children's rights. There are cases, however, as the discussion in chapter seven will highlight, where the interests and wishes of the child are not coterminous with those of the parents and where it may be necessary to consider the child's rights and needs in isolation from those of the parents. For, as Cullen (2002) notes, it is essential that situating children's rights in a network of family and other relationships empowers rather than undermines children.

[57] For example: Article 14 provides for a right to education; Article 21, a prohibition of discrimination on grounds of age; Article 32, prohibition of child labour and protection of young people at work; Article 7, the right to respect for private and family life; and Article 5, a prohibition on slavery, forced labour and trafficking in human beings. For a general analysis of the impact of the Charter on families, see McGlynn, (2001a) and Cullen (2002).

[58] See for instance A-G Jacobs' Opinion in *Z v EP*, Mar. 22, 2001, C-270/99 P; A-G Geelhoed's Opinion in *Baumbast,* Jul 5 2001, C-413/99; A-G Leger's Opinion in *Wouters,* Jul 10 200, C-309/99. The Charter has also been considered in proposals for new EC legislation such as the Directive on tobacco advertising, COM (2000)1) 283, the Direcive on environmental crime, COM (2001) 139, on the Regulation relating to asylum responsibility, COM (2001) 447, and on the adopted Regulation 1049/2001 relating to access to documents, OJ 2001, L 145/43.

Conclusion

This chapter has documented the evolution of the concept of 'family' in Community Law and the extent to which this reflects and potentially reinforces traditional models of the 'functional' nuclear family. The empirical and legal evidence presented above raise some serious concerns about the extent to which this definition effectively represents and accommodates the situation of 'real' migrant families in Europe today. As it stands, ECJ interpretations of Article 10 Regulation 1612/68 imply a distinction in legal entitlement (and thus citizenship status) between those families that 'conform' to the traditional model and those that fall outside of it.

However, in spite of the continuing ambivalence of the ECJ towards adopting a more progressive approach to the family, more judicial positive steps have been taken, particularly throughout the latter part of the 1990s, towards advancing the concept of 'family' and 'child' beyond the parasitic free movement formula. Perhaps the most promising and fertile developments to have occurred in this respect are in the context of the Union's increasingly prominent human rights agenda. The Charter of Fundamental Rights in the European Union, in particular, clearly articulates a commitment to safeguarding and enhancing family and children's rights in ways that are no longer conditional upon furthering the interests of the migrant worker and, ultimately, the economic interests of the Community. The extent to which this will pave the way for a more inclusive and substantial sense of EU citizenship, however, remains to be seen.

5 From 'Best Interests' to Participatory Rights: Children's Involvement in Family Migration Decisions[1]

Introduction

We referred, in chapter three to the limited body of research on family and migration decision-making focusing on the involvement of partners (wives) and the issue of dual careers. Previous work (Ackers, 1998; 2001) has considered in some detail the nature of migration decision-making processes in this context of reconciling partnering and career progression with a focus particularly on the involvement of female partners in these life-course decisions. This chapter builds on that work to focus specifically on the experiences of migration decision-making processes in families with children. Some of the tensions between partner's careers emerge once again but so too do issues concerning the children. While the phenomenon of the 'trailing wife' or 'tied mover' raise complex issues around the relationship between economic roles and their influence on family decisions, no-one would question the fundamental notion that both partners should be involved in the process. The idea that children might be actively involved in family or migration decision-making is more contentious. The chapter first sets the context for a discussion of children's engagement with these processes within the emerging framework of children's rights and moves on to discuss how respondents talked about the involvement of children in migration decisions.

The Legal Framework: Children's Participatory Rights

The United Nations Convention on the Rights of the Child (UNCRC) (1989), now ratified by all EU Member States, is based upon three fundamental and interconnected principles; the 'welfare' or 'best interests'

[1] This section of the chapter is based on a previously published paper (Ackers, 2000).

principle (Article 3), the 'non-discrimination' principle (Article 2) and the 'participation' principle (Article12). Article Three states that:

> In all actions concerning children, whether undertaken by public or private social welfare institutions, courts of law, administrative authorities or legislative bodies, the best interests of the child shall be a primary consideration.

Article 12, refers to the need to, 'assure to the child who is capable of forming his or her own views the right to express those views freely in all matters affecting the child'.

Whilst early attention focused on the implementation of the best interest principle, concerned primarily with safeguarding children's interests (as the passive victims or beneficiaries of policy), recent years have witnessed something of a policy shift, identifying some tensions between the need to protect children's welfare and the extension of participatory rights. As Franklin (1995, p.3) notes,

> Legally, the notion of the 'best interests of the child' increasingly came to be supplemented, if not superseded, by the principle that where appropriate the wishes of the child should inform legal decisions.

Eekelaar (1994) attempts to reconcile this tension by asserting that the best interests principle should be properly understood to accommodate an opportunity for the child to determine what these best interests are. He proposes that children's views should be permitted to influence the outcome of the issue in question subject to the condition that it is compatible with the law and interests of others and, more controversially, is not contrary to his or her self-interest in terms of physical or mental well-being and integrity.

Recent legal developments within the UK have sought to articulate children's rights in these terms by focusing increasingly on the voice of the child and mechanisms to promote child participation while taking into account the child's individual characteristics and needs (in terms of age and maturity) and balancing these with the parents' responsibilities to act in the child's best nterests. The Children Act (England and Wales) 1989, for instance, with its emphasis on 'listening to children' states in Section One that the wishes and feelings of the child must be taken into account in the light of the child's age. The Children (Scotland) Act 1995 (Section 6) further provides that the views of children over twelve will be taken into account in relation to any 'major decisions' involving them.

This, according to Jeremy Roche (1996, 1999), has given rise to a different kind of debate at the core of the children's rights movement; a debate which questions how effective and real (as opposed to superficial or tokenistic) participation can be achieved and whether children themselves will perceive this as in any way meaningful to their lives. It also raises concerns around the operational strategies practitioners, policy-makers and families can adopt to make children's participation a reality compatible with parental roles.

In the main, practical discussion about children's participatory rights has largely taken place at judicial and administrative level, at the interface between the family and the public arena. The family itself, as the context of decision-making processes, has only been brought into the analysis when 'dysfunctional' elements exist and external, typically public, bodies have been brought in to regulate family relationships. The involvement of children in important areas of decision-making continues to be viewed as unimportant in 'functional' family units. The assumption would seem to be that such families operate with children's best interests in mind; only when consensus breaks down is the presumption rebutted.

There are two reasons for turning our attention to decision-making processes within families. Firstly, the legislation theoretically encompasses such situations. While the wording of Article 3 UNCRC (1989) implies a fairly narrow concern with public bodies, the reference to 'all matters concerning the child' in Article 12 could be interpreted more constructively. The Scottish Law Commission (1992, paras 2.62-64, cited in Roche 1999, p.490), when considering the possibility of extending participatory rights beyond the state to parents, made the following observations:

> The question as we saw it was whether a parent or other persons exercising parental rights should be under a similar obligation to ascertain and have regard to the child's wishes and feelings as a local authority was in relation to a child in its care ... There are great attractions in such an approach. It emphasises that the child is a person in his or her own right and that his or her views are entitled to respect and consideration. On consultation there was majority support for a provision requiring parents in reaching any major decision relating to a child, to ascertain the child's wishes and feelings as far as practicable and give due consideration to them having regard to their age and understanding.

The commitment, expressed in this statement, to the symbolic potential of constructing the child as citizen is referred to by Roche (1999) who suggests that focusing greater attention on the family unit itself as a forum for change, rather than pushing for change from the 'top' down, forces one to examine how power relationships within the family unit are conducive to effective child participation.

Academic debate over the past few years has focused on the need to establish the case for children's rights at the theoretical and conceptual level. The success of this approach can be witnessed not simply in terms of the extension of formal legal rights, but also in its emphasis on children's subjectivity drawing children into the debate around inclusivity and citizenship (for a recent summary of EU developments see Stalford, 2000). Echoing the recent campaign organised by the European Children's Network (EURONET),[2] Roche (1996, p.24) outlines the objective as one of 'taking all children seriously and as seeing them as citizens too':

> Rights are not just about state-citizen relations but about how civil society should imagine itself; in this context the imagery of social conversation and participation is central to the rethinking of citizenship (Roche, 1999, p.475).

Notwithstanding the symbolic importance of these debates it has proved difficult to understand the implications of them for the everyday lives of children and parents. As Franklin (1995, p.6) cautions, 'in the effort to address these general and theoretical considerations practical suggestions for change have often been overlooked'. Roche (1996, p.26). similarly encourages us to move on from theorising to:

> ... rethinking the contexts in which issues of children's rights arise ... the issue now is not one of establishing the principle of children's rights but of extending the range of situations where the language is perceived as legitimate.

Migration Decision-Making

This chapter explores some of the issues raised in the debates around children's rights in the context of family decision-making and considers the impact of the children's rights discourse on social values and parenting within migrant families. International migration research rarely, if ever, considers the role of children in migration decision-making processes. To the extent that research has attempted to deal with migration decisions, this has typically taken place within a cost-benefit (or rational choice theory)

---

[2] EURONET is a coalition of networks and organisations campaigning for the interests and rights of children. The recent campaign was entitled 'Children are Citizens Too'.

approach focused on 'measuring the returns to migration'.[3] Underlying this approach is the presumption that 'voluntary' migration (as opposed to 'forced' moves) represents the outcome of decision-making processes based upon predictable economic returns. The notion of voluntarism and economic advancement also implies a consensual male breadwinning family model and a broad commonality of interests within the migrant family. The lack of research on the impact of migration on children makes it difficult to evaluate mobility in terms of children's 'best interests' or the impact on their quality of life and future life chances.[4] Limited research on the returns to wives reinforces the notion of migration decision-making as 'rational household strategy' since the economic returns to male breadwinners generally outweigh the costs to women of career dislocation (given their secondary labour market role). Given these narrow economic terms, it then becomes 'rational' – from the point of view of the family as a whole – for the unit to relocate.

Certainly, this was the view of some of the children interviewed who appeared to accept, unequivocally, the 'logic' of father's career progression. In many cases children accepted the necessity of moving and the determinacy of their fathers' decision: it was not so much a conflict of choice between family members but the overall expediency of the decision (and their understanding of it in those terms) that precipitated the move. In these situations, children 'echoed' the inherent rationality in the household strategy:

> None of these moves was a choice of any family member. My father had a very good salary and many benefits from his job. It would be foolish to risk a removal from the Company. We had a big apartment free of charge, a car that all its expenses were paid by the Company, which also paid the fees of our schools. Anyway, none of us was unhappy with these moves from country to country. They gave us the opportunity to have a nice, comfortable and interesting life [431].

> My father needs to work in different countries sometimes and if it is for a long time we follow him. We all move to the country where he works. It was the same here. He had to work in the construction of the metro in Athens [433].

---

[3] As distinct from the type of more anthropological or sociological study designed to evaluate the experiences of migrant groups in the 'diaspora'.

[4] This is the case, in practice, for many post-colonial migration flows – it is generally the more highly skilled social groups that have the resources to effect a move.

In fact, the majority of moves (67 per cent) were motivated primarily by parental (and mainly paternal) employment considerations. The importance of work as the principle motivation behind the movement of families can be contrasted with the findings of a previous project on gender and migration where women identified a far wider range of factors. These included the desire to travel and learn languages, to study or to join partners abroad (Ackers, 1998).

It is important to remember, however, that in these kinds of 'voluntary' mobility, the concern is typically with social or career mobility as opposed to economic necessity: it is not a zero sum game. The point at which such a cost-benefit analysis is made is also important: it is rather too late to evaluate the respective impact on partner's careers when the wife has already assumed a secondary labour market role prior to migration.[5] Detailed evaluation of the returns to migration, for children, would thus demand a life-course approach capable of encompassing a series of decisions as children's lives unfold, career trajectories develop, families form and caring relationships evolve. One young woman expressed her anger at the constant moves, initiated by the demands of her step-father's career, which she felt effectively undermined both her mother's autonomy (she had worked full-time in a good position and now cared for the siblings) and, in consequence, her own economic autonomy. Evaluating this case, in terms of the economic gains to the family as a whole, is therefore highly misleading:

> [My mum] used to work and she has lost independence through that and I resent him for making us have to move ... I have been told that when I have done my A levels Alan doesn't want to support me anymore – that's another reason why I am going back to Ireland. I've got to get out of home. My grandpa is [supporting me] – he's got a lot of money in the bank for me for University. I think Alan will support [her three half-siblings] through college but like my mum says, why should he support me with the attitude I have towards him – that's fair enough really – I just say, 'you can't say that, you're not my dad'. It's hypocritical! [004].

The young woman in this case, aged 16 at the time of interview, illustrates the complex issues involved in her migration history and the difficulty in attempting to evaluate the process in terms of her 'best

---

[5] In practice, previous research on gender and intra-Community mobility has indicated that the initial economic returns to EU migrant women (most of whom were single at the point of migration) are high: it is post-migration partnering and family formation that promotes downward career mobility for this group of women (*cf.* Ackers and Perista, 1998, pp.183-223).

interests'. At the point of interview she weighed up the whole scenario in quite positive terms and demonstrates an ability to reflect in a surprisingly rational way on her experiences. Some months later she returned on her own to Ireland.

Accordingly, a key difficulty in assessing the impact of migration on children's welfare lies in the presumption of shared interests and the failure to acknowledge the 'multiplicity of (competing) interests within families'. It is precisely this 'ideology of family privacy' that Roche (1999, p.478) contends 'results in family members being seen to 'volunteer''. This point, so relevant to migration decision-making, is also raised by Franklin (1995, p.4) who refers to the impact of the high profile and tragic deaths of Jasmine Beckford and Kimberley Carlisle which:

> ... exploded the myth of the family ... The perception of the family as a place of quiet sanctity increasingly became disrupted by a reluctant acknowledgement that children's interests and rights could not be presumed to be identical with those of their parents; indeed children's and parent's rights might be antipathetic.

Moving from theoretical prescription to practical policy demands consideration of various issues including the range of decisions in which children should be involved, identification of the group of 'eligible' children and, finally, the consequences of participation (in terms of outcome). Failing to deal with these issues, albeit within a specified context, runs the risk of participation becoming an empty and tokenistic gesture. Of course we need to listen to children, but how do we move from that to actively involving them in decision-making?

Treseder (1997, p.6) contends that, with the right kind of input, it is possible to involve children in 'just about any decision that affects them...so long as the process is properly thought out, is appropriate to the environment and suitable resources are available'. In emphasising the importance of context and a clear operational strategy (the absence of which will 'almost certainly lead to failure'), Treseder develops Hart's (1992) 'ladder of participation' model as the basis of an operational tool to promote child participation. Hart's 'ladder' usefully demonstrates alternative forms and consequences of child participation. The first three rungs of his eight-rung ladder are referred to as 'manipulation', 'decoration' and 'tokenism' representing the denial of participation and, indeed, the potential dangers of the rhetoric of participation. The remaining five represent shades of participation and include projects that are 'child designed and directed', 'adult designed with shared decisions with children' or in which children are 'consulted and informed' with their opinions taken seriously. The inference of a progressive hierarchy of levels of participation, moving towards some ultimate goal (in rung 8) has led Treseder (Figure 5.1) to adapt the metaphor, referring instead to a circular layout with the five rungs of participation presented as five different, but equal, forms of good practice:

Figure 5.1 Degrees of Child Participation

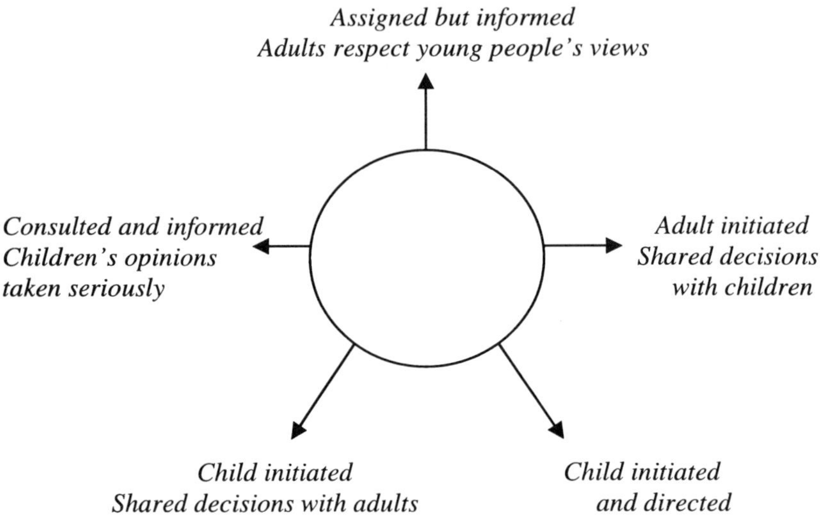

Source: Treseder, 1997.

Through the adoption of this model, the objective now becomes one of selecting the option that 'has most benefit in a specific environment'. Noticeably, it is a model that provides an interesting framework within which to establish relevant objectives and evaluate child participation in a given context.

As we have seen above, the relative balance between children's welfare and respect for their participatory rights is, to some extent, context-bound and varies according to the importance of the issue and the range of interests at stake. Consequently, operationalising participatory rights implies some consideration of the decision in question. Freeman (1983) recommends a distinction between 'major' and 'minor' decisions and Scottish law refers to, 'any major decisions involving them'. Article 12 (UNCRC) simply refers to 'all matters affecting them'. Franklin (1995, p.10) suggests that the denial of rights occurs across the board, encompassing children's involvement in the private realm of the family and ranging from relatively unimportant matters such as decisions about 'which clothes to wear or what time to go to bed, to more significant concerns'. Rather than attempting to specify particular conditions under which participation is appropriate, however, Franklin (1995, p.10) proposes a presumption of entitlement – effectively a reversal of the burden of proof on the basis that, 'The burden of proof always rests with those who wish to exclude others from participation; children should not be obliged to argue the case for possessing the same rights as everyone else'. We clearly need to rethink the contexts in which children's participation could be meaningfully raised. Family migration would certainly qualify as a major decision involving a complete change in children's lives at both a public and private level (for more discussion see Ackers and Stalford, 1999). In practice the decision is likely to involve a range of actors including a child's parents and siblings. Families move at various stages in the life cycle; in some of the examples given children were very young at the time of the move or were even born in the host state (in those families contemplating a return). In others they were much older, perhaps in the final years of schooling or contemplating employment.

One of the criticisms of the existing legal framework promoting child participation is the unitary concept of child underlying the law. In practice there is no such thing as a 'child' in the abstract sense; socio-economic, cultural and gender characteristics, amongst others, render assumptions based upon some asocial model of 'child' overly simplistic. Perhaps the only acknowledgement of diversity within the population of children can be seen in the debates around chronological age and competence.

The relationship between a child's age and citizenship status forms a long-standing debate that has informed discussion around participatory rights. In operational terms, it would clearly be administratively expedient to 'link' entitlement to chronological age. In this vein, Section 6 of the Children (Scotland) Act 1995 offers the guidance that, 'children aged 12 or over are presumed to be capable of forming a view'. To some extent, the notion of linking age to participatory rights fits quite well with the findings of our research that suggests a link between the impact of migration on children and their ages. Respondents with pre-school children generally reported fewer problems for the children themselves (although they refer to the problem of childcare). Difficulties appear to arise when children are of school age and particularly when they are entering secondary school at the age of 11-12 (depending on the school system).

The purpose of ascribing limits according to chronological age is, however, based upon notions of competence and the capacity for rational thought: in order to participate in decisions a child must be able to understand the issues at stake and be able to arrive at an informed view. The problems in assuming a relationship between age and competency, given the inherent diversity that exists within the category of 'child', has lead to more 'subjective' conditions. Section 1(3)(a) of the Children Act 1989 thus requires a court to consider 'the ascertainable wishes and feelings of the child concerned (considered *in the light of his age and understanding*)'.

Article 12 UNCRC similarly refers to the child's '*capability* of forming his or her own views'. Whilst there is undoubtedly some wisdom in Roche's (1999, p.483) contention that 'The arguments for the increased participation of children in decision-making affecting their lives are both practically and theoretically more compelling the older the child is', the problem of deciding when a child achieves an appropriate level of competency remains. When underwriting the reversal of the burden of proof argument, Holt (cited in Franklin, 1995, p.14) places the onus on children themselves to determine the level of participation in a given context arguing that, 'children, without regard to age, should participate when their interest and knowledge of affairs motivates them to do so…it seems probable that very young children would abstain'.

Franklin (1995) goes further, questioning both the inference that children lack a capacity for rational thought and the logical corollary of that, that all adults are fully informed, rational and competent. Certainly some of the children in our research presented very rational and objective appraisals of their situations. In practice, the kind of relativism implied in the competency argument is highly problematic. What weight does one attach to prior experience, for example? In the following case the father suggests that his superior experience, following numerous international moves, effectively relieves him of the need to involve his children in migration decisions:

> I don't think they ever have really decided. They don't have the same view as [my wife] and I. We have been around the world and so we can visualise it. 'We have been here so maybe we would like to go there' – you know? So their experience is far less [087].

Following the competency argument through might imply that the children, in such cases, would never achieve the 'track record' of their parents and as such would always defer to their parent's more extensive experiences.

The mother in the next example said that they had not encouraged participation because the children were unable to anticipate the consequences. She knew that they would object and, in any event, they had already made the decision. In that sense, it wasn't so much that the children could not express a view but that she was not prepared to allow that view to influence the decision:

> Actually the children didn't know anything about our plans to move until we reached a decision. But even when the decision had been made and they were informed about the plans, I don't think that they could realise the changes that were expected in their lives. I suppose that we didn't involve children in the decision making because we knew that they wouldn't want this change [411].

Arguably, the frank approach of this mother avoided the pitfalls of tokenistic and manipulative participation seen in other cases. Whilst concerns expressed within academic literature suggest an increasing dissatisfaction with boundaries structured rigidly according to chronological age, the sentiments expressed in the interviews suggested that parents often felt age was a key defense – their children were too young to be able to appreciate the consequences and potential benefits of a move (and therefore unable to act as fully informed and mature actors in such major family decisions). Typical responses were as follows:

> Peter was 12 at the time he had to follow us. I didn't give him a choice, did I? [081].

> Interviewer's Summary: The decision to come to Portugal was the couple's. She doesn't remember talking to her son about that decision, 'He was too small (3 years old)' [316].

> My sons were too young to participate in the decision making, but they were happy when we came. They didn't complain [417].

The children themselves sometimes expressed resentment at their exclusion from family decision-making, particularly when the views of older siblings were taken into account. The parents in the next example were given three opportunities to involve their daughter in migration decisions; on each occasion they felt that she was too young to participate. Her exclusion from decision-making must have been felt particularly acutely given that her older siblings were apparently involved:

> As I was the youngest in the family, I was never asked … I was just two years old when I came to Greece and seven when I left. I returned again to Greece when I was thirteen [422].

The following case involved a family with three daughters and the degree of choice exercised by the girls depended both on their age and educational context. In practice, the parents felt that one child was too young to make a choice to stay behind, another (the eldest) was established at college and therefore had little choice but to remain:

> Our first daughter was studying at that time. Obviously there was not a question if she would come with us to Greece. The younger one knew that she should stay with us as she was too small to stay behind alone. If you asked her, she will answer that she didn't want to come. Actually, only our second daughter had a choice about her residence. At that time she was at the end of her training course. She decided to come with us and look for a job in Greece [408].

In this case, the decision about whether to involve the child appears to turn on the age at which the child could be safely left behind (at college or in employment) and not in terms of a child's ability to exercise rational and informed decision-making. To the extent that the child had autonomy, it was in its capacity as an individual to physically break away from the family; she could become an independent individual (and 'fly the nest') but was not permitted to exercise relative autonomy within the family unit. This 'Hobson's Choice' scenario constituted a relatively common way of dealing with the participation issue and is discussed in more detail below. The following section describes some of the justifications parents adopted when discussing the exclusion of their children from the migration decision.

Parental Strategies in Migration Decisions

Operating in their Children's 'Best Interests'

The needs of the child were uppermost in the following parents' minds when making migration decisions:

> We need to see if the children settle here, but that was the intention when we came back this time [085].

> And because of our daughter, I think we really needed to go back. She didn't have a lot of friends and ... It seemed like a good time to go back [220].

In the following case the move was precipitated by family breakdown (with the child's father moving to Italy). The mother's description of the situation, however, suggests that she considered the return to her home country as beneficial to her son, enabling him to avoid the tensions she experienced as a migrant child in the UK:

> I always wanted to return in Greece. I was unhappy in England. I didn't like and I wasn't identified with British people. I wanted to reach a decision to go back as soon as my son was small because I didn't want him to go through the difficulties I experienced from my own migration when I was a child [406].

Some parents suggested that whereas a temporary stay and the experience of living in another country may be good for their children, longer periods may prove more problematic. This may connect with concerns about their social and educational integration:

> They offered us to stay for another five years, but we thought that it would be too long. If they had offered my husband a job for another two years, we would have considered staying. But you never know what will happen with your children, and how they'll react [222].

These statements perhaps provide evidence indicative of the kinds of 'peripatetic' careers that the European Commission refers to in its paper on the European Employment Strategy (CEC, 2001) with employees and families moving repeatedly over the life-course in response to employment opportunities. Migration, in that context, is an on-going process rather than a single move followed by 'settling' in the host state. Certainly, this picture of on-going mobility connected with career progression was reflected in a parallel project concerned with the mobility of scientists throughout the European Research Area (Ackers, 2001).

Another group of respondents, all living in Portugal or Greece, were motivated by the desire to find a good quality of life in which to bring up their children:[6]

> We decided to come to Portugal because we thought that this still was a peaceful country and every parent's fear is crime, isn't it? And people are generally friendly and mostly and we liked the atmosphere [301].

---

[6] These arguments were also identified in the previous study, particularly by women migrants living in Ireland (Ackers, 1998).

> I would like them to grow up in a warmer environment, not only physically but also socially. So we decided to come to Portugal [320].

> … to give the children a really nice childhood, free of fear and danger and weird people and violence and all the rubbish you get in the UK [334].

For others, the move was made as part of a wider concern to broaden their children's horizons. In the following case, the children's education would not be disrupted (as they could attend the Greek school where their father worked) and they could return after a short period (which they did):

> We wanted to move to Austria for the children. It would be beneficial for them to live in another country apart from Greece. My husband mentioned that as a teacher, he could apply to teach in a Greek school abroad. I thought that it was a great opportunity [437].

Concerns about their children's well-being evidently motivated parental decisions in the above cases. Although most of these parents had not consulted their children, as such, they believed that they were operating with their children's interests in mind. In the following case, the mother suggests that the parent's decision to override the children's objections to moving was taken with their 'best interests' in mind. This point illustrates quite nicely the potential conflict that exists, in the parent's minds at least, in achieving a balance between what is 'good for the child' (the welfare principle) and respecting children's autonomy (the rights principle):

> Interviewer's summary: The mother told me that the children's refusal to go to Greece for good did not affect their decision as they believed that, 'it would be in the children's best interests' [418].

A similar view was expressed in the following case. The parents saw no need to consult as the primacy they attached to the family unit and the presumption of shared interests meant that they felt they were operating in their child's best interests simply by ensuring the family stayed together:

> She was always with us. She was there in China, then in Hong Kong and now here in Portugal. Well, there was no need to talk about the subject. These are things that we live together, among us, every day. In fact, the most important thing is that the family may be a meeting point, a nucleus, which never changes [302].

A number of different strategies were employed by parents to secure compliance with the migration decision, each offering various degrees of participation and coercion. A variant on the 'welfare' approach to child participation can be seen in a number of cases where parents suggest that, while the child may not consent at the point of the decision, they would reflect positively on the decision in later life (the future-oriented consent approach). In other cases children were able to exercise choice within parameters ascribed by their parents (the 'Hobson's Choice' or 'children's menu' approach). In the final group of cases presented below, parents adopted strategies of persuasion, typically underplaying the long term consequences of the decision and encouraging children to believe that the choice was reversible.

Examples of 'Future Oriented Consent'

In the examples below parents expressed the view that, even though it was inappropriate to attempt to involve the child in the family decision at the point of migration, the child would, in the longer term, see the value of the move and reflect upon it positively. This approach to decision-making is based upon two linked notions: firstly, that the parents can operate in the child's best interests (taking his or her welfare into account in an objective fashion) and, secondly, that children, at least up to a certain age (and typically this is interpreted by parents as being the age at which they could remain without their parents) lack the experience and foresight to be able to make rational, informed, decisions.

Franklin (1995) has referred to this kind of justification for denying participation rights to children as based upon 'future oriented consent' or Archard's (1993) 'caretaker argument'. A key problem identified by Franklin (1995, p.13) concerns the tendency for such strategies to become self-justifying to the extent that, 'the consent of the child at some future date may simply be a product of the very process of intervention'.

The potential for this self-justification can be seen in quite a tangible way in the context of migration decision-making and particularly in the experiences of children who have undergone a series of moves.[7]

Our next case involved a boy who moved from Sweden to Greece with his family and then returned some years later. It illustrates a number of common themes. Firstly, the difficulty of moving children aged around twelve when they are well established in their own social circle and beginning to develop some independence from the family. Nevertheless, it also shows the change in attitude over time as children reflect on the move some years later and realise the benefits of it. Arguably it underwrites the

---

[7] Some 40 per cent of the sample interviewed made more than one international move (including returnees).

priority his parents attached to a long term, 'future oriented consent', perspective:

> I was extremely rebellious. I absolutely didn't want to move and they almost had to force me. This was my reaction. It was much easier for my brother. He just went along. I'm not sure that he understood that much. He must have been five or six years old by that time ... [My parents] said that it would be such a good opportunity for me, to learn the language and to meet people from different cultures and things like that. They told me that I ought to look at it as an opportunity instead of something that I had been forced to do. That I should look at it as something good, instead of something bad. At that time I didn't value it at all but today I do. Today, I think it's one of the best things I've done in my life. It gave me an opportunity to learn the language, and that's something incredible [205].

Another boy was similarly persuaded:

> Last year we moved to Greece permanently. I didn't want to come. I didn't want to leave my friends in Holland. My parents said that it will be nice here and that I'll make new friends [421].

In the following case, the family had moved repeatedly and the children grew accustomed to it. The parents also felt that the lack of problems associated with moving reflected the children's ages and the fact that older children (aged 12 or more) became very attached to their friends:

> Mum: I think because they are still young it is easy for us [to move]. I have seen other families with kids in their teenage years. I guess from twelve and up it gets more difficult.
>
> Dad: They are more emotional. Teenagers seem to be more emotional about the bonds they create with peers and stuff. I mean the kids make very close friends too. It is very traumatic. Katy, with the last few moves we have had, we had several cry sessions saying 'I don't want to move, I don't want to move', and when we get to new locations very quickly they make new friends [087].

The research emphasizes the importance of exercising caution when making generalizations about the impact of moving on children. In very many cases they refer to very difficult initial phases, of concerns about losing friends and having to completely re-build their lives. Some years later, though, the majority of cases are able to reflect on the move in a more positive light and, in retrospect, appreciate the experiences gained. To that extent, the 'welfare principle' has been realised and the priority attached to children's welfare over and above participatory rights vindicated.

In practice it is very difficult, in a migration context, to imply a child's consent, however. The extent to which a child may indicate consent (or at least a positive appraisal of the move) depends to a large extent on the point at which they are asked and how we interpret their response. Asking a child immediately before or after a move is likely to reveal a high level of dissatisfaction, dislocation and loneliness. On the other hand, speaking to them some years later (as we did) often results in more positive responses as they have re-established new social contacts and settled into school and communities. Nonetheless, an expressed reluctance to return 'home' should not be misinterpreted as implying consent; in most cases it simply reflects their memories of the initial move and their fear of any repeat. The majority of children 'prefer' the status quo (in this context). To that extent the views expressed by some parents, that children are unable to make a decision until they have experienced the move (suggesting that they may then return if they are not happy) smacks of self-justification.

Restricting Options: A Children's Menu?

Roche (1999, p.487) defines a series of criteria essential to ensure that participation amounts to more than simply 'consulting in order to persuade him or her of the rightness or inevitability of a certain outcome'. These include demands that the child is furnished with accurate information, that this is effectively communicated; that alternative strategies are fully explored and that they are listened to and 'treated seriously'. In addition, whilst the views of one child may not be determinative, careful and honest debriefing should take place.

This issue of consultation as persuasion arose on a number of occasions in the research with many children presented with a limited range of options. In practice this typically meant that they were offered the option of remaining in the home country (either staying with family or friends or attending boarding school) or accompanying the parents on the move.

The process of family decision-making described in the cases described below typically represent an element of choice within parameters tightly defined by parents. To the extent that parents felt able to respect their children's views, the children were often presented with a kind of 'Hobson's choice' – either come with us or stay on your own. In other words, they may be permitted at a certain age to 'opt out' of family decisions but not to influence them. There were no examples of entire families deciding to return together in response to children's choices.[8]

In the following case, the family had moved several times as a result of family breakdown and re-marriage. There were four children in the family, the eldest of which, the interviewee, was not the biological child of the father. The mother said that they had not involved the younger three children in the most recent decision but had given the older girl, who was fifteen at the time, the choice of whether to accompany them or remain in boarding school:

> I had the choice of whether to stay on – I could have gone to the boarding school because there was a boarding school joined onto our school. I don't know why I didn't because when I first moved over here I sort of regretted that I hadn't stayed on but I'm glad I came now but I don't know, I have really mixed feelings. I really miss Ireland but I love it over here. They have never ever made me a part of the moving – like, 'where shall we go' – it's just they've gone and I've had to follow on except in the case of Ireland I could have stayed [004].

The interviews identified a group of mainly older children who either remained or returned 'home' following a period spent living abroad. These were often older children returning in order to re-integrate socially or to ensure that they did not experience progression problems in the transition from school to higher education:

> Interviewer comments: The mother tells that the whole family wanted to move to Italy except for the son who decided to stay to finish his studies. They never really hesitated to go [220].

The experiences of the young woman in the following case illustrates some of the problems of assuming that children will come to appreciate the benefits of moving. At the age of nineteen, one respondent returned to Sweden leaving her mother, stepfather and younger brother in Belgium:

> I was very negative towards the decision to move, and I didn't really want to change my mind either. I was very determined not to like it. I really wanted to move back home. When I started my last year at school, I said to my parents, 'I'll move back to Sweden after I've graduated'. It didn't matter whether I had anything to occupy myself with or not. After graduation, I hadn't, and I became unemployed. But I moved back to Sweden and

---

[8] The sampling technique would not have identified cases in which families had decided not to move at all.

arranged a place to live ... I didn't go back to my old way of living, but started up a new life [224].

Another interviewee also decided to return to Sweden on her own even if this implied boarding school. Her brother subsequently decided to return and attends the same school. They are able to spend time with their aunt in their family home at weekends:

> My parents always return to Sweden in the summer, and then I meet them. And we were writing to each other ... to me, this wasn't a problem. I didn't think that much about it. We have always kept our house in Sweden. During the years we've been living abroad, our aunt has been taking care of it, or living there herself...Otherwise, we would have to stay with our relatives ... It has been rather important to us...especially now, when we're in a boarding school and we want to go home at the weekends. Then it's nice to be able to go home to our own place [227].

Family separation,[9] as a response to the pressures of reconciling children's and parent's needs, was quite common:

> The next move will include only myself and my husband. Our two children are adults now, living in the Netherlands. My youngest son will join them very soon [450].

The decision in the next case also involved the question of whether and when to return home. The mother had gone to some effort to ensure that practical options existed and also that the girl (aged 17 at the initial move) could exercise some choice at least to the extent of her own movement, if not the rest of the family:

> Mother: After a year, Chloe still didn't know if she wanted to stay for another year. She was allowed to choose whether she wanted to stay in Belgium, or whether she wanted to return to Sweden to graduate. She didn't make up her mind until the last minute, but she has always found it difficult to take a decision ... I took her to Sweden one week before the semester would start, so that she would make up her mind. She even went to school the first day. We had planned that she would live here, together with her brother. One of the other students was planning to move, and the room was still empty. So she would have stayed here. I suppose she missed all her friends. And you [addressing to the father], you weren't even here. We stayed with a friend in Stockholm, and spent a whole night talking about it. Finally, she made up her mind [216].

---

[9] A subject we return to in more detail in chapter seven.

In one case the impact of separation from siblings was felt quite keenly by the child who remained with her parents. Her objective was thus to study hard in order to be able to join her brothers in their school:

> When my first brother left for France, it was awful for me. When the second one left too my life changed. I felt very alone. Home is different now! I miss them a lot and I very much looking forward to joining them. I am very much concentrating on studying because I want to definitely pass my exams. Therefore my typical day is schooling and studying even at weekends!
>
> Mother: She very much wants to return to France. We will stay in Greece at present and then we hope that we will be transmitted to a country close to France. We want to be close to our children but we don't wish to return to France yet [434].

The mother in this case is clearly concerned to respect her daughter's wishes to return and live with her brothers. Nevertheless, she is not prepared to allow these concerns to alter her own plans. Arguably, the choice framework open to these children presents them with very difficult decisions indeed when a desire not to move or remain in the host state implies separation from their parents and siblings and, most commonly, attendance at boarding school.

Parental Persuasion - The Reversibility of Decisions

In many cases parents had developed an interesting strategy as a means of reconciling these tensions, at least in their own minds. On the basis that children were either too young or inexperienced to be able to weigh up the relevant factors involved in the decision, they 'persuaded' the children to move with the assurance that the decision was both potentially reversible (they could return) and further that the child's interests might precipitate the decision to return. Of course, in practice, this situation is far more complex than many of the other, more straight forward, 'suck it and see' decisions people make in life. Contemplating a return home following a lengthy period abroad can, in itself, create many dilemmas for children who have both begun to establish themselves in the host state and lost contact with the home country. To the extent that parents are prepared to 'honour' this commitment, in most cases, as we shall see, they are referring to the child's right to return alone. In that sense it is not a case of reversing a decision but making an entirely new decision.

The following family returned home to Ireland from Holland when their daughter was fourteen. The mother and child present somewhat different perspectives:

> I always say to them in arguments, 'why did you move here and make me come with you?'. They just told me and what could I do? I was only 14 at the time. They told me about two weeks before we were due to move. We were due to come back for Christmas but it took a long time to sell the house. I didn't really have much time to get used to it though. It was just leaving the cat behind...When I got here I just sat and cried and cried [052a].

The mother described the situation in a slightly different way, suggesting that they presented the choice as being a temporary, potentially reversible one:

> We did have a family meeting. We sat down with them and told them all the plus and all the minus points. I mean they knew we were coming over on holiday to decide did we want to stay or did we want to go. Then when we got back they kept asking us what we were going to do but we hadn't made up our minds by then. I was a bit worried you see in case [my husband] didn't want to come home as well. It would have been really difficult if both of us hadn't have wanted it but luckily we did. Obviously the girls didn't want to move – they wanted to stay although there was a stage when they found it very exciting but when it sunk into them that they were coming over here and not going back, they really didn't want to come over. But I explained to them that, well, when they're older, they can go back to Holland if they want – that's their choice – and to treat it as though they were only coming over temporarily to help their English and if they want to go back later they can [052b].

This example illustrates a number of issues. Firstly, the importance of involving children during the formative stages of decision-making and providing them with the information necessary to express an informed preference at that point. Clearly, the tactic of leaving consultation until the very last minute (when arrangements have been made) suggests a very hollow kind of participation – perhaps reaching only the first rung of Hart's (1992) ladder (manipulation). Secondly, the mother presents a variant of the 'future oriented consent' idea. In this case, rather than expressing the belief that they are doing the right thing, as parents, in moving the children, she suggests that their respective life-course positions actually presents them with a wider framework of choices; the daughter has time on her side and can, if she wishes, go back on her own when she is older. In asserting her own right to return 'home', it would seem that the mother is failing to take responsibility for the initial migration that effectively uprooted the children in the first place. For the children, in common with many others interviewed, the concept of 'home' lacked the certainty ascribed to it by parents. It was also interesting to witness the mother's concern at the potential dissent of her partner compared to that of her children.

The experiences and approach of the following mother, another returnee, and the extent to which she attached primacy (at that point in time) to her own preference was very similar. Once again she did not appear to reflect on the original decision to move away but rather asserted her own right to return 'home' (but not her children's right to stay 'home'!):

> They hated it. It's understandable from their point of view because we took them away from their best friends. We took them away from their country. We took them away from their home really. I mean this is our home but that was theirs. But the way we look at it is that they've got a choice to go back there when they're 18 if they want to. I think Lucy would go back tomorrow if she had the chance [055].

The extent to which the mother in the previous example contemplates the possibility of her child exercising choice in future migration decisions, demonstrates how, once again, the range of options are tightly framed and there is no question of the daughter's preferences influencing the family as a whole. It is rather a case of the child 'opting out' of the parent's migration decision and returning alone.

Some parents were better able to reflect on the implications of return migration and the complex effect of migration on a child's identity:

> My son was twelve years old, and that's a difficult age. Once he got an outburst of rage, and said that we would destroy his life. But then, when we were about to move back home to Sweden, he didn't want to move. Then you start to think about what you've been up to [205].

The parents in the following two examples also employed the persuasive 'tactic'. In the first case, the child clearly resented the fact that her older brother was able to exercise choice and remain in the home country while she had to accompany her parents. In the second, the parents evidently did respect the girl's wish to return home some time later although, once again, she made the move alone and not as part of the family group:

> Interviewer: What was your reaction when your parents told you that were going to move to Belgium?
>
> Respondent: It was a bad reaction, I suppose ... I wasn't really prepared for it ... I absolutely didn't want to move. The whole year I spent trying to persuade my parents that I could stay in Sweden. My brother was allowed to stay and I wanted to stay as well. I thought about going to a boarding school in Sweden. Finally, we decided that I should come along, but that I only had to stay for one year. If I didn't feel at home after half a year, my parents promised me that I could move back home to Sweden [221].
>
> I didn't want to go, because I enjoyed living in Sweden. I objected to the decision, a lot. I told them that I would run away if I wasn't allowed to stay, and so on. I had a boyfriend and a lot of friends, and I didn't want to leave them. My mother and stepfather told me that I had to go for half a year, and give it a try. If I didn't like it, I was allowed to return to Sweden. I wasn't allowed to stay by myself in Sweden. It was very unfair, because I've always been very well-behaved [224].

This approach, of suggesting to the children that the stay was temporary and potentially reversible, was referred to by one child as a deliberate 'tactic' to ensure compliance:

> My parents never really told me that, 'we'll stay in Belgium, and we'll never go back to Sweden'. It was more like, 'We don't know for sure, but we will at least stay for another year'. This was the kind of tactic they used, and I think it worked. After a while, you got used to it, and one day I realised that we wouldn't go back [225].

The parents in the case above, clearly attempted to 'persuade' the son to view the move positively and took steps to inform him of the consequences of the move (in terms of showing him the school) but evidently exercised some deception in the process. It illustrates the error of assuming our children to be less competent or aware than we really know them to be!

Another child told a similar story. It is difficult to know in these cases whether there was a deliberate attempt to 'persuade' the child or whether the parents were genuinely uncertain about the future. In either case it meant that the children lacked the knowledge on which to make an informed decision:

> I don't even think I really understood that we would stay for such a long time. At first, my father told me that we would only stay for two or three years. But then we just stayed [230].

In some cases the impact of age and the length of residence in the host state meant that the return move was more traumatic than the initial migration. The boy in the next case appears to resent the repeated nature of his father's work-related moves and the continual pressure on him to re-construct his life and establish new friends:

> My reaction to the change, to the travels, varied. In the beginning, in Brazil, I sort of expected it. I didn't mind, it was good. But I didn't like the idea [of moving to] Spain because I had already adapted to the place. To leave my friends, to start everything all over again [328].

As we have seen above, the prospects of a return migration do not present so much a reversal of the initial decision but rather an entirely new decision and dislocation, often in practice more difficult than the initial move (to the extent that the child was older and experienced the social dislocation more acutely). It is simply not possible to reverse a decision as profound as an international move without serious consequences for the children.

The introduction has already suggested that the acceptance of the notion of child involvement in decision-making was more firmly established in cases of family breakdown where legal requirement or professional practice established the possibility of enhanced participation for the children affected. The 'best interest' or welfare principle would thus appear to hold in the case of 'intact' families. It is interesting, in that context, to compare the nature of child participation in migrant families which have either temporarily separated for some reason or undergone a permanent breakdown. In many ways the range of options, in terms of which country to live in, was greater in those cases where the parents had either temporarily or permanently separated.[10] Of course the decisions in these cases must be particularly difficult for children. The fact that her parents were themselves exercising different choices gave the girl in the next example, more options, although she did not, of course, have the option of the family remaining together:

> My mother and my brother moved back a year before me and my dad, but I didn't want to move then. I wanted to graduate in Italy, because otherwise it would have been rather complicated [216].

In the example presented below the boy had little choice in earlier moves but, since family separation, his range of options had increased:

---

[10] 21 per cent of the children interviewed (38 cases) had experienced family breakdown and many more were separated from parents and siblings for periods of time.

> Interviewer Comments: The boy said that he has spent five years in Bermuda, one year in Guernsey and six years in London roughly. The last year he has been living in Greece. He hadn't participated in earlier decisions for 'dad's work', 'we had not a choice actually but the third time I really had a choice to stay in England with my dad and my sister or to come to Greece with my mother and my stepfather' [409].

The following girl had made a series of moves all of which were determined by family separation. In common with the previous example, the child was very much a passive 'victim' of her mother's migration decision (in fact an abduction) but subsequently exercised some degree of 'choice', making her own decisions about where to live:

> I was very small when I left Greece and went to Germany first time. I was just three and a half and my brother was five. I don't remember many things. We went to my mother's home-town … I don't remember the time that my brother came to Greece with my father … having some problems in Germany, I decided spontaneously to stay here with my father. I'm happy that I had a free will and my parents didn't try to prevent me or force me to stay somewhere [412].

In the end, the girl returned to Germany. Since leaving Greece she lost her ability to speak Greek and was subsequently unable to communicate with her grandmother and experienced problems integrating. As older children, the last two examples illustrate the potentially greater choice, in terms of residential location, open to children in some cases of family breakdown. In such circumstances, it seems that parents are more prepared to respect the notion of child participation. In practice, these choices were particularly hard for a child to make, however, as alternative courses of action involved geographical separation from parents, siblings and extended family members.[11]

Acting on Children's Views

Article 12 UNCRC only provides for the right of children to express their views. The extent to which the views of a child, once expressed, are permitted to influence decisions will necessarily depend on the context and, in particular, upon the respective balance of interests involved. Whilst a child's views about what clothes to wear, the choice of friendships or even

---

[11] Again, this case and the issue of family breakdown is discussed in more detail in chapter seven.

perhaps whether to use contraception (following the Gillick ruling)[12] should, arguably, be determinative, in the context of migration decision-making, as in many other family decisions involving parents, siblings and family members, the paramountcy principle (or veto) is unlikely to be appropriate. In practice, some form of shared participation, in advance of the decision to move, with children informed of alternatives, permitted to express their opinions and then fully briefed on the outcome and rationale behind the outcome is, in most cases, the preferred approach. This corresponds with two potential rungs on Hart's (1992) ladder. The fifth rung, 'consulted and informed', perhaps represents the optimum achievable level of participation in the majority of migration decisions (and requires that children's opinions are given serious consideration). The sixth, on the other hand, implying genuinely shared decision-making may be appropriate in certain circumstances, perhaps when the parents have a number of alternative options or when the children are themselves facing serious decisions in their lives (over schooling, for example).

Lansdown (1992, p.4), referring to Article 12 UNCRC, details the conditions required for effective and genuine participation:

> Consulting with children means more than asking them what they think. It means ensuring that they have adequate information appropriate to their age with which to form opinions. It means being provided with meaningful opportunities to express their views and explore options open to them and it means having those views listened to, respected and *considered seriously*.

This commitment to serious consideration encourages children to participate, to learn the principles of democracy and shared decision-making as the basis of active citizenship and counters the paternalism leading to passivity implicit within the future oriented consent approach.

Roche (1996, p.33) concludes his paper stressing the importance of achieving a balance between autonomy and support and understanding the 'interconnectedness' linking the three principles underpinning the UNCRC and the lives of parents, children and adults. In practice the objective must be to achieve a balance, in any given context, between the promotion of autonomy and support. In most situations children's views cannot be determinative; the extension of participatory rights, however, promotes

---

[12] The child's right to determinancy depends on her reaching a 'sufficient understanding and intelligence to be capable of making up his own mind on the matter requiring decision', *Gillick v West Norfolk and Wisbech Area Health Authority* [1985] 3 All ER 402 (HL).

agency and the self-definition of needs and desires. And, most importantly, as Minow (1987) suggests, it allows individuals to make claims.

Conclusion

The objective of this chapter was to consider the relevancy and implications of recent theoretical debates, highlighting the tensions between the welfare principle and children's participatory rights in a specific empirical context. It has discussed the strategies adopted by parents in one of the most serious areas of family decision-making. The empirical evidence presented underwrites the limitations of using chronological age as a criteria determining participatory rights and also of assumptions, so pervasive in migration theory, of the family as a consensual unit. Where parents were influenced by the age of their children, it was more a case of achieving a level of competency with which to maintain independence from the family. As such, the relationship between age and the ability to make rational and informed decisions was rarely considered by parents. To the extent that children are permitted to engage in migration decision-making, it is usually within a restricted framework of choices, with children able to choose whether to remain physically located within the family unit or to develop some independence outside the family. In no cases were children permitted any influence on decisions guiding the family as a whole. In cases of family breakdown, children had a wider range of choices available to them, at least in terms of residential location. On the other hand, family breakdown, in the context of international migration, presents children with some very serious decisions.

In a more general sense, the discussion has emphasised the importance of moving forward from theoretical reasoning to consider children's participatory rights in specific decision-making and empirical contexts.

6 Negotiating Kinship Transnationally

Introduction

This chapter considers the impact of the dispersal of families over space on family contact, 'care' and kin relationships.[1] Chapter three has already described the nature of the migration processes in which the children have been involved, the incidence of children's repeated mobility and the existence of on-going 'active' links with kin across two or more countries. Baldassar and Baldock (2002, p.64) use the term 'transnational' to describe the situation of migrants who 'live their lives across borders and develop and maintain ties to two or more homes, even when the countries of origin and settlement are geographically distinct'. Speaking some time earlier, Basch and colleagues (1994, p.7) refer to 'transmigrants' as:

> people who take actions, make decisions, and develop subjectivities and identities embedded in networks of relationship that connect them simultaneously to two or more nation-states.

Whilst the language of transnationalism is relatively recent, all migrant families will have faced the challenges of managing relationships across national borders. The changing contexts within which these processes are taking place will, however, shape their experiences as opportunities for communication and travel change over time. Certainly the changes in employment patterns highlighted in chapter three are having a significant impact on family dispersal. As Mason (1998, p.4) suggests:

> the geographical discourse of kinship is likely to be becoming a more central feature of everyday life ... as family, kin and personal relationships on the one hand, and patterns of migration, residence and co-residence on the other, are said to be becoming more complex, more variable and less predictable.

---

[1] We have chosen to focus on family here and not on friends as such. Although we collected considerable material on children's friendships there is insufficient scope in this book to specifically develop these issues.

The level of international partnering and parenting and the increasing incidence of family breakdown identified amongst our sample would support this contention. In all, ninety-six of the 180 children (53 per cent) interviewed in the children and migration project lived in 'international families',[2] reflecting the migratory patterns of their parents and the level of post-migration partnering (as outlined in chapter three). Baldassar and Baldock's (2002) sample of academic migrants also reports high rates of inter-marriage. Of the sample of 12, six were single when they first moved and subsequently married host nationals. Of the six who moved with partners, three had subsequently divorced and re-partnered with host nationals (2002, p.73).[3] Family breakdown also emerged as a major issue that shaped the migration decisions as well as the lives of children in our study. As we saw in chapter three, some 21 per cent of our sample of families (38 cases) reported some form of family breakdown. Divorce and separation, particularly in cases of international partnerships, has an impact both on the physical dislocation of kin but also on moral reasoning in relation to kinship.[4] In addition to these changes in family structure and form, patterns of migration are also in the process of rapid change reflecting shifting employment patterns in European and global labour markets. We have already drawn attention to changing patterns of employment, particularly for the highly skilled, and the emergence of 'career-long peripatetic lifestyles' in chapter three. This implies an expectation and tolerance of repeated mobility and emphasises the importance of understanding migration as an on-going process rather than as a one-off event.[5]

This chapter examines the impact of these forms of intra-EU mobility on family relationships and the 'doing' of transnational kinship. The chapter opens with a review of some existing work concerned with the relationship between distance, proximity and kin relationships and assesses the relevance of this work to the current study. In particular, it considers the value of the analytical handles developed in Jennifer Mason's work on kinship and geographical reasoning (1998) and Baldassar and Baldock's

---

[2] The majority of women interviewed in the preceding Gender and Migration project (Ackers, 1998) had also met their partners and subsequently married in the host state. This resulted in high levels of inter-marriage and 'international families'.

[3] These findings, although based on a very small sample, support the results of parallel research with migrant women and scientists, both of which identified a very high rate of international partnering (Ackers, 1998 & 2001).

[4] These issues, as well as the legal consequences of divorce and separation and its impact upon the lives of parents and children, forms the specific focus of chapter seven.

[5] The notion of migration as a peripatetic process is also referred to in the context of retirement migration, as in the work of O'Reilly (2000) and Ackers and Dwyer (2002).

(2002) study of migration and care. Having discussed the relevance of other research we move on to present some of our own empirical findings in relation to how parents and children talked about the impact of migration on family dispersal and relationships.

The Importance of Proximity to Kinship and Care

Baldassar and Baldock (2002, p.62) refer to the tendency of 'family studies' to emphasise geographical proximity as 'one of the most important variables in the maintenance of inter-generational care-giving practices'. As evidence of this approach, they cite the work of Rogerson, Burr and Lin (1997, p.122) who conclude their review of research on the impact of proximity on caring relationships with the statement that, 'distance is the strongest predictor of assistance exchanges among family members that require a physical presence'. In another paper, Lin and Rogerson (1995, p.304) point to the close connection between caring relationships and geographical proximity arguing that, 'because care-giving often requires close proximity, it is important to understand the demographic and geographic availability of adult children'. Warnes' (1986) study of the relationship between residential proximity and intergenerational relations, based on large-scale survey work, found that although advances in communications (such as the telephone or the internet) had a compensating influence and facilitated the maintenance of intergenerational contact, nevertheless distance had a 'dampening effect' on visiting frequency (Warnes, 1986, p.1593). Indeed, even 'very small increments of distance' had a restraining effect on contact. Warnes reported that for those relatives living within 2 kilometres, between 5 and 20 kilometres and at least 100 kilometres away the percentage of respondents visiting their parents at least once a week drops from 81 through 47 to 1.6% across these groups (p.1593/4).

It is, of course, important to consider not only the frequency of contact but also the quality and nature of these exchanges. Whilst Rogerson and Lin (1995) distinguish 'exchanges that require physical distance', they do not develop this point in any detail. Warnes' (1986) study did not consider this dimension and the impact of distance upon the nature or quality of support provided and received. Johnson (1988, p.171) goes a step further, however, in promoting this presumption of 'distance-decay' when she suggest that with increasing kinship distance, 'the support becomes more perfunctory and consequently less reliable over a prolonged period of time'. Distance, then, would appear to not only reduce the frequency of contact but also changes their character and, more widely, the reliability of the migrant family as a caring resource.

Baldassar and Baldock (2002) take issue with the assumption that older people who have no proximate adult children lack support and access to caring relationships and that adult children are 'free from the sense of moral obligation towards their parents' (2002, p.62). Rather, their own findings suggest that 'transnational migrants continue caring and care-giving relations with their parents notwithstanding great geographical distance' (p.62). Other research with migrant women, scientists and retirees similarly highlights the tenacity of kin relationships across physical space and the importance of understanding the relationship between mobility and care in the lives of migrants at all stages in the life-course (Ackers, 1998; Ackers, 2002; Ackers and Dwyer, 2002).

For Mason (1998, p.2), distance has a 'malleable' quality and people respond to it in different and changing ways:

> both geography and kinship are inextricably linked, yet also negotiable in their relationship and subject to change and to multiple interpretation.

Whilst distance inevitably modifies kinship, the reverse may also be true – kinship modifies distance, or at least perceptions of it and people interpret distance in different ways and in response to different circumstances. For some people at some points in time, very short distances constitute major obstacles to kin relationships, whilst for others, long distances are easily negotiated. In attempting to move beyond the 'either-or' approach and understand the complexities of the relationship between distance and kin relations, Mason identifies a range of different forms of geographical reasoning.[6] First she found evidence of what she terms 'distance-thinking' (p.25). Distance thinking encompasses those people who 'do not see kin relationships as particularly significant to their own lives' (and may in fact prefer not to live too closely to at least some of their relatives), and those who take a 'can-do' approach to distance and kinship and are prepared to 'make kin relationships work over long distances' (p.16). In this latter situation, distance was 'malleable' and living at a distance from kin could be managed, in some cases, not 'because kin relationships did not matter, but because distance was not prohibitive to their functioning' (p.9).

This malleability was reflected in the readiness of some distance thinkers to contemplate on-going mobility. Here, distance was not

---

[6] She makes it clear that reasoning is not the same as action.

prohibitive in any final sense as it could always be reversed.[7] This links to the ideas discussed below about 'cultures of moving'.

A second form of reasoning identified by Mason is 'reluctant distance thinking' (p.19). Reluctant distance thinkers are able to contemplate and tolerate living at a distance for at least some time in an attempt to balance a range of factors and agendas (such as career trajectories and the needs of children). Mason also refers to evidence of 'local thinking', reflecting that group of people for whom kin relationships were highly significant but demanded proximity (they simply could not function in any meaningful way over long distances).

Mason's work thus provides a theoretical framework for analysing the impact of distance upon families. There clearly is a relationship between distance and kinship but it can work in complex ways – in some cases distance can strengthen kin relationships whilst in others there is evidence of 'distance-decay'. The point is to consider the relationships more carefully and attempt to identify and understand the factors involved.

Factors Mediating Geographical Reasoning

Geographical reasoning in relation to kinship is not context-free – such reasoning is shaped by the situation. Factors potentially influencing this relationship might include the migration histories of family members both historically and at the present time (the existence of a 'culture' of moving, for example); socio-economic and legal variables and employment conditions (of both partners and other family members); family structure and relationships including marital status and the presence and characteristics of children or other 'dependant' kin; and the geography of dispersal and the impact of culturally-transmitted values.

We also need to be clear about what we mean by kinship and care as some circumstances or, to put it another way, forms of 'need', may shape responses to distance in different ways. To that extent, the nature of the 'care context' and its evolution over time and space will influence geographical reasoning. The emphasis in the existing research discussed above is firmly upon care and, in particular, upon the impact of distance on the informal support given to elderly relatives by their adult children. This emphasis constructs the flows of intergenerational support as one-

[7] Evidence of this kind of thinking in relation to their children's mobility was presented in chapter five. Similar ideas emerged in the retirement migration study with many respondents showing themselves prepared to delay moves, move abroad or return home in order to provide care and support to families (Ackers and Dwyer, 2002).

dimensional and presumes simple patterns of dependency based upon chronological age. Elderly people are thus characterised primarily as recipients of care and not as care providers.[8] In order to understand, in a more holistic sense, the relationship between migration and family, we need to embrace the intergenerational dynamics more broadly (to specifically include children) and consider both our conceptualisation of care and of kin relationships. Existing research in this field is highly limited and the literature which does exist focuses primarily on the geographical separation of the 'nuclear' family from wider kin networks and the impact of proximity, within that context, upon relationships. Our own research has identified a level of separation both from the extended family but also within the nuclear family itself (of parents and children on the one hand, and between siblings on the other). Our understanding of how people 'do' kinship transnationally thus encompasses transnational parenting and partnering and geographical reasoning in relation to these more immediate family relationships. We have, therefore, approached the intergenerational dynamics in this study from a different trajectory and have also provided the opportunity to consider children's perspectives.

The following section discusses some of these issues in more detail before moving on to consider our respondents' accounts of the impact of moving upon their family relationships.

A 'Culture of Moving'?

Warnes' research (1984, 1986) focused on inter-regional moves within the UK and their impact upon the nature of contact and care between adult children and their retired parents. This work highlighted the importance of residential location, the occupational status of adult children and previous mobility history as factors shaping responses to distance. The impact of previous mobility upon migration decision-making and kinship emerged as a key issue in other work with migrant scientists (Ackers, 2001). These findings indicated a clear link between previous family and personal mobility and the propensity of respondents to make career-related moves later in life (some 62 per cent of respondents had previously lived abroad). One respondent referred to mobile scientists as 'birds of a feather' who are 'all interested in being mobile' (quoted in Ackers, 2001, p.61).

Similarly, work with retirement migrants identified a cohort of people for whom moving had become 'normal' and expected (Ackers and

---

[8] Previous work with retired migrants challenges this presumption providing considerable evidence of elderly migrants moving in order to *provide* care (Ackers and Dwyer, 2002).

Dwyer, 2002). For those people who had spent much of their working life abroad, the experience of moving between countries (in the Forces or other peripatetic careers) significantly broadened their perception of distance and the potential range of retirement locations. Mason (1998, p.28) also points to what she calls a 'culture of moving', reflecting families' migration histories and experience of geographical dispersal (and managing kin relationships in that context) which then shaped attitudes to proximity. The sample of academic migrants in Baldassar and Baldock's (2002, p.73) work provides further evidence of an acceptance and expectation of mobility:

> Most had already been away from their families for many years: they had left home to study at university and this had led onto jobs, and several had lived and worked in other countries before coming to Australia.

Many of the respondents in the current study described a similar situation, although their accounts perhaps provided more evidence of ongoing mobility, with some respondents referring to their repeated moves over the life-course as a 'way of life'.[9] To that extent, as we shall see, the existence of a 'culture of mobility' would seem to shape responses to distance. Another factor, referred to briefly above, concerns the nature of the relationship and the kinds of care involved at any point in time.

Family Needs and the Level of Dependency

Echoing the feminist literature on caring,[10] Baldassar and Baldock (2002, p.83) distinguish between two forms of caring relationship – those which involve *caring about* someone and those which involve *caring for* someone:

> Not being in close proximity, they cared about rather than cared for their parents, although their involvement in decisions about matters of health, finance and housing, and their continuing supportive letters and phone calls certainly had considerable similarity to what one would expect of a care-giver living in closer proximity.

Caring about someone generally refers to forms of care that are less susceptible to distance-decay (at least in the context of the forms of labour

---

[9] Some of this material was presented in chapter three in the discussion about career-related moves.

[10] See, for example, Finch and Groves, 1983; Ungerson, 1987, Graham, 1991; Glendinning, 1992; Twig and Atkin, 1994.

migration within the EU that we are dealing with in this study). They encompass contact and emotional support (the 'emotions of caring' or caring 'about') and are exemplified in the frequency and nature or quality of contact. Notwithstanding the financial implications then, these forms of contact and support include communication by telephone, letters, and/or email, visits, participation in family decision-making and financing the purchase of care. Here, physical distance is not a barrier to *caring about* family. *Caring for* family, however, refers to the concrete, 'hands-on' care-giving on a more personal level, implying physical presence and potentially challenging family location decisions (typically implying return moves or extended visits).

Johnson (1988) refers to a similar specialisation of function, with some relatives specialising in *emotional functions*, connected with sociability, advice, comfort and self-validation, and others engaging in *instrumental functions* which refer to the kinds of daily tasks involved in caring for someone such as transport, household assistance, meal preparation and shopping. Distance may influence the nature of the tasks in which kin are involved with an inevitable shift in favour of the 'emotional functions' rather than the 'instrumental functions'. It is unfortunate, however, that Johnson demeans the 'sporadic contacts' and 'ritualised support' that take place at distance. She is somewhat dismissive of the role of these forms of contact through letters, telephone calls and visits which she suggests 'might intermittently boost one's morale [but] do not necessarily handle the practical aspects of daily living' (1988, p.172).

Although Mason challenges the simplistic distinction drawn between non-active *caring-about* relationships and active, *caring for* relationships, she also shows how periods of intensive need or 'care crises' can transform attitudes to distance, thus underlining the malleability or fluid nature of migration decisions:

> It is, undoubtedly, easier to become a distance thinker if one's time living away from kin does not overlap with any period of intensive need of oneself, or of kin for whom one feels responsibility (Mason, 1998, p.29).

The example she provides is of a woman, a 'distance' thinker, who had demonstrated a clearly 'can-do' approach to managing kinship at a distance until her mother began to need 'practical care of the kind which was difficult to provide or arrange over the telephone' (p.10). At this point there was some evidence that her views on distance were being 'scaled down a little' (p.10).

Our own research suggests that, even in such circumstances, migrants review their situation and often show a very high degree of commitment to their families, perhaps returning either temporarily or permanently to care for family members. In some cases, this might take them away from partners and children. This supports the conclusions of another study of elderly return migration which found that 'the main reason for return was a desire to be near family and friends or to care for relatives' (Malcolm, 1996 p.27). While the current study found less evidence of care crises precipitating a return move and a greater inclination towards 'distance-thinking', this was often because of parents' immediate caring responsibilities towards their own children which might influence their sense of obligation and ability to care for more distant relatives.

The Impact of Resources on Geographical Reasoning

The economic imperative determining the timing and geography of many of the families' moves is also an important factor affecting their responses to distance and kin relationships. Speaking in the context of inter-regional mobility and with a focus on the migration decisions of adult children, Rogerson and colleagues (1997, p.124) note the importance of labour force behaviour and the 'economic status of the child' in explaining the distance between generations:

> ... the fewer financial resources the child has, the more likely the older parent will be to move closer allowing the child to provide care locally rather than purchase professional help.

Access to resources thus facilitates distance-thinking in a very direct way. The importance of resources figures not only in decisions about the financing of care, however, but also in relation to the cost of maintaining contact in a more general sense. As Mason (1998, p.29) puts it, 'Maintaining supportive kin relationships over long distances can cost money and require access to resources, like a car for instance'. Of course, in a transnational context, the resource implications are even more pronounced. In previous work with women migrants, the location decisions (as opposed to migration decisions as such) were often motivated by a desire to live as close as possible to relevant and efficient transport networks (such as airports and ports, for example) and post-migration internal moves were often made to secure this advantage (Ackers, 1998).

Baldassar and Baldock's (2002) work also identifies the importance of resources to maintaining kin relationships. Their study incorporates two separate samples, one of Italian migrants in Perth (the majority of whom moved in the 1950s and 60s), together with a small pilot study of 12

European or North American academics. This latter sample has more in common with our own respondents. The motives for migration are identified as primarily 'individual' and linked to career progression and not, as in the Italian sample, 'the outcome of a tradition of migration based on family and community strategies of survival' (Baldassar and Baldock, 2002, p.73). None of their academic sample envisaged the move as permanent, reflecting the 'expectation of mobility' characteristic of many academic careers and their respondents highlighted the importance of resources to kin relationships in two different senses. First, managing kin relationships over such long distances implied some considerable sacrifice in terms of both time and money, as this quote from one of their respondents illustrates:

> ... the problem is a lot of your paid leave seems to go on these what are often obligatory visits ... I'd love to just go to a little holiday home or just something, you can't afford it, because it [the money] all goes over there (Baldassar and Baldock, 2002, p.80).

Managing kinship at a distance thus involves some considerable investment, with a greater obligation to visit placed upon the migrants themselves. The second way in which their respondents highlighted the importance of resources to kin relationships was in their discussion of some of the key advantages associated with academic careers – advantages which facilitated their ability to manage kinship at a distance. These included the flexibility of working and potential for extended periods away from the workplace together with opportunities to defray some of the costs associated with long-distance travel. One of their respondents describes the 'benefits' as follows:

> The long Christmas university break in the southern hemisphere allowed return visits at that time, and sabbaticals, conference and research travel, as well as long service leave offered opportunities for travel back home (Baldassar and Baldock, 2002, p.76).

Other work with mobile scientists revealed similar forms of reasoning (Ackers, 2001). In addition to the flexibility afforded by extended vacations and fellowship opportunities, respondents also referred to some of the benefits intrinsic in the nature of their work which positively facilitate distance-thinking. In some areas, such as more theoretical work or where fieldwork is being increasingly replaced with computer simulation, scientists were less tied to laboratories and more able to travel to visit partners and family. In that sense, research may be either very inflexible (particularly when it involves continual observation of experiments), whilst in others it offered highly flexible opportunities. In the following case (quoted in Ackers, 2001, p.99), the respondent's partner was a scientist with a permanent position in another country:

> He's also a researcher at university and that's good, because as a scientist you're pretty flexible and … you can organise your own working time. So, in periods when he doesn't need to teach, he can come here for one week and work here – and I can do the same, of course. 'Cause I can simply bring my computer and ... so, this makes it a little bit easier, because therefore we can be together anywhere. But, not all the time.

Although this project was confined to a study of scientific careers, the extension of flexible and home-based working is arguably extending to other areas of work and is further supported by access to communication via the internet and other forms of communication technology.

The extent to which there is distance-decay then might depend upon the costs in terms of both time and money of continuing to visit and the ability of the families concerned to absorb these. Whilst Mason's (1998) study involved primarily internal migration within the UK, Baldassar and Baldock's (2002) involved considerably greater moves across the globe which even for those with the most advantageous careers is likely to be prohibitive of regular short-term visits. The more limited evidence of active caring in their research may thus reflect the sheer distances involved and financial costs of visits.[11] Moving around the EU, as our respondents have done, is clearly much easier and less expensive and, in many cases, amounts to no greater problem in terms of time and money than extensive internal travel.[12]

Understanding the resource implications of mobility also demands consideration of the EU legal framework which shapes the rights of mobile Community nationals and, importantly, the welfare claims they and their families can make in the home and host states. This is of particular significance in relation to the kind of 'caring for' activities discussed above. Our previous work has discussed at some length the legal valuation of unpaid work, the failure of European law to recognise informal care as work and the consequences of this in terms of the citizenship status of mobile carers (Ackers and Dwyer, 2002; Ackers, 2002). Unpaid carers do not have access to the panoply of welfare benefits open to Community

---

[11] In fact their respondents make this point in referring to the costs of financing visits across the globe.

[12] In many cases one or more members of a family had, at some point, moved further afield, perhaps to Australia and Africa.

workers and moving in order to provide care may thus result in serious personal risk. Whilst 'dependant' children and ascendant relatives have a legal right 'to join' their citizen-worker parents or children, our work has also revealed the difficulties of exercising this kind of legal entitlement and moving elderly dependant people transnationally in order to access informal care. A positive legal and resource framework is likely to promote distance-thinking to a greater extent than one which denies citizenship status to, for example, cohabitees or unpaid carers.

The previous section has identified from previous research and literature a number of variables shaping family responses to distance. In the next section we present some of the findings of our work with EU migrant children and their parents. We focus first on the impact of migration on wider family contact and the 'caring about' dimension. The material presented here considers relationships between the migrant family and their wider kinship networks and the impact of separation upon these. We then move on to consider an issue not raised in previous academic work – separation within the nuclear family group itself. Finally, we discuss the impact of distance on family relationships that demand a physical presence (Rogerson, Burr and Lin, 1997). We focus here on the issue of care for elderly dependant relatives and also childcare support to mothers.

The Geography of Separation: Migrant Children's Contact with Wider Family Networks

Families and the value attached to family networks featured prominently in the migration experiences of children and parents, both in terms of the impact of moving on 'active' practical support and in terms of the emotional and cultural bonds associated with and nurtured by kinship. This is particularly evident in cases of family breakdown[13] or the death of a partner when individuals may instinctively look to their extended family for practical and emotional support. The interviews provided a strong sense of family commitment with family featuring prominently in almost all of the interview accounts. Only in 13 cases did respondents report having very little contact with either their paternal or maternal relatives (in 3 of these cases the family had lost contact with both sets of relatives). It is difficult to assess whether this loss of contact was attributable to the migration or whether it would have occurred anyway, since these interviewees generally referred to other factors such as divorce and remarriage or the death of a central, binding figure in the family as a contributing factor. This reference

[13] Chapter seven is devoted to the issue of family breakdown.

to the role of 'kin-keepers' in maintaining contact within migrant families is also raised by Baldassar and Baldock (2002). They refer to the importance of 'kin work' and the extent to which this kind of activity was mainly conducted by women, both in the early post-migration years and also later on when migrants were more financially secure: 'Women were still the ones who did the 'kin work' – writing cards and letters and phoning both their own and their husband's kin' (2002, p.69).

Respondents in our study reported regular contact with family by telephone, email, fax and letters[14] and 126 respondents visited extended family during the summer or over the Christmas holiday period, in some cases up to four times a year. Responses consistently emphasised the importance of the family and of maintaining regular contact with them despite the distance and, indeed, *because of* the geographical distance. This was seen as important in terms of sustaining and developing emotional ties but also in terms of family as an important forum in which to preserve and express personal and cultural identity:

> It is indispensable this regular contact with my culture, essentially with my family. I'm with my family every year. One year I didn't go and I was resentful of that. We think the family is important, as well as the relationship with everybody [323].

> [The ties with France are important] ... not only because of the family, but also to have contacts with another country, with another culture, to travel more. They have the chance to travel further with the grandparents. Or to visit the grandparents when they are in a more distant country [324].

Opinions were divided as to whether the migration had either a positive or a negative impact upon their relationship with their wider family. Many felt that it affected only the frequency of contact and not the quality of relationships:

> The distance, of course, prevents our frequent contacts with the relatives in Spain. However, it only affects the frequency of our contacts, not the quality of our relationship [445].

Apart from holiday visits, the majority of respondents made regular telephone calls, sent and received letters or had other forms of contact with their families. Many respondents demonstrated a very pragmatic approach

[14] It would seem that the 'art' of letter writing is in decline as respondents referred more commonly to the use of telephone and increasingly email as the preferred medium.

to living away from kin whilst accepting the limitations of these forms of contact:

> The visits are not very frequent, but the relationships are close. We write to one another, we always know what's going on ... As technology advances the communications develop, things are easier. We often communicate by fax and lately by e-mail ... we speak to one another when we want to, there's not that obligation thing. And if we miss them we have the fax and the telephone helps too [328].

Others felt that living in a different country actually made them more appreciative of their family networks and they valued the opportunity provided by the holidays to spend concentrated, 'quality' periods of time with distant kin. Indeed, some commented on the fact that they actually made more of an effort to keep in contact since they had moved away:

> I like it when you don't see your relatives every day. If you see each other too often, you miss that special 'magic'. I like it when we only see each other at Christmas, because then you have a lot of things to talk about [205].

> Both my family and my husband's family were against our decision to get married and stay in Greece. They wished we would stay close to them but I couldn't stand the idea of living close to my mother-in-law [430].

Whilst the child in the previous example expressed the relatively unusual view that distance and infrequency of contact made visits more 'exciting', especially at Christmas, adults were generally more inclined to see the benefits of distance to family relationships. In particular, they talked positively about how distance enabled them to maintain a sense of autonomy from the wider family unit and allowed them to avoid family conflict and the kinds of tensions that were seen to characterise proximate family relationships:

> Being away from your relatives helps to avoid any negative interaction. They become in your memory people without any fault, full of qualities, ideal persons. The lack of the everyday association prevents the damage of a relationship and preserves its best characteristics. The conflicts are less and consequently the damage is small [431].

Mason (1998, p.1) makes a similar point in her acknowledgement that, for some people, 'local and everyday familiarity with each others' lives can feel intrusive as well as friendly and supportive'. Furthermore, the support of parents and the fact that the family took the time and effort to visit, 'in some ways added rather than subtracted significance from their relationship'. Attitudes or responses to distance might thus be interpreted as a kind of 'test' of kinship and people who were apparently not prepared to make this investment and 'work at' long distance relationships could be seen as 'taking kin relationships less seriously' (p.16).

Other respondents presented a different view, however, suggesting that distance affected the quality of their relationships with kin in other countries:

> My parents, my elder daughter and my sister with her family are living in England. I've seen them only once since I left. It's not easy for us to travel frequently. I believe that this is the problem with migration, the family. You have to live away from the persons you care about. Telephone contact never replaces personal contact! [408b]

This example underlines the importance of resources to the management of kinship at a distance and the inadequacy of more impersonal forms of communication. Many parents referred to the practical difficulties and particularly the financial burden of visiting relatives in a different country, especially when they had a number of children. To overcome this, children often visited their relatives unaccompanied by their parents during the holidays or, instead, relatives travelled to the host country.

In general, children were more likely to express the view that distance restricted the quality of their relationships with family. Eight children expressed the sentiment that the emotional bond between them and their extended family was weakened by the geographical and/or cultural distance between them with some expressing a sense of isolation or exclusion in relation to their cousins who, living in close proximity to each other, could share everyday experiences:

> I think that I would like to visit my relatives more often. They see each other pretty frequently, and whenever I come to Finland a lot of things have happened that I haven't heard of. It makes me feel a little bit left behind [201].

Many of the children interviewed regarded the contact they had with family abroad as somewhat artificial and expressed a desire for a more 'normal', routine-based relationship:

> But of course you miss the everyday life. I talked to my grandfather on the phone the other day, and then I kind of discovered that there are certain things that we never talk about. He asked me how long time it takes me to

> get to school, and I've been going to that school for six years now! We never talk about these things when we're in Finland because we've got a lot of other things to discuss. But you kind of miss it ... You would like them to be familiar with the things going on. All the concerts and exactly what it looks like at home ... You really miss this [209].

A father in the following example expresses similar sentiments about the lack of regular, 'everyday' contact and the personal costs of living away from home. Reflecting on the question of how family contact would be different if he lived closer to his family, he says:

> I get really upset at times about the fact that because they have so many cousins that we see every so often, but if we had been back home we would have been at everybody's birthday. We would have looked each other up at the weekend and had a stronger relationship. I would have wanted that for our children and for us as well. It is fun being a family and living this far away we don't have the opportunity [087].

The respondents' comments above suggest that living abroad may encourage idealised notions of family life and contact 'back home'. Certainly this was a reality for a number of the children interviewed whose snap-shot of family life during the holiday period was extremely active and generally harmonious. It may be that whilst migration does not necessarily adversely affect family relations in the sense of limiting physical contact to any greater extent than family life conducted in a non-migration context, the children's perceptions of it are otherwise.

Echoing the findings of Baldassar and Baldock's (2002) work, seven of our adult respondents referred to the attitudes of their family towards their moves as factors shaping the impact of moving on post-migration relationships. Most commonly, this conflict reflected grandparents' responses to the migration of their daughter or son:

> It's been quite traumatic. She [her mother] has taken it as a punishment to be honest – and because I am the only child she had no-one else to give her attention to. It was like I deserted her – people were telling her all sorts of horrible things. It wasn't a positive experience, she just felt abandoned. It was a big responsibility, forever you have to think, well, do I choose my life or do I stick by them. It doesn't mean you don't stick by them – it's the physical break [001].

> We think we've betrayed our family. It's always hard for a family to watch a son leave after raising him for 25 years [327].

Mason also notes the importance of relatives encouraging and supporting the 'migration project', seeing this as a major factor promoting 'distance thinking'. She cites a case in which the respondent's parents-in-law expressed disapproval of the move on the grounds that 'they didn't want to not have their grandchildren around' (1998, p.15).

Some interesting comments were made by our respondents regarding the impact of cultural perceptions of the role of the family and family relationships, many of which reinforce certain cultural stereotypes and provide an interesting insight into the way in which young people's lives are moulded around their family ties. In the first two examples presented below, the statements about the value of family in Italian social life speak to the centrality of the family in the Italian system of social welfare. This is defined by Langan and Ostner (1991, p.131) as an example of a 'mother-daughter economy' when compared with the more socialised, social-democratic approaches of Nordic welfare states. However, in the last quote, which compares Ireland unfavourably with Italy, the respondent suggests that, in some cases at least, these comparisons may not correspond to empirical reality but rather provide an example of 'looking back through rose-tinted spectacles' and reinforcing social and cultural stereotypes:

> In Italy, the whole family lives together. Their family ties seem to be very strong. In Italy, the children don't leave their parents until they are about to get married. Sometimes, they are like 35 years old, and still living with their parents. But we are talking about two different societies. In Italy, the family is very important, and people care a lot about the family. When a child finally leaves his parents, they usually buy him a flat or an apartment for two reasons ... They want their children to have a good start in life, but they also want to make sure that they'll be looked after in the future. In Sweden, we don't act that way. As soon as a child starts at university, he or she is supposed to support him or herself. To take study loans and all that ... In Italy, this isn't the case. People support their children as much as possible ... the family is very important in Italy. Family, family, family ... and then friends [217].

> I felt a bit sorry leaving my cousins, because we are really close. I suppose this was the worst part of it. They are like our sisters. In Italy, family is much more important than in Sweden though [222].

> For us family is the most important thing you can have. We love family. Italians are very close, not like here [in Northern Ireland] [056b].

Family Relationships across Linguistic Boundaries

The work we have referred to above says little about the impact of language on communication within the migrant family and the extent to which this affects transnational kinship. Although Baldassar and Baldock (2002) mention language proficiency as a variable affecting contact, they are referring here to the literacy levels of their Italian migrant sample as opposed to their linguistic competence. The incidence of inter-marriage was high in their academic sample, as in ours, but it is worth noting that in their sample the couples, children and relatives generally shared a common language. Language for the Baldock and Baldassar's academic respondents and for most of Mason's sample was, therefore, not an issue. In our own sample this was often not the case and language added new challenges in terms of kin-keeping and maintaining communication between grandchildren and grandparents and, in some more difficult cases, with separated parents.[15] Language thus emerged as a key variable shaping responses to distance in our work and the ability to maintain relationships at a distance. The incidence of inter-marriage and international partnerships, family breakdown and the age at which many children moved were also important variables in this respect.

The impact of migration upon family life and relationships is evidently more profound when it occurs across linguistic boundaries. Eighty one per cent of our sample (148 respondents) made reference to language and its impact on family relationships. The ability to communicate effectively is central to any relationship with language differences within the family obviously adding a new dimension to kinship communication. Seventy-nine children interviewed spoke a first language which was different to that of at least one side of their extended family. Despite this, the majority could communicate on at least a basic level with family members and managed some form of interaction particularly with other kin of the same generation. For the remaining children interviewed, language did not pose a problem at all either because they were bi-lingual or because all of the family shared a common mother tongue. The children in the following examples display a 'can-do' approach to situations which would pose a serious obstacle to adult relationships:

> I can understand what they say because Italian sounds like French but I have some difficulties to speak so I communicate with my cousins using

---

[15] Discussion of the impact of language on communication between children and parents in divorced and separated families follows in chapter seven. Language also forms the focus of discussion in chapter nine in the context of children's education.

> sign or I write it or I ask my father to translate. None of them speak French at all. When they speak to me I can usually understand it [005].
>
> She [her cousin in Australia] is a year older than me. I remember that we couldn't communicate when I arrived in Australia because she didn't speak Portuguese and I didn't speak English. We played together but each one spoke her own language. Then we became best friends [407].
>
> We [him and his cousins] just played games anyway – between kids it's fine [063].

For some children with limited or no ability to communicate, the experience compounded their sense of isolation from the wider family and their sense of geographical, social and emotional distance. Perhaps unsurprisingly, language was most frequently mentioned as a problem with respect to relationships with grandparents.[16] Other research has referred to the impact of migration upon inter-generational relationships between grandparents and their grandchildren. Baldassar and Baldock (2002, p.69 and p.77) emphasise the importance of visits in promoting relationships between children and their grandparents with respondents in both of their samples talking about visits organised specifically to support these forms of relationship.

Other research, in a non-migration context, emphasises the increasing importance of grandparents as providers of support to their grandchildren and children. Wilk (2000) refers to the importance of intergenerational relationships between grandchildren and their grandparents and the increasing prevalence of these forms of relationship, suggesting that never before have so many people had a grandparent or grandchild for such long periods of their lives. Echoing the criticism of the 'distance-decay' model referred to above, Wilk questions the view put forward by Kornhaber and Woodward (1981) that economic development has cut the vital connections (i.e. time and proximity) of a good relationship between grandparents and their grandchildren. Wilk challenges this interpretation, pointing to the impact of demographic trends and the instability of marriages and partnerships which have:

---

[16] In previous research into gender and migration this was raised as a problem in relation to the relationships between partners and their in-laws, with migrant women expressing frustration at their role as translators (Ackers, 1998). We did not find evidence of this in this study.

turned grandparents into important representatives of stability and continuity, thus making their relationship with grandchildren more significant than in former times (Wilk, 2000, p.26).

Some respondents referred to the fact that grandchildren gave meaning to their grandparents' lives. Certainly other work with retired migrants (Ackers and Dwyer, 2002) adds weight to this view with clear evidence of their role in supporting both their children's (and mainly daughters') endeavours to combine parenting with paid work and their grandchildren, particularly in situations of family crises and breakdown.[17] Grandparents in our research have proved to be important in both *caring for* and *caring about* activities.

The language barrier has proved to be an impediment to kin relationships, however, and grandparents often feel distanced from their grandchildren because they do not speak the same language as their grandchildren. This can serve to exacerbate the legacy of isolation caused by migration. In some instances, grandparents' only means of communication was through a third person (perhaps the parent) who had to translate conversations making it difficult for them to establish an independent and more personal relationship. The children in the following examples explain the impact of language upon their relationships:

> I think they [the grandparents] would like us to speak Dutch with them, but we don't know. They have a much closer relationship with my cousins because they live there and they speak Dutch very well. I think that my grandparents, my mother's parents, feel a bit disappointed that my mother did not teach us Dutch and that she moved here [320].

> The grandparents don't like it when we speak Portuguese. They don't understand it either. They are suspicious of what we say. In France I can't speak French to my sister. I speak Portuguese and the grandparents hate it [324].

Some parents also commented on the fact that language differences had prevented their children from developing a relationship with their grandparents:

> My mother hasn't ever seen my last daughter since she has never been in Greece and they have never communicated since they have not a common language. The language barrier caused problems in my children's

---

[17] Rogerson and colleagues (1997, p.121) also refer to the increase in the amount of childcare provided by grandparents in two-worker households.

> relationship with the extended family. My third child cannot have any relationship or even communicate with her grandmother in Greece [412].

> I have told them that if they try harder with the language it will make things easier for them to understand their family. They will have a better relationship with them [077].

> I mean the situation is that we are both bilingual so the children had to be bilingual. Both grandparents don't speak the other language so the onus was on us to educate the children so that they were both bilingual [068b].

The solution to these problems as far as many parents were concerned was simple: bi-lingualism. Parents did not seem to view this notion with any trepidation, notwithstanding the lack of bilingualism amongst the general non-migrant population and the difficulties many people experience in learning another language. To them it was a practical problem capable of resolution and the onus was on the children (and not the non-migrant relatives) to rise to the challenge. The children were thus strongly encouraged by their parents to learn the language of their relatives in order to promote communication. Seventy-five children (41 per cent) were attending or had attended supplementary language classes or had made efforts to learn the language at school.[18] In many cases parents adopted fairly complex routines to enable their children to practice their language skills. A number of parents for instance only spoke to their children in one particular language at home or at particular times of the day and often children spoke to their mothers and fathers in different languages:

> When we were small, she [their mum] always spoke Italian to us and if we spoke English she'd just ignore us. She would pretend to not hear us and say 'I don't know what you're saying, bla bla' so we had to speak Italian [061].

Children's eagerness to actively engage with relatives on a social level and the sense of frustration and exclusion experienced when they were unable to take part in conversations due to the language barrier is highlighted by the following examples:

> With the other relatives they usually speak in English or they speak in Dutch using some English words. But they manage, they are so greedy to have communication they are forcing themselves, if it's not correct Dutch, never mind, they all laugh, we have a lot of fun, but we communicate [303].

---

[18] See chapter nine on language, learning and EU migrant children.

> I felt pissed off during the lunches and dinners and everyone laughs and I used to really annoy my mum and say, 'What did they just say?' [063].

So far, the examples have focused on the impact of distance on relationships between the migrant nuclear family and its wider kin networks. Perhaps because of the nature of this sample of EU migrant families and the impact of peripatetic and dual career situations, coupled with the prevalence of international partnerships and incidences of family breakdown, our work has identified a relatively high level of separation *within* the immediate nuclear family. A parallel could perhaps be drawn here between the kinds of traditional economic migrations from the colonies which typically involved periods of family separation as male 'pioneers' made the first move to be subsequently joined in a sequence of moves by partners and children. These forms of family separation (although often involving female pioneers) and subsequent re-union (at least with children) are also evident in Anderson (2001) and Phizacklea's (2000) work on Filipino domestics. The following section examines the responses of children and parents to these processes and their impact on the nuclear family unit.

The Impact of Migration on Families: Separation within the Nuclear Family Group

Migration may both reflect and precipitate changes taking place within families. In some instances, moves are precipitated by changes in family structure or relationships – the formation of a new partnership, the arrival of a new baby or the need to care for someone. In other situations, the relationship works in the opposite direction – migration generates changes in family structure and relationships. It may lead to new relationships with host nationals or cause tensions between partners, or it may shape attitudes towards parenting. In research with mobile researchers, for example, we found evidence of women delaying or forgoing motherhood in order to progress in 'mobile' careers (Ackers, 2001).

The following section considers the impact migration has had on relationships within the nuclear family itself and, in particular, the extent to which it results in the geographical separation of family members.

Some of the most serious examples of family separation occurred in the context of parental divorce and parental separation which often resulted in a second phase of migration and the physical, cultural and, on occasions, linguistic separation of children from one or more of their parents. A more detailed consideration of the effect of family breakdown on the families and children interviewed is presented in the next chapter. The interviews reveal, however, that this experience of geographical remoteness is not restricted to children in these circumstances. In very many cases, 'intact' families experienced at least some form of temporary dislocation. A total of 67 families reported a period of temporary or more long-term separation as families managed the tensions between paid work and caring and between the needs of adults and children within a migration context. Of these, around two-thirds involved the separation of one parent from the rest of the family (with children typically living with the mother). The remaining third (24 cases) reported a period in which the child or children were living away from both of their parents.

We talked at some length in chapter three about the nature of parents' careers and the changing characteristics of European labour markets and employment trajectories. In most cases, family separation arose as a result of the father's employment situation (and, to a lesser extent, the tensions implied in dual careers), either because his job required him to make repeated moves, because the moves were temporary or simply because the migration process was 'staged' in some way. This form of separation was often only temporary with the father moving initially for work and the rest of the family subsequently joining him. This situation was quite common and usually involved a delay of only a few months while the children completed their year or term at school and the father made some practical arrangements to facilitate the family's move. The following examples were typical:

> Our father moved half a year before the rest of us [215].

> My husband went to Germany a month earlier in order to find a house for us [429]

> Our father lived in Geneva for a couple of months, before the rest of the family moved [from Sweden] to join him in Brussels [214].

On some occasions, it was the mothers who moved in advance of the father to settle children in schools or, conversely, returned home in advance of the father. Many of these women were similar to Mason's (1998) 'reluctant distance thinkers' in that they accepted the necessity of moving but saw it as a temporary and necessary compromise:

> I came first with the children because it was the opening of the school year. My husband came some months later [433].

Whilst these periods were quite short, the experience may be repeated several times as fathers moved again. In some cases, however, the period of separation extended to several years, as these comments – first from a father and then from a mother – illustrate:

> Well I worked for three years here on my own before my family came here. There was no work in Italy and they came here when I found some work [056].

> [My husband] came to Athens in order to find a job, restore the house, find a good school for the child, etc. We came two years later. [Our son] had missed his father and he wanted to be with him. Consequently, he wanted to come to Greece [443].

For one of the families in the sample, the pressures of the father's job demanded frequent moves which amounted to a period of over seven years of constant moving. Originally, the family – father, mother, daughter and son – moved to Spain from Sweden and stayed there for two years. However, the parents wanted the children to go to a Swedish school and to learn the language so the mother returned to Sweden, with the children, and the father stayed working abroad. They stayed in Sweden for seven years and the father continued to work abroad, taking jobs in Iceland and Saudi-Arabia. Eventually, after he had worked in Saudi-Arabia for one year, the rest of the family decided to join him.

In some instances the families attempted to 'manage' these kinds of situation by maintaining two homes and moving between them during the year. In one example, the family had moved away together but then returned to establish a base in Greece whilst the father continued to move for work, as he explains:

> We returned to Greece last year but I will spend six months per year in Holland and my family [will join me for the] summer vacation [421].

In another example, the family underwent a number of separations over the course of three years. The father was offered a job at short notice and consequently his family was unable to join him immediately and so he moved to Italy six months before the rest of the family. The family joined him but then, after one-and-a-half years, the mother and son moved back to Sweden while the father and daughter stayed in Italy for another year. The mother stated that her fear of losing her job motivated her decision to return to Sweden.

In some situations, the temporary separation of family members was reflected upon quite positively, as providing time for planning and preparation. The mother in the following case reflected upon the relative advantages of 'staging' the migration and the extent to which this facilitated the children's integration in the host state. Once again, the family clearly moved repeatedly:

> My husband had to be in Athens in November. The children were in the middle of the school year in France. We didn't want to interrupt their education. Therefore my husband came alone to Athens and we joined him next year. It was difficult for everyone to live separately! However, it had some positive aspects. Each time we go to a country, we need to find accommodation, school for the children and any other facility. This time, my husband had the time to make inquiries, enroll the children at school etc. This was the first time that the children knew in advance something about the conditions where they would live in for the next five years; information about their school, the neighbourhood. They had the opportunity to have answers to their questions about the country — that helped a lot in their preparations and their adjustment later [436].

Just as initial out-migrations were often planned around jobs and school terms, so too were return moves. Once again, this resulted in temporary separations with – mothers often remained behind with their children to minimise the disruption to children's schooling and ensure progression. In one case, a mother remained in Ireland with her children whilst her partner returned to England for work. She stayed until the end of the school year since her son was doing the equivalent of GCSEs.

What is remarkable about many of these interviews (together with those discussed in chapter three) is the matter-of-fact way in which parents and children tacitly accepted the employment imperative and the necessity of family separation. Very few parents openly acknowledged any problem with this 'way of being' for themselves or their children and openly reasoned about the respective needs of the working father and, on occasions, the mother and their children.[19] Taken at face value, such responses would suggest that the parents at least were 'distance-thinkers' and firmly believed that family relationships, even within the nuclear family group, could or had to be effectively managed at a distance.

In an exception to this, and notwithstanding the very temporary nature of the separation in this case compared to others, the following mother acknowledges that her son clearly suffered as a result of this period

---

[19] These points are discussed in more detail in chapter five.

of separation (despite the short time apart) and the fact that they did not discuss the situation with him beforehand:

> His father went before, 1 or 2 months and [the child] showed to be missing his dad. He almost didn't eat. It was bad for him. Then he recovered but we did wrong really. We should have prepared him [323].

In some instances, factors other than children's education precipitated the move. In one case, a mother referred to her desire to have her baby back home:

> We already had our first daughter when the Company asked my husband to go to Finland for a year. We all went ... but I returned to England with my daughter before my husband. I was pregnant and I preferred to have the delivery in England. We were living with my mother until my husband's return. [They then moved to Greece together] [403].

In another, the child's health and the mother's unhappiness[20] were key factors precipitating a move:

> Sarah (the daughter) was unwell as well. She suffers from Asthma and had a serious attack. I had to go back, although there was no boat going back because of the weather and then the boat went in for its annual refit! So I had to drive for 18 hours, and with Sarah getting unwell I said to [my wife] that, as you have always hated it, why not stay here then. She said, 'all right I bloody well will'. I still had 9 months to do on my contract with them [086].

The Separation of Children from Parents and Siblings

In the examples given above the children had been separated for a period of time from one parent (usually the father). In addition to these forms of separation, we also found evidence of children living apart from both parents and sometimes siblings too. The reasons for this form of separation included concerns about progression and schooling; efforts to immerse children in other languages (by encouraging them to spend periods alone abroad); periods spent with grandparents, relatives and/or family friends to relieve parents of caring obligations; and the commencement of paid work or military service by older children. Finally, in some cases – and this was

[20] Many more examples of the impact of 'missing home' on migration decisions were cited in chapter three.

predominantly the case for children from Sweden – older children remained in their home country simply because they did not want to move.[21]

The group of cases presented below includes situations in which the separation of children from their parents reflected concerns about education and progression.[22] In the first example, the child's father was English and the mother, French. The father was working in France immediately prior to the interview and lived there with the mother whilst the children lived in England. The son explained how he came to the UK because he had found the French education system too formal. At the time of the interview, he was boarding at an international school in England:

> *Son*: "My dad works away a lot."
>
> Q: *When did you come over from France?*
>
> A: "Almost two years ago."
>
> Q: *And your parents are still in France?*
>
> A: "Yes, I have a brother, who came here before me. I then heard about it and he is at University."
>
> Q: *How often do you speak to your parents?*
>
> A: "At first I spoke to them every Monday, but now my dad has a new job in England and they have bought a house in Cambridge, so I am living there on my own in this house, but dad often comes for a night or two, and my mum comes sometimes with him ... In France, ... we had exams all the time, I had four hours of exams per week. I fell very ill in the end and that is why I came here" [088].

The child's father in the next case is an engineer who lives in Ghana with his wife. The child, who lives in England, describes his family as 'basically all over':

---

[21] This point was developed in the discussion in chapter five in the context of the participation of children in migration decision-making. The fact that these respondents were mainly Swedish reflects a 'quirk' of the sampling strategy – an example of the kind of compromises in method common in collaborative research. In the UK and other countries we generally avoided making contacts in boarding schools as we wanted to interview parents and children. A few 'slipped through the net' in the Swedish sample. In the event, however, they proved highly interesting insights.

[22] These issues are discussed in more detail in chapters eight and nine on education.

> I have a sister and she lives in Ghana. We have a house in Germany. My sister has been staying in Germany. My mother will be coming over to Britain soon, my father will still be in Ghana

The decision to attend a college in England reflected the child's concerns about progression and his wish to maximise his options by following the International Baccalaureate (IB) system in an English-speaking country:

> I thought that I couldn't go back to the German system because I failed one year when I went to the States, so if I went back I would have to study in class ten or something like that, therefore it was ruled out, and so I hated the school in Ghana and they were doing A levels which I didn't want to do but I wanted to continue the IB. I couldn't do it in Germany – everyone says you get a higher standard of education under the IB. It is international, so I looked about to see where else in Europe I could study for the IB – an English speaking country [094].

The following cases were also quite typical and show how migration and, in particular, repeated migration resulted in separation within the family group and 'phased' moves as some siblings were 'left behind' in order to continue with their education or employment:

> In these moves, the family wasn't always together. They went together to England but the sisters have stayed there to study. So, they didn't live in Spain or in Portugal [349].

> The father, the mother and the younger daughter came to Greece 18 months ago. Their second daughter joined them some months later. The older one studies in England [408].

> We moved again, to Germany where we have been staying for four years and then we returned to Greece. Well, not all of us! My older sister had been already in England for studies [431].

The upheaval associated with moving to a new country and securing new employment resulted in many parents leaving children temporarily with family in the home state. Of course, this form of separation usually occurred in dual career situations. In the next case, the father had employment ties in more than one country and the mother worked in the travel business, as the mother explains:

> It was impossible at that time to settle down in a country. I continued working in the travel-agency and he [her husband] had business both in Greece and in Spain. For several years our home was the plane. The child

> was living at that time mainly with the paternal grandparents in Athens. But he also spent a lot of time with us in Spain.

The child described the situation as follows:

> My parents were traveling in the beginning and I was living with my grandparents in Greece. Sometimes, I lived with them in Spain; not very often because they were busy [445].

In another case, the mother was of Swedish/Italian descent and the father was from the Czech Republic. They had four sons and lived briefly in the United States when the boys were very young. Since returning to Sweden, the three older boys had spent three weeks every summer in England studying at an international language school. Their eldest brother, who was 16, had already lived in England for three years at the beginning of his teens where he attended an English public school and stayed with friends of the family – a move which his parents said was 'entirely his own decision' [204].

Another group of mainly older children returned home following a period spent living abroad. In this situation, the older children were often returning in order to re-integrate socially or to ensure that they did not experience progression problems in the transition from secondary school to higher education. In one of the cases, a child returned to Sweden at the age of nineteen where she has remained for the past four years. Her mother, stepfather and younger brother are still living in Belgium:

> I was very negative towards the decision to move, and I didn't really want to change my mind either. I was very determined not to like it. I really wanted to move back home. When I started my last year at school, I said to my parents, 'I'll move back to Sweden after I've graduated'. It didn't matter whether I had anything to occupy myself with or not. After graduation, I hadn't, and I became unemployed. But I moved back to Sweden and arranged a place to live ... I didn't go back to my old way of living, but started up a new life ... I already knew the city, and that's an advantage. And then, I started all over again. But I definitely didn' t want to return to Brussels. My mother tried to persuade me that I could take a course at the international school in Brussels. But I was very determined that I didn't want to go back, and I still am. [224].

In another case, a child also decided to return to Sweden three years previously on her own where she attended a well-known boarding school. Her younger brother had also recently decided to return to Sweden and became a student at the same boarding school:

> My parents always returned to Sweden in the summer, and then I'd meet them. And we wrote to each other ... to me, this wasn't a problem. I didn't think that much about it. We always kept our house in Sweden. We've never sold it. During the years we've been living abroad, our aunt has been taking care of it, or living there herself. She still does. My parents didn't want to sell the house, because they wanted us to be able to go back to Sweden. Otherwise, we would have to stay with our relatives. It has been rather important to us ... Especially now, when we're in a boarding school and we want to go home at the weekends. Then it's nice to be able to go home to our own place [227].

Similar situations were reported by parents, many of whom appeared to accept the 'necessity' or expediency of separation as part of their life-course and as a necessary compromise in attempting to reconcile individual needs and wishes. In many ways they took a 'matter of fact' approach to these forms of separation:

> My daughter plans to leave for France next year. Currently, she studies a lot in order to pass her Baccalaureate. She very much wants to return to France. We will stay in Greece at present and then we hope that we will be sent to a country close to France. We want to be close to our children but we don't wish to return to France yet [434].

In one case, the impact of separation from siblings was felt quite keenly by the child who remained with her parents. Her objective was thus to study hard in order to be able to join her brothers in their school. The separation from her brothers was evidently more painful than her anticipated separation from her parents:

> When my first brother left for France, it was awful for me. When the second one left too my life changed. I felt very alone. Home is different now! I miss them a lot and I very much looking forward to joining them. I am very much concentrating on studying because I definitely want to pass my exams. Therefore my typical day is school and studying even at weekends [434].

Caring 'for' Family at a Distance[23]

We have already referred to the ways in which the emergence of forms of dependency demanding more intensive practical support can transform

---

[23] For more detailed discussion of the relationship between care and mobility, see Ackers, 1998; Ackers and Dwyer, 2002; and Ackers, 2002.

geographical reasoning. In some instances, an effective response to these kinds of need may be achieved through the organisation and financing of care by the migrant family (and require only a short visit or other forms of communication). Baldassar and Baldock (2002, p.70) refer to the significant financial contribution migrants made in terms of purchasing equipment (such as washing machines) or funding nursing care: 'Perhaps the most significant example of caring at a distance is evident in the widespread practice of the migrant forgoing their inheritance'. They suggest that this practice could be interpreted as an acknowledgement of their responsibilities to their families and the burden of care imposed on non-migrant sibling carers.

Although their university sample did not indicate a significant involvement in direct 'care-giving' tasks (at least at the point of interview), they did find a number of cases involving temporary return moves in order to care for dying relatives and support siblings. The incidence of these moves increased significantly in the case of sole surviving parents and also when other family members were not available to provide support.[24] Rogerson and colleagues (1997, p.124) also point to the importance of 'sibling structure' on intergenerational contact:

> ... daughters are more likely than sons to provide informal support to elderly parents and it is not family size but the presence of a daughter that affects the level of parental help.

This situation is supported by the findings of research with migrant women of working age which identified situations in which migrant daughters, on occasion, assumed a primary caring role (at least in terms of organising care and managing care crises) even in circumstances when male siblings lived much closer to the dependant relative (Ackers, 1998). This did not always prove to be the case, however, and other factors, such as the family status and situation of proximate sibling carers may mitigate this effect. Subsequent work with retired migrants (Ackers and Dwyer, 2002) found the gender of the carer to be less significant, but this is perhaps because we were dealing with retired people. To that extent, the tension between paid work and unpaid caring roles was less evident and the incidence of spousal and intra-generational care was much greater.

Baldassar and Baldock's (2002, p.84) research leads them to question the validity of a 'simple gendered construct of caring from a

---

[24] Return moves motivated by the desire or obligation to support sibling carers and the impact of the availability of other family carers on migration decisions were also reported in Ackers, 1998 and Ackers and Dwyer, 2002.

distance'. Male migrants were in a similar situation to females in terms of their ability to rely on siblings back home. What they did find, however, was a gendered division of caring labour with males more likely to be involved in economic support and assistance with repair and maintenance work whilst women provided more emotional and personal support.[25]

Returning to the current project, in ten of the families interviewed, respondents referred to the care needs of an elderly relative as a key factor precipitating a move. In all ten of these cases, at least one of the parents was a returnee. Collectively, these cases illustrate the complex interplay between life-course events (such as family (re)formation, bereavement and caring relationships) and mobility. In one of these cases, a child's father had died suddenly when he was only four and the child subsequently developed behavioural problems and was diagnosed as having Attention Deficiency and Hyperactivity Disorder. The father was a German national and met the boy's mother in the UK when they were students. They returned to Germany for his national service, when they had their first son, and then moved back to the UK until he died:

> We moved [to Germany] after he [her husband] died, his mum also had a heart attack so they needed someone to be close to her. She was in quite a bad way losing her son and had a heart attack due to the shock so I moved out there temporarily really to keep an eye on her and give her some support and also as part of the grieving process. I needed something too and I hoped that we'd settle down there and I thought that Peter might enjoy it ... We came back after about fifteen months to England and a lot of it was to do really with the school system and the fact that he wasn't very happy in the kindergarten [074].

This example raises many interesting issues. Firstly, it illustrates some of the problems (referred to in chapter two) of relying exclusively on the reports and memories of children. Clearly, the child was too young to remember accurately the sequencing and reasoning behind the family's moves. Secondly, in the context of the current discussion about care, this example also highlights the importance of understanding care as an evolutionary and reciprocal process and the inadequacy of legal and policy distinctions which tend to assume one-way flows of caring resources and a discrete population of care providers and recipients. The child's mother was clearly in need of support herself when her partner died but nevertheless responded to the needs of her mother-in-law and moved in order to help her cope with her bereavement. Her subsequent return to the UK was, she

[25] This is supported by the findings of recent Time-Use surveys (Perista, 2002).

suggests, motivated by another dimension of care - the need to access good childcare for her younger son who himself had special needs. Distance, in this case, was not a barrier to contact and the mother's moves on a number of occasions were motivated by care issues. In this case the lack of sibling support for her mother-in-law in Germany was clearly a factor, and this was common in other respondents' accounts:

> My husband was a lecturer in a [British] University. We've been very well settled. In 1989 my mother got seriously ill and she asked us to be with her. I am an only child. My parents wanted my support [414].

> My parents were getting old and I was their only child. We couldn't stay on the island where they live, but I had to be in Greece. Australia was too far! [407]

The reference to distance in this last example suggests that perhaps managing kin relationships in the European context (and moving between Germany and the UK or Germany and Greece was often the case) did not present the same kind of obstacle to care as moves from places like Australia. We have already noted how migration decisions are rarely, if ever, dominated by one factor. Typically a cluster of issues are 'in the pot' and at any one point in time the increasing salience of one issue might tip the balance in favour of a move in one direction or another. This is particularly the case as migrants reach 'middle age' and career progression is tempered by other concerns and exerts less influence. The following two examples reflect this tendency and also the 'dovetailing' of two specific factors – the increasing levels of dependency amongst kin back home and their own need to return home at this point in their lives:

> We came back to Greece in 1996. There were two reasons this time. My husband's father, who is very aged and ill, needed our care. Besides, we were getting older and we wanted to spend the rest of our life in Greece [422].

> My husband has always dreamt of returning to Greece. He was home-sick, his parents became old, we had a home in Athens [408].

It is possible that the age structure of Baldassar and Baldocks' (2002) sample meant that some of these processes had not yet emerged. Certainly in the work with retired migrants these factors figured with increasing impact in the later stages of the life-course. Some evidence of the impact of the 'collapse' of traditional life-course phases upon the migration decision-making processes of migrant women was evident in the gender and migration work, however, as women and, in particular, professional women have children later and the population of retired people increasingly encompasses two generations.

The impact of bereavement on surviving family members, as we have seen above, was evident in other cases:

> [We returned to Portugal] because my grandfather died, my mother's father, and we wanted to provide support for my grandmother [310].

In another case, the family had managed to 'care at a distance' for sometime before a crisis situation arose precipitating an immediate migration:

> I met my husband in France where he had migrated in the early seventies in order to work. We got married and we had a comfortable life. We both have had good and profitable jobs and a nice family. My husband is an only child. His only relative, an aged father, refused to come and live with us in France. My husband was very concerned about him. The only thing we could do was to visit him as much as we could. In the summer of 1984, we visited Greece as we did almost every year. My father-in-law was already old and ill. At that time he had a serious stroke. My husband couldn't leave him alone [401].

This case illustrates the impact of 'care crises' upon geographical reasoning. Whilst certain forms of contact and care can be managed at a distance the emergence, sometimes quite suddenly, of caring needs may emphasise the importance of proximity. The respondent in the case above also alludes to the influence of the attitude of the elderly relative on this process. We have already referred to the problems, in practice, of exercising the Community law right of ascendant relatives to move to join their citizen-worker carers. In all of our research, we have found very few examples of effective exercise of this entitlement – it was far more common for the care-providing relatives to return in order to care than for the dependant family member to be shipped out to join them. In practice, moving very elderly and frail people transnationally risks isolating them from their social contacts and also from the support of local voluntary, informal and statutory welfare systems.

Distance and Support with Child Care

The importance of informal support to mothers is highlighted in Finch and Mason's (1993, p.164) research which concluded that despite growing evidence of changing family patterns, such as the increase in rate of divorce and trends in favour of cohabitation, the existence of stable and supportive family networks remains paramount in people's lives. Indeed, as Finch (1989, p.30) states earlier, 'small scale practical support, given either on a regular or occasional basis is often sees as the essence of kin relationships'. Cornwell (1984, pp 86-90) similarly emphasises the importance of familial support to working mothers, arguing that the increasing participation of women in the labour market has necessitated a reorganisation of domestic obligations such as child care and a growing dependence upon family support:

> It seems that it is of continuing importance for women to be able to call upon relatives to assist them with child care and that this still is a key element in women's organisation of their daily lives, as it has been in the past.[26]

Yeandle's (1984) research in the UK found that about two thirds of the women studied had relied upon female kin at some stage for assistance with child care, principally from mothers and mothers-in-law as well as from sisters, sisters-in-law, aunts and grandmothers. Jensen (1989, p.119) similarly notes the gendered nature of informal support with childcare suggesting that, 'almost without exception, [the children] will be taken care of by women, either their own mothers or women who get paid for the work' or, indeed, by their parents' mothers or other female relatives.

Our research indicates that this is very much the case. There is also some evidence that kind of kin support it is of particular importance when women (and less frequently men) are left as the custodial parent following divorce.[27] Migrant mothers generally lack access to this kind of support. The reference to the nature of support in this context and, in particular, to its regular and on-going nature as a key element in the organisation of women's daily lives distinguishes it from the kinds of care situations we have referred to above which demand immediate and intensive, but often relatively short-term, interventions. If this kind of daily support constitutes what Finch (1989) has termed the 'essence of kin relationships', then

---

[26] See also the work of Yeandle, 1984; Boh, et al., 1989; Bernstein and Brannen, 1996; Jones and Millar, 1996; and Drew, Emerek and Mahon, 1998.

[27] See for further discussion chapter seven.

distance is likely to have a significant impact upon the lives of migrant mothers.

The central focus on gender issues and the relationship between women's public and private roles in the previous gender and migration project (Ackers, 1998) demanded more detailed attention to these issues than the current project which has focused on children. The interviews with migrant women revealed high levels of isolation amongst mothers who frequently lacked any informal support in the country of residence. One woman put the point succinctly saying simply that, 'You have no family if you are a foreigner' (quoted in Ackers, 1998, p.284). These problems were felt particularly keenly amongst single parents and mothers caring for disabled children. In all of our projects, including the work with retirement migrants, respondents have talked extensively about care for children and grandchildren as a factor shaping their location decisions and feelings about living at a distance. When parents in the children project were questioned about the practical implications of migrating to another country many (predominantly mothers) referred to the importance of support from family members (usually mothers or mothers-in-law) when their children were young and the extent to which migration had deprived them of this. Thirty two of the children interviewed were cared for at some point on a part-time basis by their relatives (usually while their parents were working) and fifteen adult respondents made direct reference to the fact that they missed this kind support following the migration. We have already referred to the high incidence of international partnerships in the sample. What this meant in practice for many parents was that one set of relatives were living in closer proximity than the other (typically the father's parents perhaps reflecting the dominance of male interests in migration decision-making). In these situations we see a mixed response. On the one hand, it was clearly beneficial to have access to family support. On the other hand, women often reported feeling upset that their own mothers were excluded from this close personal contact with their grandchildren. The context in which many migrant women are receiving family support and the nature of the kin relationships involved is evidently somewhat different from non-migrant mothers who, in the absence of state support or independent resources, rely first and foremost on their own mothers and often sisters for mutual support:

> [My] husband's mother looked after Sarah a lot and that was good. But I would have liked my mother to have looked after her as well and shared it ... it was a struggle not to have her near [001].

> Since my husband's parents are living pretty close, they've helped us with the children and stuff like that ... This was very important when the children were small. Of course I would like my own family to be closer, for the children's sake [201].

> It's very intensive being a parent anyway, but being a parent and not having this family support around you makes it extra difficult [211].

> My parents-in-law, as I told you, live in the same building. They have been always been around and they help a lot in the children's care and upbringing. They are second parents for the children, not only grandparents [405].

> I missed that more than anything, because you find you can't trust people like you can your family. I really missed not having my family although I had a good friend who helped me out. But at the end of the day, you feel you're imposing. With your own family, you're not taking liberties [067].

In the last example above, the issue of family obligations and the extent to which women felt they could more easily turn to family for support without feeling that they were exploiting the goodwill of friends is raised. The pressures on migrant mothers and the impact of moving upon the level of assistance they received (and the impact of this on their ability to combine mothering with paid work) depends not only on the availability of kin but also on the domestic welfare system and the nature and costs of accessing public and voluntary sector provision. The situation is particularly problematic for those women who have migrated to countries and regions which are characterised by a 'familistic' model and, as a consequence, offer little in the way of support to families who lack access to informal networks.[28] The transition to a new country potentially presents

[28] Papadopoulos (1998, cited in Drew, et al, 1998) notes that in child care provision for children up to 3 years of age a clear case of divergence emerges between the Member States. On the one hand countries such as Austria, Germany, Greece, Ireland, Luxembourg, Spain and the UK have minimum provision for only 2 to 3 per cent of children in this age group. Italy and the Netherlands offer marginally higher levels of support to 6 and 8 per cent respectively. Finland is likened to France in the assistance it provides in this area followed by Belgium and Sweden which accommodates over one third of children in this age group. At the top end of the scale Denmark covers up to 50 per cent of child care for children under 3. Provision is significantly higher for children between 3 and 6 years of age, with Finland and Portugal at the lower end (43 and 48 per cent respectively) followed by Ireland (58 per cent), Luxembourg (55-60 per cent) and the UK (60 per cent). Spain and Greece with 64 per cent are closer to the average. At the upper end of the continuum are the Netherlands (72 per cent), Sweden (72 per cent), Austria (75 per cent), former West Germany (78 per cent) and Denmark (79 per cent). Italy, Belgium, France and the former East Germany are at the top, all providing more than 90 per cent of support for this age-group of children. Overall,

practical problems for those families who had previously either relied heavily on kin support or benefited from extensive social support from the state or voluntary sector. In this situation, migrants are likely to be left with neither family nor state assistance with child care. This was highlighted in the report of the European Commission Network on Childcare (1996, p.13) network on child care:

> People who have left their countries of origin, for whatever reason, may have achieved gains in terms of employment, or of physical security, but there are also losses. They are out of reach of their own families and other familiar networks.[29]

Chapter three emphasised the fact that the free movement of persons provisions – and the extension of social rights in the Member States – was based upon the principle of non-discrimination rather then harmonisation. To that extent, citizenship status, in terms of access to social resources, depends not only on the formal legal entitlement under the free movement provisions, but on the interplay of that with the framework of material provision available in individual Member States. The impact of moving on citizenship thus depends on the geography of the move. As such, significant variations in forms and levels of provision persist with important implications for the migrating family. The organisation and funding of childcare in countries such as Ireland, Portugal, Germany and Greece, for instance, is still very much based on the idea of a home-based, dependent, wife and mother with principal responsibility for child care and home-making. To that extent, these countries provide little in the way of socialised childcare and family support (Drew et al, 1998, p.28). Drew and colleagues note that the research of Papadopoulos (1998) confirms this point noting that:

> In Greece, as in most southern European countries, the key welfare provider is the 'family'... A comparison of family composition in the European Union countries reveals the strong attachment of Greeks to the nuclear family form ... The centrality of family as a social institution in Greece is clearly manifested in ideological and symbolic terms in the social values and attitudes held by Greek men and women (Drew et al., 1998, p. 54).

Denmark, Belgium, France and Sweden boast the most comprehensive child care provision in the European Union (Drew et al., 1998). Marked differences also exist between rural and urban areas.

[29]See also Commission of the European Communities, 1990; Simpson and Walker, 1993; Daycare Trust and National Childcare Campaign, 1994; and Ruxton, 1996.

Papodopoulous notes, however, that despite the alleged strong attachments of Greeks to 'the family', welfare state support for families is almost non-existent. This inconsistency is illustrative of the socio-economic role that the nuclear family performs in Greece as welfare-providers for its members in both affective and material terms. Thus Greek family policy, through it's commitment to non-intervention, implicitly nurtures and reproduces the ideological assumption that the family (essentially the mother) is the main provider of welfare in society. A number of respondents in Greece made reference to the inadequacy of Greek state provision in this area and the impact of this upon their lives:

> Greece is not famous for its supportive system for families! [435]

> Actually I had nobody around to help me with the children. My mother came for a while when I gave birth to the children but then I was alone. My parents-in-law were unable to take care of the children, as they were old and ill. In fact, they are in need of our help. It was very difficult for me to bring up my children. I did not have any help since everyone had his/her own duties ... I stayed at home with them every day until they were three and a half years old and could be admitted in the Child Care school. We couldn't afford to send them to a private Child Care school that admits younger children. And now, I can only work in the mornings, when the children are at school [423].

> My mother-in-law was living with us and she was indeed very helpful to me not only in the children's bringing up. She took care of the children every time that I was away on business. My own parents were away and busy with their own occupations. In Finland when a child is going to be born, the parents are entitled to have, free of charge from the State, all material that a baby needs. Families in Finland have great support from the State for the children's upbringing. This way they are encouraged to have many children. In Greece the social policy is formed by a different mentality. The State does not offer much and this way there is a limited authority of public agencies in family life [441].

> Having four children, the mother especially is really very busy. It is impossible for somebody to succeed in this without support and assistance. In my case the support was coming from my husband and the assistance from my mother. If a mother in Greece has not a mother or a mother-in-law to help her with the children's care, she is lost. Greece does not provide solutions for few hours. For example if you want to go for shopping, you have to carry the child or the children with you if they are too young to go to school. This is a real need in Greece [432].

Additionally, the implications of the inability to rely upon informal support depends to some extent on the level and take-up of material support available within the host society, which itself is shaped by cultural attitudes towards different forms of support (Ackers, 1998, p.223-271). So, even where statutory support exists, migrant mothers may not feel able to utilise it.

In several interviews, women refer to the temporary support they received following the birth of their child when their own mothers travelled out to help them. This was a common situation and relates to a point we made early about the distinction between definable periods of crisis or intensive need (circumstances in which kin may be able to overcome the distance barrier for a limited period), and the kind of day-to-day, less intensive help, like picking children up from school, which often prevents mothers' complete withdrawal from paid work. It is these kinds of care practices that seem so susceptible to distance-decay and this has serious consequences for the women concerned. These women also made reference to the prohibitive costs of publicly available childcare.

Conclusion

The findings of our research suggest that whilst distance transforms relationships and relationships shape perceptions of distance, migrant families do not eschew their kin obligations but invest significantly in maintaining family relationships across geographical space. The impact of distance on kinship reflects a whole range of variables. At some stages in the life-course, kin relationships are 'do-able' with minimum amounts of intensive personal contact, and the effects of distance are increasingly mitigated by the development of ever faster and cheaper forms of communication via telephone, email and visits. To some extent, visits in this context hold an excitement and expectancy that actually supports good relationships.

Our research has underlined the importance of understanding both the impact of family formation and parenting upon migration processes and wider family relationships and also the impact of migration on the children themselves and their relationships with family. We have found evidence in our sample of the two elements of 'distance-thinking' referred to by Mason (1998). On the one hand, we found examples, particularly amongst parents, of the notion that proximate living might be 'too close for comfort' and restrictive of personal autonomy. On the other, we found many cases in which respondents, and particularly parents again, felt that meaningful kinship relationships could be successfully nurtured and maintained at a distance. The children in our sample were generally more inclined to be 'local thinkers' in this respect, however, and missed the kind of day-to-day contact with grandparents, cousins and wider kin. Mason refers to the fact that her sample included people who had, at some point, lived in close proximity to their family prior to their move. It may be that this experience of proximate living allowed sufficient intimacy and friendship to develop prior to the migration. The challenge of distance then was to maintain those relationships. Many of the children in our sample did not have this initial intense experience to build upon and faced the challenge of actually forming relationships transnationally.

As Mason points out, the nature of the caring needs and caring context also shapes the way people think about distance. Whilst the kind of intermittent visits supported by other forms of communication may be sufficient to promote 'non-dependent', affective relationships between children and their extended family, the emergence of forms of dependency and care needs may imply a very different response. Our findings indicate two different kinds of situation here – first, situations where some form of temporally-limited 'care crisis' or episode emerged which may be responded to by a temporary return or extended visit; and second, the on-going, less intensive and more routine kinds of practical support provided to mothers with young children. The former kinds of situation, whilst posing serious challenges to migrant families, may nevertheless be consistent with 'distance-thinking' approaches. The kinds of small-scale but on-going practical support provided to working mothers is more or less impossible to sustain in a migration context. The consequence of this lack of support is evident in our research. On the one hand, it impacts dramatically on the labour market participation of EU migrant women, resulting in temporary or permanent withdrawal as women, dislocated from sources of informal support and with limited access to other forms of statutory or voluntary sector assistance, struggle to combine unpaid caring work with employment. On the other hand, if and when relationships within the migrant family break down and the only support she has in the form of her citizen-worker partner dissipates, most of these women return home to access informal care networks. Distance, in the context of motherhood, and particularly single parenthood, thus has a significant impact on kin relationships and geographical reasoning.

In another important way, however, the other studies discussed in this chapter can be distinguished from our own. These studies are, in the main, looking at the impact of distance on relationships within the wider 'extended' family – with ascendant relatives and adult children. As such, they do not consider the dislocation which migration often brings within the immediate nuclear family itself and the potential for separation. In these situations the kind of gradual evolution of relationships is replaced by often immediate changes in family circumstances with members of families moving at once from co-residence to geographical separation. Kinship, within the context of our study, not only demands consideration of relationships within extended families but also within the nuclear family itself. The prevalence of this kind of situation emerged as a feature of our study, perhaps reflecting the experiences of an increasing number of European citizens given the impact of changing labour markets, the growth in peripatetic and dual career situations, of international partnering and parenting and, its corollary, international family breakdown.

Our research has identified many situations in which employment circumstances or concerns around educational progression result in the separation of parents from children or the separation of siblings from each other. In such situations, the nature of geographical reasoning is quite different between the parents and children (depending on their age and perspective and perhaps the extent to which they have been involved in the decision) displaying very much a 'can-do' or 'have to do' approach to distance.

Arguably the forms of intra-Community mobility identified in the course of this and our related work suggests that migration, particularly of the highly skilled within the EU, has more in common with forms of inter-regional mobility than 'traditional' international migration. The limited geographical scale of moves within the EU, the increasing availability of regular flights between regional airports reducing the costs of travel in both a financial and temporal sense, perhaps lays the foundations conducive to distance-thinking. On the other hand, the nature of the care required at any point in time may play a role – whilst supporting children's education is clearly a dimension of 'care' it may be a form of care that can be provided at a distance. This is not to suggest that it is, as Johnson (1988, p.171) suggests, more perfunctory and less reliable, but rather that it can be successfully managed in some contexts for some children. As such, it is perhaps important to distinguish these forms of care from the practical, hands-on caring of dependant elderly relatives which forms the focus of much of the previous research referred to above.

Whilst the geography of the moves may have a significant impact on the management of kin relationships transnationally – with moves within Europe proving more manageable than those to Australia, for example – language emerged as a considerable barrier to kin relationships even when distances themselves are not quantitatively great. Linguistic competence and the encouragement of bi-lingualism amongst children thus supported distance-thinking. However, many children resented the pressure to remain bilingual particularly in adolescence or after lengthy residence in the host state. In such cases, the inability to even talk to relatives on the telephone or participate in family discussions during visits rarefied the impact of distance on kin relationships.

Baldassar and Baldock (2002, p.86) refer to the importance of seeing migration and care as intergenerational and transnational *processes* rather than as 'one-time events ending in settlement'. This emphasis on process and the evolutionary and often unpredictable nature of migration decision-making and the life-course is certainly echoed in all of our work. To that extent, it is important to recognise the importance of context, its constantly changing nature and the influence of this upon geographical reasoning. A person may be a distance-thinker in one context but a local thinker in another reflecting, perhaps, the quality of relationships, changes in family structure and responsibilities as children are born or leave home or parents become ill, thus changing financial circumstances or the need for social support.

The following chapter continues to examine the relationship between migration and families, this time focusing on the particular problems raised in the interviews in cases of relationship breakdown.

7 Divorce, Separation and Parental Responsibility: The Status and Experiences of EU Migrant Children

Introduction

Chapter four has highlighted the inadequacies inherent in the Community law definition of the family and its failure to keep pace with changes in family structure, marriage and partnering practices. The report of the High Level Panel on the free movement of persons presented to the European Commission in March 1997 (European Commission, 1997) recommended two changes to the concept of family – specifically to the requirement of dependency and the concept of spouse – on the grounds that filling these two main gaps will allow families to remain together. The rationale for further intervention in the family sphere is thus grounded firmly in notions of functional 'intact' family units and family reunion as a mechanism to facilitate mobility and, ultimately, to achieve the internal market objectives. The wording of another section in the main body of the report (1997, p.51) reinforces this objective:

> It may … be concluded, from the point of view of family interests, that the objective of free movement has, thanks in part to the case law of the Court of Justice, been attained. However, several problems remain concerning family reunification and access to social advantages. The panel has opted to deal with the question of social advantages under this heading, dealing with family status in so far as access to those advantages is a means of achieving the objective of the preservation of family unity and of fostering integration in the host country.

This conceptualisation of the limitations of Community law and the protection offered to families exercising their rights to move, whilst welcome, nevertheless ignores the prevalence and consequences of family separation and divorce in particular for the partners and children of Community workers. It is now universally acknowledged, for instance, that the sequence of life events such as 'partnering', marriage and childbirth are no longer prescribed: becoming a parent is no longer coincidental with being a partner or a spouse; and, moreover, phases of family and relationship formation can be repeated throughout the lifecycle, for example through divorce, remarriage and reconstructed families (Ackers, 1998; Dumon, 2000; Stalford, 2002). The European Observatory on National Family Policies (1997, p.23) notes in this regard:

> As adults' behaviour in relation to family formation and dissolution has changed over the last few decades, so too have children's experiences of family forms. At any one time, there is now a more diverse range of family types in which children may live. Thus while the majority of children in the EU live with both their natural married parents, a significant and increasing minority live within an alternative set of arrangements: with one of their parents only as part of a lone parent family, with their non-married parents in cohabiting couple families, and in re-constituted families, for example ... Moreover, as a result of trends in relationship breakdown and re-partnering, we can expect that the likelihood of an individual child directly experiencing more than one family type in the duration of his or her childhood has increased.

Such patterns create more complex challenges to 'international families' since they often lead to the migration of one or other party to a different Member State or back to their country of origin (or elsewhere). This has undoubtedly led to more elaborate parenting arrangements in a migration context contributing to the incidence of complex cross-national residence, contact and maintenance disputes and, at the extreme, international parental child abduction.

Building on the discussion of the concept of family under the free movement provisions in chapter four, this chapter considers the legal effects of post-migratory divorce and separation on spousal and family rights. It focuses in particular on the legal prospects of divorcees who have relied solely on their status as a spouse to derive initial entitlement under the free movement provisions. The chapter then moves on to examine the impact of marital breakdown on the children of EU migrant workers, noting the specific difficulties involved in negotiating divorce, contact, residence and maintenance arrangements across legal and geographical boundaries. It will refer particularly to the significant legal developments that have taken place in the last two years at EU level to address problems associated with determining jurisdiction and enforcing recognition of divorce and parental responsibility arrangements across Member States and consider the nature and extent of children's involvement in such processes.

The Legal Impact of Separation and Divorce

There is very little ECJ case law concerning the effect of divorce and separation on a spouse with Community citizenship. The cases discussed below all involve spouses of third country nationality and some uncertainty exists over whether a spouse with Community nationality would be dealt with similarly. A spouse already holding Member State nationality may derive an independent right of residence under Council Directive 90/364 as an 'EU Citizen' provided he or she is financially independent. While protecting such a spouse from the risk of expulsion, however, this directive does not provide for access to the panoply of social rights available to migrant workers and their spouses, for example under Article 7(2) Regulation 1612/68.

One of the first cases in which domestic courts have considered the impact of divorce on the rights of a non-Community spouse was that of *Grewal.* The English High Court decided that the plaintiff, a divorced third country national, had relinquished his right under the free movement provisions to remain indefinitely in the UK at the point of the divorce. This approach was reaffirmed in the subsequent case of *Sandhu.* Sandhu was a male of third country nationality who gained entry into the UK by virtue of his status as the spouse of a Community migrant worker. Some years later his German spouse left to return (apparently permanently) to Germany, along with their son. Mr Sandhu then applied for unrestricted leave to remain in the UK where he held a full-time job. The High Court judge, Comyn, J. (in what is regarded amongst those of the legal profession as a characteristically humane approach which may not have been adopted by other members of the judiciary) described the issues as follows:

> Can an EEC national admitted to this country as such together with her non-EEC husband deprive him of EEC protection by, for example, deserting him, separating from him, by going to live elsewhere in this country, by going back to her native State or by going somewhere else abroad? If she can automatically and over any interval of time do that, it would ... add a new terror to marriage (para. 11).

Comyn, J. continued to argue that there cannot be a hard and fast rule either way; it must always depend upon circumstances – whether it was a marriage of convenience or whether the parting took place after a fairly short period of time – in which case, 'it might well be proper to say that the EEC protection was lost by the non-EEC member' (para. 12). He then referred to the commitment of the EU, under the free movement of persons provisions, to:

> take into account family and other commitments of the person involved ... in particular as regards the worker's right to be joined by his family and the conditions for the integration of that family into the host country (para. 31).

This commitment, he argued, should not be:

> construed as meaning that there is a permanent cloak thrown around the non-EEC partner; a cloak of a general permanent condition. But it gives him a status of which, in my judgement, the other party by a unilateral act cannot deprive him (para. 33).

Despite constant reference to the 'family', however, neither secondary legislation nor the judiciary attempt to define the term. We are, therefore, left to assume that by 'family' reference is to some notional 'nuclear' family norm; a family form which is more of an ideological construct than a reality and has been in steady decline across Europe for many years. Comyn J. argued, by analogy to the right of family members to remain following the death of a worker, that divorced or separated spouses should be entitled to remain. Referring then to the preamble to Council Directive 73/148 on the abolition of restrictions on movement and residence, he notes, 'that is again a clear indication of the EEC law gathering the family of a spouse under its cloak, not the spouse's cloak.' At first instance, therefore, the Court held that Mr Sandhu should be allowed to stay indefinitely and permanently and that separation and divorce did not automatically extinguish spousal rights. The Court of Appeal ([1983], 3 CMLR 131), however, took a different view on the grounds that, 'put the other way around', the worker's less generous right to be joined by his family did not imply,

> the family's right to join the worker. There is a right given to a spouse as a member of the family, it is a right not to come here independently of the other spouse, but a right to install themselves with a worker who ... and note it is in the present tense … is employed in the territory of another member state...in the present case the husband can only make a claim to a right for permission to stay in this country as long as the wife herself is exercising it.[1]

[1] Clearly this position has been challenged by the proposed directive on the right to family reunification, COM (1999) 638 final, amended by COM (00) 624 final. This seeks to harmonise domestic legislation to grant a right to family reunification to all third country nationals legally resident in the Member State (including refugees) (Kostakopolou, 2002, pp.13-14).

Steiner (1996, p.257) suggests that if the matter had been referred to the Court of Justice, its conclusions would have been closer to those of the English High Court on the grounds that:

> Policy reasons in favour of giving some security of residence to divorced or abandoned spouses of a bona fide marriage, especially when there may be children of that marriage who will still remain members of the worker's family surely require that the law be construed to ensure that a spouse's EC rights do not necessarily cease on divorce or when the worker leaves the country.

In any case, even if the Court of Appeal had granted Sandhu an ongoing right to remain in the UK independently of his wife, his status in other Member States, namely his right to visit his son in Germany, would have remained uncertain.[2]

The ECJ considered the impact of separation in another case, *Diatta v Land Berlin,* involving the Senegalese wife of a French Community worker living in Germany, who had separated with the intention of seeking a divorce. The question of whether the spouse of a migrant worker is required to live with the migrant worker in order to retain her rights was referred to by the Court of Justice. Ms Diatta claimed that the provisions of Regulation 1612/68 (Article 10) do not impose an express obligation to cohabit. The requirement of a migrant worker to make available to his family housing 'considered as normal ... in the region where he is employed' (Article 10(3)), is based on requirements of public policy and does not infer that married couples should live together. Moreover, a worker who is a national of a Member State cannot be allowed to cause the expulsion of a spouse in whom he has lost interest merely by refusing to continue to share his accommodation with her. As such, the Court interpreted EU law to the effect that the marriage subsisted until divorce; there was no requirement to live under the same roof to enable Ms Diatta to be regarded as a member of her husband's family. The ECJ based its decision on the view that the primary objective of Regulation 1612/68 was to facilitate intra-Community mobility, that Article 10 Regulation 1612/68 extending free movement rights to family members was instrumental to establishing this freedom, and that having 'regard to its context and the objectives which it pursues, that provision cannot be interpreted restrictively' (D'Oliveira, 1993, p.300). The same approach was adopted in

---

[2] It is likely that he would have been treated simply as another third country national with rights pertaining only to the UK and losing the more privileged mobility rights attached to his previous EU migrant family status.

the subsequent decision of *Commission v Germany* which applied the Article 10(3) Regulation 1612/68 conditions only at the initial stages of the migration (in which case the 'spouse' would presumably have to fall within the traditional confines of the definition on the point of entry into the host country) and did not require the family to live indefinitely under the same roof.

D'Oliveira (1993, p.31) comments that the consequence of these decisions,

> is that the ECJ has retained marriage as a formal condition for being treated as a 'spouse' under Community law, but that this condition may be devoid of any substance ... the existence of which continues only for the convenience of the advantages of Community law, which are withheld to unmarried couples living in stable relationships under one roof.

This was confirmed in the case of *R v IAT and Surinder Singh* where the spousal residency right of an Indian national who had been living with his British wife in Germany was not affected by the issue of a *decree nisi*.[3] The Court concluded that Community law protected a spouse up until the point at which the marriage was finally dissolved. The Singh case was of particular interest as it involved an Indian national who had married a British citizen and then travelled with her to Germany where they worked for some years before returning to the UK. In other words, it took place in an 'internal situation'. The Court, however, found that the period of working in Germany 'made all the difference' and qualified Singh as a Community worker thereby extending important rights to him in the UK (which he would not have had if he had not migrated) presumably up until the issue of the *decree absolute*.[4]

The case of *Eyup v Landesgeschaftsstelle* provides a more recent example in which the ECJ has mooted the impact of divorce on third country national spousal rights. This involved two Turkish nationals – a

---

[3] The Commission proposed, following the report of the High Level Panel on the free movement of persons (Veil, 1997), that the law in relation to divorce be brought in line with Community law in the event of bereavement in which case the rights of the family are not extinguished (*Commission v Belgium*).

[4] The importance of a Community 'link' was emphasised in *Morson and Jhanjan v Netherlands*, where the Court ruled that two Dutch nationals resident in the Netherlands, 'who had never exercised the right to freedom of movement within the Community' had no rights under Regulation 1612/68, to bring their Surinamese parents into the Netherlands. This decision can be compared with that in *Dzodzi v Belgium*, where the ECJ confirmed the right of a non-Community spouse to install themselves with a Community worker with full access to social advantages in the host state. In such cases a non-migrant national may be in a less favourable position than non-national migrants who qualify as family members.

migrant worker and his spouse – who were both legally resident in Austria. The couple divorced after two years but continued to cohabit in Austria and later had four children. The couple then remarried after a further eight years. Mrs Eyup's status as a family member, however, was challenged when she applied for a permanent work permit from the Austrian authorities under Article 7 of Decision 1/80 of the EEC-Turkey Association Council. This provision entitles family members of duly registered Turkish workers, after three years of lawful residence, to respond to offers of employment and, after five years of lawful residence, to take up any employment of their choice. Her application was rejected on the grounds that Article 7 of the Decision applied to spouses, not cohabitants and that, taking as a starting point the date of the second marriage, Mrs Eyup did not yet fulfil the five year requirement. Moreover, her previous marriage to Mr Eyup, which had lasted for only two years, was also insufficient.

On referral to the ECJ, Mrs Eyup challenged the Community definition of 'family' under Regulation 1612/68 and the *Reed* decision[5] concerning the status of cohabitants in conjunction with Article 8 ECHR concerning a right to respect for private and family life.[6] Her challenge, she argued, was supported by the 'general social developments' that had since taken place in respect of family life and modern patterns of family formation since the Regulation was adopted and the *Reed* judgement pronounced. The ECJ, while failing to acknowledge that such changes were of sufficient currency to override the economic imperatives of Community law, and indeed, the social and moral norms of the less permissive Member States, it did concede that given the specific circumstances of Mrs Eyup's case and the nature of her relationship with Mr Eyup, the two periods of marital status (albeit separated by a period of cohabitation) could be aggregated to meet the five year requirement of Article 7 Decision 1/80.

Thus, despite its positive outcome for the plaintiff, this decision fails to satisfactorily address or significantly advance the status of divorcees (or indeed cohabitants) under Community law. Indeed, the ECJ appears to have only overlooked the divorce and period of cohabitation on the basis that the couple had since brought themselves back within Community protection by remarrying.

Whilst recognising the potential vulnerability of partners under Community law (and protecting those affected by separation), the persistent failure of the Court to consider the ultimate effect of divorce where such proceedings had already commenced may reflect its reluctance to deal with

---

[5] The *Reed* case is discussed in detail in chapter four.

[6] For an in-depth comparison of the status of the family under the EU and ECHR systems, see Stalford, 2002.

this issue. The problem is clearly most acute where the spouse is not a national of a Member State as in the above cases. The restrictive interpretation of the 'spouse' concept perpetuated by these decisions thus produces a number of legal dilemmas which carry serious consequences for children. First, the legal implications of separation and divorce depend on the nationality status of the non-working partner. Where this person is a Community national they will retain a right of residence, subject to the resources requirement, and may, therefore, be unable to claim extensive entitlement under the social advantages formulae restricting their material status.[7] Where the partner is of third country nationality, however, they may be unable to claim either a residency entitlement or the right to work.[8] This situation may well precipitate a return (either voluntary or enforced) to the non-qualifying parent's country of origin. Although the child retains its status in the host state as the child of a migrant worker, such cases raise serious issues concerning the applicability and enforceability of domestic legislation, with implications for child maintenance, contact and residency. These issues will be discussed in turn in the following sections.

Regulating Family Life following Divorce and Parental Separation: An increasingly 'European' concern

The sample of families interviewed for the current project suggest a separation/divorce rate of approximately 14 per cent (that is 26 cases including 15 cases of divorce and 11 cases of separation).[9] In all, 21 per cent of the sample (38 cases) reported some form of family breakdown. This figure is greater than the number reported as divorced or separated as in some cases new partnerships had subsequently formed resulting in a change in reported status. There were 5 cases in which the child's parents had separated having never married (and in some cases never cohabited either). In 3 of these cases, the mother had had a short term relationship with the biological father which broke down before or shortly after the child was born. The children concerned had no further contact with their father. In the remaining 2 cases, the mother had lived with the father for

---

[7] The scope of the social advantages formula enshrined in Article 7(2) Regulation 1612/68 is discussed in detail in chapter four.

[8] Extended to spouses of Community workers under Article 11, Regulation 1612/68. Very recently, the ECJ has endeavoured to address this issue in the case of *Baumbast and 'R'*.

[9] It is important to note when comparing this figure with national figures that the sampling strategy adopted excluded partnerships with no children.

some years before the breakdown of the relationship. In these cases, the children had maintained contact with their fathers.

While it is clearly unreliable to draw any statistical inferences on the basis of this sample size, it is important to note the potential implications of Community law on this group of 'non-traditional' families.[10] The disparity between the current EU legal position and trends in divorce and separation is further highlighted when viewed in the context of recent European statistics (although the rate of marital breakdown amongst 'international' couples is not recorded). Certainly liberalisation of legal processes has made divorce much more accessible than in the past,[11] and changing social attitudes and the diminishing influence of the Church have alleviated much of the stigma attached (Boh, 1989; Smart, 1999). Consequently, the period 1960-1985 saw a more or less uninterrupted rise in the number of divorces. By 1995, the divorce rate had risen such that it is estimated that nearly one third of marriages ended in divorce across the EU. A look at an overview of the divorce rate across the Member States (EUROSTAT, 2000) reveals three distinct geographical groups: the Nordic countries, England and Wales where the rate is maintained at over 40 per cent; the Central European countries where it is between 30 and 40 per cent; and the Southern European countries where it is below 20 per cent. Most recently, the Council of Europe (2001) reported that between 1960 and the mid-1990s, the number of divorces across the EU quadruped from 170,000 to 677,000. In the years 1999/2000, the number of divorces in the UK was estimated as 159,000 (43 per cent) in stark contrast to 21,502 reported divorces in Sweden (55 per cent) and 19,104 (17 per cent) in Portugal. While the past two decades have witnessed a 'levelling out' in the rate of marital breakdown in some countries, this is most likely due to the growing tendency to cohabit rather than increased stability in marriage.[12]

Aggregate data at European level recording the number of children living in 'reconstituted' families is lacking, although national sources indicate that in Sweden 6 per cent of under-17 year olds, 4 per cent of

---

[10] Ackers and Dwyers' (2002) research has indicated the limitations of lifecourse perspectives which imply a simply linear and chronological sequence of events. In practice, people move between legal categories over the lifecourse in a less predictable manner. Previous work on women and migration (Ackers, 1998) identified a series of cases in which women experienced on-going changes in their post-migration marital status. To that extent, the potential impact of Community law is likely to be much higher than any static picture of marital status presents.

[11] With a shift in emphasis from matrimonial offence, guilt and punishment towards one based on irretrievable breakdown, mutual responsibility and need.

[12] It is only recently that the breakdown of cohabiting relationships has been officially recorded and data is only available for a few Member States.

under-17 year olds in France and 8 per cent of dependent children in Great Britain live in step-family set-ups (European Observatory on National Family Policies, 1997, p.24).

The socio-legal and economic impact of relationship breakdown on parents and children has been well-documented, particularly in terms of maintenance contact and residence arrangements (Trinder, 1997; Roche, 1999; Douglas et al, 2000; Piper, 2000; Smart and Neale, 2000; Lowe and Murch, 2001). A number of EU countries such as Portugal, Belgium, the Netherlands and the UK have amended and simplified divorce procedures and the availability of mediation services with respect to the rights and needs of children.[13] The disparity between individual domestic procedures, however, highlights the potential problems inherent in co-ordinating post-divorce arrangements across geographical boundaries. Indeed, a number of interviewees' experiences illustrate the need for greater convergence to ensure parity of treatment across Member States and to ensure that agreements reached in one country are enforceable (both in theory and in practice) following one or other parent's migration to another country with or without the child. It is only in the past decade that the EU has made any significant strides to implement concrete, enforceable provisions to supplement the vague and incidental family rights available under the free movement of persons provisions. Previously, cross-national family disputes have been resolved either informally, nationally, through bi-lateral agreements or by reference to a minefield of complex, overlapping international law with the EU institutions demonstrating a steadfast reluctance to engage in any attempt to superimpose uniformly applicable family measures on Member States' domestic frameworks.

Certainly, there remains fervent opposition by policy-makers and legal practitioners alike to the recent flurry of EU activity in this respect. Arguably the subsidiarity principle would support the contention that supranational measures are ill-disposed to the significant divergences in Member States' family law systems, which are themselves informed by potent cultural, religious, economic and social norms. This point was made clear by the ECJ in the *Hofmann v Barmer* case (para 25) involving a father's claim for parental leave under the Equal Treatment Directive. The Court found that it was not in contravention of the directive to restrict such leave to women on the grounds that 'the Directive is not designed to settle questions concerned with the organisation of the family, or to alter the division of responsibility between parents' (para. 24).

[13] For an outline of divorce procedures in the individual Member States, see Ruxton (1996).

As far as imposing harmonised equal opportunities laws is concerned, it seems that the impact of the EU is largely restricted to the regulation of public dependency and the protection of paid workers. Nevertheless, we have seen in chapter three how the importance attached to achieving uniformity in the interpretation and application of the free movement provisions, as one of the fundamental principles of European law, has necessitated a more substantial EU incursion into areas of family policy. Thus, that which was functional to subject to the 'subsidiarity principle' in a non-migration context becomes dysfunctional when economic expediency demands 'footloose' labour. Given the Court's interpretation of the purpose of free movement as essentially one of 'facilitating mobility' and its assessment of migration behaviour (and perceptions of barriers to labour mobility), such incursions into the family policy may be justified on the grounds that the migrant worker's family provides the essential 'infrastructure for men's mobility' (Scheiwe, 1994, p.251).

Further arguments justifying EU intervention in the family law arena, as opposed to exclusive action by Member States relate to the fact that the role of the EU in creating or supporting the dynamic – to the extent that it constitutes an 'unintended consequence' of free movement policy – implies some direct responsibility on the part of the EU to ensure its resolution. Additionally, action at national level is unlikely to prove efficient or effective in dealing with a problem which 'spills over' national boundaries in much the same way as environmental pollution. As such, the renewed surge of EU activity in this respect can today be legitimised on the basis that, as Commissioner Gradin (29 April 1998, p.62), responsible for Justice and Home Affairs, stated:

> the free movement of persons is an objective which today has largely become a reality. More and more citizens are marrying citizens from other Member States ... Matrimonial and custody disputes are both often heart-rendering for all those concerned. It is therefore particularly important that these disputes can be resolved without being complicated by procedural difficulties.

In response to the family-related legal and judicial demands created by the increasingly common cycle of cross-border migration, relationship and family formation, divorce and then re-migration, the Treaty of Maastricht 1992, through the implementation of Articles K1 and K3, provided the necessary legal and institutional basis for enhanced intergovernmental and inter-judicial co-operation between Member States in civil – including family – matters (under the Justice and Home Affairs Pillar Three). This yielded first of all the Brussels II Convention of 28th May 1998,[14] the aim of which was essentially to introduce uniform rules for determining jurisdiction and ensuring enforcement between Member States in relation to annulment, divorce, separation and decisions concerning parental responsibility. Although it was initially envisaged that activities pursued under the Brussels II Convention would be intergovernmental and thus non-binding in nature, it has since acted as an important catalyst for the development of a series of focussed European measures to address family-related problems exacerbated by free movement. An important step in this process came about as a result of the Treaty of Amsterdam 1997, which relocated certain matters relating to free movement from Pillar Three to the Pillar One realm of EC competence. Consequently, the Brussels II Convention was almost immediately translated into enforceable, uniformly applicable law[15] through the implementation on March 1st 2001 of EC Regulation 1347/2000 of 29 May 2000.[16]

The main objective underpinning Regulation 1347/2000 is expressed in its preamble and recalls the concerns raised by Gradin (1998, para. 4):

> Differences between certain national rules governing jurisdiction and enforcement hamper the free movement of persons and the sound operation of the internal market. There are accordingly grounds for enacting provisions to unify the rules of conflict of jurisdiction in matrimonial matters and in matters of parental responsibility so as to simplify the formalities for rapid and automatic recognition and enforcement of judgements.[17]

---

[14] The Convention on jurisdiction and the recognition and enforcement of judgments in matrimonial matters O.J. C221 16.07.1998.

[15] This was achieved on the legal basis of Article 61(c) EC which states that in order to establish progressively an area of freedom, security and justice, the Council shall adopt measures in the field of judicial co-operation in civil matters. This is supported by Article 65 EC which provides *inter alia* that such measures must have cross-border implications, be necessary for the functioning of the internal market and include measures for 'improving and simplifying…the recognition and enforcement of decisions in civil and commercial cases, including decisions in extrajudicial cases'.

[16] Regulation (EC) No 1347/2000 of 29 May 2000 on jurisdiction and the recognition and enforcement of judgments in matrimonial matters and in matters of parental responsibility for the children of both spouses. OJ L 160, 30/06/2000, pp. 0019-0029. The Regulation is directly binding on all Member States with the exception of Denmark (see Hedemann-Robinson, 1999).

[17] Interestingly, although the legal basis is not the same, the rationale behind Regulation 1347/2000 echoes that supporting the extension of valuable workers' rights under the 1960s free movement provisions, namely to facilitate intra-community mobility, and more importantly, to remove any potential obstacles to the functioning of the internal market.

Like its 'parent' – the Brussels II Convention – Regulation 1347/2000 regulates matters concerning jurisdiction, recognition and enforcement of judgements both in matrimonial matters and in matters of parental responsibility. The main provisions as they currently stand apply to two types of civil proceedings: (a) divorce, marital separation and marriage annulment (Art.1); and (b) to the residence and contact rights of parents over the children of both spouses in the context of events specified under (a).[18]

Although the interviews for our study were conducted prior to the implementation of these measures, the empirical data presented in the following sections indicates, on the one hand, the nature and extent of recognition and enforcement-related problems experienced by some migrant families following divorce and, on the other, the reluctance to resort to existing formal legal mechanisms of dispute resolution at both international and domestic level. This leaves room for some speculation as to whether or not the developments subsequently made in the European family law arena will provide a more expeditious, participatory mechanism for regulating migrant family relationships in the future.

Recognition and Enforcement of Divorce across Member States

One important and obvious difficulty arising out of divorce and separation in the context of migration relates to whether such legal measures enacted in one Member State are recognised in other Member States to which either party subsequently moves. This issue has in the past been regulated with relative ease by a range of international and bi-lateral agreements.[19] Most of these have now been superseded by the provisions of Regulation 1347/2000.[20] Article 2 of Regulation 1347/2000, for example, sets out the criteria for determining jurisdictional competence in issuing divorce, separation and annulment proceedings, listing a series of preconditions such as habitual residence and domicile. Essentially, a Member State is deemed competent to exercise jurisdiction provided it fulfils at least one of the criteria and has been seized before any other competent Member State.

---

[18] These provisions will be considered in detail in later sections of this chapter.

[19] See for instance, the Luxembourg Convention of 8 September 1967 on the Recognition of Decisions Relating to the Validity of Marriages; The Hague Convention of 1st June 1970 on the Recognition of Divorces and Legal Separations; and the Convention of 6th February 1931 between Denmark, Finland, Iceland, Norway and Sweden.

[20] By virtue of Article 60, in so far as they concern matters governed by the Regulation. See further, Stalford (2003a).

This is perhaps the most controversial feature of the Regulation. It essentially states that where a party issues proceedings for divorce, legal separation or marriage annulment, the court of the Member State in which proceedings are first issued shall have exclusive jurisdiction. This rule, referred to as *lis pendens,* dictates that another Member State is precluded from considering the case if proceedings have already been initiated elsewhere by the other party. Apart from a few very limited exceptions,[21] there is no discretion to change jurisdiction from the one first seized. Previous legislation which favoured the *'forum conveniens'* approach (common sense assessments made on the balance of fairness and convenience as to the most appropriate jurisdiction) are no longer applicable.

Articles 13 and 14 of the Regulation provide that any orders made in respect of divorce, legal separation and annulment will receive automatic recognition and will thus be enforceable in any Member State to which either party moves.

Legal practitioners have expressed concern that these provisions will trigger a race between couples to seize the jurisdiction of the Member State that offers divorce laws best suited to their needs. The perception is, for example, that wives will flock to the UK to secure the most favourable financial and child custody orders while husbands will prefer the more 'husband-friendly' German or Swedish systems (Hodson and Green, 2001; Truex, 2001). The choice of jurisdiction affects also the speed with which the divorce will be processed and could potentially be used as a method of delaying proceedings. Such is the case for countries like Italy or Ireland where the only grounds for divorce is a 3 or 4 year period of separation respectively. The likelihood is (although there is as yet no supporting case law) that this would prevent the commencement of divorce proceedings within such a period in any other jurisdiction (Mostyn, 2001). Truex (2001, p.8) comments in this regard:

> There is great consternation about Brussels II in the Republic of Ireland. It must be remembered that divorce has only been allowed there since 1997, following a referendum to repeal a constitutional prohibition against it. Although the Family Law (Divorce) Act 1996 allows no-fault divorce, it requires 4 years separation ... [Will] it be fair in circumstances where, for example, the English resident spouse of an Irish domiciled applicant must

[21] These exceptions are set out in Article 15 and rest on the notion that the proceedings in one jurisdiction must be manifestly contrary to public policy, irreconcilable with an earlier judgment, or that any children involved have not had an opportunity to be heard.

then wait 4 years for divorce when English law might allow a quickie divorce based on adultery or unreasonable behaviour in just a few months?

In practice, knowledgeable opportunists' capacity to pick and mix from Member-States' family law systems is limited by the domicile/habitual residence test applied by Article 2 of the Regulation determining jurisdiction. First and foremost, they would have to demonstrate more than a mere commercial link with the country in which they sought to obtain their divorce and the Regulation imposes a minimum time limit in which the individual is required to live in a country before attaining the status of habitual resident.[22]

Within the sample of families interviewed for our research, there was only one case in which a parent recounted problems relating to recognition of her divorce. This involved an English woman who had married her Dutch partner and lived with him in Holland until he left her to live with another woman. Within 6 weeks of leaving, he had already filed for divorce. On returning to England with her two children, the woman discovered that her Dutch divorce was not recognised in England and, as such, could not pursue formal procedures to secure child maintenance payments by the father. At the time of the interview, therefore, the woman was seeking a 'proper' divorce in England.

In this case, it was less the formal recognition of the divorce itself which posed a problem (although it clearly would have implications for the woman's capacity to remarry) but rather the obstacles it posed to ensuring acknowledgement and fulfilment of the father's parental responsibilities towards the children.[23] Indeed, it was the wider problems, created by uncertainty over mutual recognition between Member States of divorce and legal separation, which prompted proposals for supra-national uniformly applicable regulation leading to Regulation 1347/2000. Problems were particularly apparent between Germany and France since neither Member State had ratified the international Convention already in place (The Hague Convention on Recognition of Divorces and Legal Separation 1970). What was initially intended, therefore, as a means of achieving simplicity and

[22] Furthermore under Article 2, in the UK and Ireland the individual has to have been residing in the Member State for at least 6 months prior to the application if they are deemed to have their 'domicile' in the same Member State; or 12 months in all other cases. For recent case law concerning the criteria applied to an assessment of 'habitual residence and domicile, see *Irvin* [2001] 1 FLR 178 and *I v I* [2001] 1 FLR 913.

[23] This case is discussed later in the context of maintenance. For examples of domestic jurisprudence relating to the mutual recognition of divorce between Member States, see *C v C (Divorce: stay of English Proceedings)* 11 May 2000, [2001] FLR 624; and *Hemain v Hemain* CA [1988] 2 FLR 388.

uniformity in relation to divorce and legal separation, spawned a more complex body of laws addressing various ancillary issues.

Negotiating Child Contact and Residence across Geographical and Legal Boundaries

Articles 3 and 4 of Regulation 1347/2000 govern parental responsibility over the children of both spouses and provide for the situation where a parent retains a child after a period of contact in another Member State. An important objective of these provisions, therefore, is to address what has been identified as an increasing problem of parental child abduction within the EU.[24] Article 3 determines the jurisdictional basis for resolving contact and residence disputes (rather than maintenance) on the basis of the child's (rather than the parents') habitual residence. It is technically possible, therefore, that matters relating to the divorce will be addressed in a different jurisdiction to those relating to parental responsibility if the child's habitual residence differs from the habitual residence of the parent who first seizes jurisdiction to issue divorce or separation proceedings.[25]

Again, Articles 13 and 14 of the Regulation ensure enforceability of all decisions issued within the scope of the Regulation. For example, rulings giving non-custodial parents access to their child in one country would apply in another if the custodial parent subsequently moves away thus precluding custodial parents from seeking alternative, more favourable child custody arrangements in another jurisdiction in order to limit the rights of the non-custodial parent.

Amongst the families interviewed for our study who had undergone or were undergoing divorce proceedings, only two of them pursued the formal legal route in the negotiation of parental responsibility, the remainder agreeing on such issues informally. As such, there were only a few cases in which the parent or child commented on the effectiveness and

---

[24] The European Council identified this as a priority area for judicial co-operation at its meeting in Tampere in October 1999.

[25] France presented an initiative on 3rd July 2000 calling for the adoption of a new Regulation concerning mutual recognition of judgments on rights of access to children, OJ No. C 234 of 15.08.2000 (commonly referred to as the 'Brussels III Regulation'). This calls for the abolition of *exequatur* (the formal declaration currently required before such decisions are rendered enforceable in other Member States) for decisions relating to parental rights of access. The proposed abolition of *exequatur* was coupled with a guarantee for the automatic return of the child at the end of any period of access and the scope of the initiative was defined by reference to Regulation 1347/2000. These proposals were adopted in January 2002 by the Economic and Social Committee (2002 OJ C80/41).

enforceability of existing legal provisions at national, EU and international level.[26] In 23 of the 38 reported cases of divorce or separation, the child remained with the mother. Of the remainder, there were 5 cases in which the father had custody and 2 cases where the custody arrangement had changed following problems in the child's relationship with the custodial parent. In 5 cases the child lived apart from both parents, for example at boarding school, university, with friends or relatives, and in 3 instances the siblings were effectively shared between the parents, as the following boy explains:

> I have a brother and a sister. My brother is 12 years old and lives here with us [in Greece]. My sister is 24 and she lives in Stockholm. My mum also lives in Stockholm with my grandmother.

Talking about his parents' separation, the boy adds: 'We always had two houses but they were both in Stockholm. Now we are split' [410a]. The boy's father talks about how the children reside with him in Greece despite the fact that the mother had already been granted official custody:

> In 1996, the children's mother – we were already separated – asked me to take the children to Greece because she couldn't cope anymore. Officially, the mother has the children's custody. We have never been married and although we have been separated the last few years, the children share their time between both parents ... Last year, [my daughter was] having relationship problems with her mother, she dropped out of school and she came to Greece [410b].

In contrast, his daughter attributes her decision to move to Greece to the fact that she missed her brother:

> Here we live together, my father, my brother, my stepmother and her son. I had really missed my brother and I'm happy that we have been living together now [410c].

The following father was in the process of a custody dispute with his ex-wife over their three children:

---

[26]This does not necessarily imply that such complications did not exist, but rather reflects the more general focus of the research of which the aim was not specifically to explore issues relating to family breakdown. This aspect of the research has since been developed by the authors (Stalford, 2003, and Stalford and Donnelly, 2003).

> The mother supports the children she has with her – and she has benefits for them – and I care for the children here. My son's custody has been awarded to me. My wife has the custody of the other children although there is not a final Court decision yet for the second child's custody [412].

Contact with the absent parent was also generally negotiated informally. Of the 22 non-custodial parents who lived in a different country to their children, 12 saw each other during school holidays, once or twice a year on average. 13 parents lived in the same country as the child, often in close proximity, which enabled them to visit more frequently, sometimes on a weekly or even a daily basis. In 7 cases, the child no longer had any contact at all with the absent parent. One interviewee explains the difficult situation she found herself in when her relationship ended. The father of her daughter did not speak English so when there was any contact between father and daughter, it had to be via the mother's translation:

> She was very young then so it wasn't so important, later on I used to write for her. When she was little I used to go to visit him in France but then he moved back to the Lebanon several years ago now and we have lost touch since then … [I visited him in France] because I wanted them to have some contact. I thought it was important for her to know who her father was. If he had stayed in France I think we would have kept on. It was unfortunate that the letter saying he was moving to Beirut arrived when we were on holiday and he didn't leave an address … she could find him if she wanted to through the embassy but … she hasn't … I think he got married and didn't tell his wife that he already had a daughter and she [my daughter] was worried about disturbing things [004].

While few families reported having experienced any problems of a specifically legal nature, the provisions of Regulation 1347/2000 are to be welcomed for providing much-needed certainty and security for parents and children alike through the implementation of uniformly applicable procedures for enforcement and recognition of matrimonial decisions and parental obligations. This is particularly important where there are concerns relating to parents' violation of child contact rights that, in a migration context, can so easily result in child abduction (discussed in the section below).

The Regulation, however, has been heavily criticised on a number of grounds. First and foremost, while it may provide an important legal source and a more expedient means of addressing the specific and more complex problems associated with transnational family disputes, its limited personal and material scope further endorses the traditional and highly exclusive characterisation of 'family' under the Community free movement provisions. For instance, the Regulation currently excludes parental responsibility towards stepchildren or children adopted by only one spouse in a previous union, thus disregarding the closeness of the relationship between the non-biological parent and the child. Furthermore, it precludes any consideration of the rights of the children born outside of wedlock to cohabitants and does not apply to third country nationals legally resident in the EU (Stalford, 2003a).

In response to this, the European Commission formulated a number of measures aimed at addressing some of these deficiencies. Notably, proposals were submitted in September 2001 to extend the personal scope of Regulation 1347/2000 in matters of parental responsibility beyond simply the children of both spouses. The proposals for a new, broader Regulation cover rights of access to children in family relationships *other* than marriage and to judgements other than those taken at the time of a divorce or separation.[27] The Commission also presented a proposal for a Council Decision authorising Member States to sign the 1996 Hague Convention which extends mutual recognition and co-operation to child contact and residence disputes external to the EU.[28] These measures have culminated in more recent Commission proposals for an all-encompassing Regulation that will amalgamate into a single instrument all of the measures described above, particularly the French initiative on rights of access[29] and the proposed extensions to the personal scope of Regulation 1347/2000.[30]

---

[27] See Commission Proposal for a Council Regulation on jurisdiction and the recognition and enforcement of judgements in matters of parental responsibility, OJ 2001/ C 332E/269.

[28] The Hague Convention on Jurisdiction, Applicable Law, Recognition and Enforcement and Co-operation in respect of Parental Responsibility and Measures for the Protection of Children, COM (2001) 680 final of 20.11.2001. See also Lowe, 2001.

[29] Described above at note 28.

[30] Proposal for Council Regulation concerning jurisdiction and the recognition and enforcement of judgments in matrimonial matters and in matters of parental responsibility repealing Regulation (EC) No 1347/2000 and amending Regulation (EC) No 44/2001 in matters relating to maintenance, COM (2002) 222 final/2, 2002/0110 (CNS). As a result, Regulation 1347/2000 will be repealed and fully incorporated into the new Proposed Regulation. This is scheduled to enter into force on 1 July 2003 and will become directly applicable by July 1st 2004 although, at the time of writing (October 2003), there was no evidence that the proposal had been adopted.

Facilitated Free Movement and the Increasing Problem of Parental Child Abduction

The sample included one reported case of child abduction by the mother. The Greek father had met his German partner in Germany as a student. They then married and moved to Greece where they had two children. Pregnant with their third child, the mother returned to Germany with the other two children without the father's consent. The father took the case to the Greek courts who awarded him custody of the two older children. He then went to Germany and returned with only his seven-year-old son. A 'long lasting fight' ensued resulting in a total absence of contact between the father and the other two children for over five years. At 14, the eldest daughter then chose to relocate herself to Greece to live with her father while the youngest child remained in Germany. The mother financially supports one child and the father the other two. They did not divorce (but were in the process of seeking a divorce). At the time of the interview, the daughter had recently left school and wished to return to Germany. She spoke very little Greek and had had problems communicating with her grandparents and stepmother.

This case illustrates some of the problems of divorce and separation in a migration context and the relative vulnerability of both parents and children left with inadequate and inaccessible legal protection. Even with legal instruments in place at international[31] level to resolve these disputes, the process is a long drawn-out one raising problems of jurisdiction and enforcement. The increasing prevalence of parental child abduction and, indeed, the extent to which fluid free movement policy serves to facilitate this practice, has provided the focus of further European Commission (COM (2002) 222 final/2) scrutiny in its recent proposals to extend the personal and material scope of Regulation 1347/2000:

> As people increasingly move from one Member State to another, and families break up and are recomposed, children need a secure legal environment for maintaining relations with persons who have parental responsibility over them and who may now live in different Member State.

The new proposals repeal part of Regulation 1347/2000 relating to parental responsibility, with a particular emphasis on simplifying and

---

[31] For instance, the Hague Convention on the Civil Aspects of International Child Abduction 1980 and the European Convention on the Recognition and Enforcement of Decisions Concerning Custody of Children and Restoration of Custody of Children 1980. Both of these have been implemented in England by the Child Abduction and Custody Act 1985.

facilitating procedures in the context of child abduction. Chapter III (Articles 21-25) of the proposed new Regulation thus sets out the conditions for determining which Member State should exercise jurisdiction in the event of child abduction. Furthermore, it lays down procedures for ensuring the return of a child once the period of contact has expired except in cases where there is a grave risk to the child's psychological and physical health.

Regulating Child Maintenance in a Migration Context[32]

In the few instances where post-divorce legal problems were recounted by the families interviewed, these occurred primarily in the context of enforcing maintenance payments where a the non-custodial parent (generally the father) lived in another Member State to the custodial parent. Certainly in the event of divorce in a single country context, the courts have a wide discretion to order financial provision between spouses, taking into account the welfare of any children involved, the individual financial and earning capacity of both parents and other circumstances surrounding the case. The ability to exercise this discretion in an informed and equitable way is more difficult where one party has moved to another Member State (cf. *Van Den-Boogaard v Laumen* and *M v M (Financial Provision After Foreign Divorce)*. For instance, it is more difficult to obtain access to information relating to the absent parent's financial assets or employment status. Evaluations of 'wealth' or income are more complicated in view of differing economic trends and the cost of living between Member States and, indeed, between regions within those Member States. In that context, it is interesting to speculate on the impact of the Child Support Act 1991 on the propensity of non-custodial parents (typically fathers) to leave England and move to another Member State to escape maintenance obligations. Indeed, the power and efficacy of bodies such as the Child Support Agency (CSA) and legal practitioners in ensuring that maintenance payments continue in the event of one parent moving abroad is questionable, particularly given the problems associated with enforcing such arrangements even in a single country context (Stalford, 2003b).

Cross-national actions are inevitably costly and time-consuming, necessitating access to legal and social services abroad to enable the absent parent to be located. Even then, as an EU national, there is little preventing the defaulting parent from exercising his/her rights under the free

[32] The issue of child maintenance is developed further in Stalford, 2003b.

movement provisions to move between several different Member States in avoidance of financial obligations towards any children. Consequently, parents left with children to care for will often have to rely on their family or the welfare state for additional financial support. The recent ECJ case of *Humer* is significant in this context. The plaintiff, Anna Humer, was born to Austrian nationals in 1987. Her parents divorced 2 years later in 1989 and her mother was awarded custody. In 1992, she and her mother migrated to France as migrant worker and child under the free movement provisions. The father remained in Austria. In 1993, it was formally agreed that the father would pay an agreed maintenance payment in respect of Anna on a monthly basis. This agreement was honoured until 1998 when the father lost his job. Six months later, Anna applied to the Austrian authorities for an advance on her maintenance entitlement for a period of three years on the grounds that her father's payments were in arrears and enforcement measures had failed. In the first instance, Anna's claim was dismissed on the basis that she and her custodial parent were no longer resident in Austria as required under Austrian legislation. On appeal, the decision was overturned in favour of Anna at which point, the Austrian authorities appealed to the court of final instance which referred the matter to the Court of Justice. The question facing the ECJ was essentially whether an advance on maintenance payments, ordinarily provided under Austrian legislation, constituted a 'family benefit' within the meaning of Community secondary legislation governing the rights of migrant workers and their families (in this instance, the Social Security Regulation 1408/71). The ECJ confirmed that such advances do constitute a family benefit for the purposes of Community law since the function of the Austrian legislation was to provide support for lone parents who were left to cope with the heavy burden of raising their children and who found themselves faced with additional difficulties in obtaining maintenance contributions from the non-custodial parent. It was thus incumbent on the Austrian authorities to pay the maintenance contributions on behalf of the defaulting father. The ECJ also confirmed that a child,

> one or other of whose parents is an employed person or is out of work, comes within the personal scope of the Community regulation as a member of the family of a worker, even if, following a divorce, the child no longer lives with the parent.[33]

---

[33] This case has important implications in terms of the child's *independent* right to claim Community benefits as a migrant family member.

An additional problem created by the absence of effective cross-national administrative co-ordination relates to the potential for absconding parents to make a parallel claim for state support with respect to the same children in another Member State. This was illustrated before the ECJ in *Burchell*. The separated parents in this case were living in the Netherlands and the UK respectively. Since the Dutch authorities provided even non-custodial parents with child support benefits (even if the children in question were living in another Member State), both sets of parents could continue issuing claims for welfare support in both countries in respect of the same children and for the same periods of time. Such a scenario can yield rather lucrative results for non-custodial parents, particularly if they fail to invest the benefits received in child maintenance payments.[34]

The notorious complexities involved in deciphering as much as enforcing existing international and bi-lateral agreements that regulate transnational child maintenance exacerbate this problem. Pre-Maastricht, Article 220 EEC had already spawned a number of Conventions, including the Brussels Convention of 27 September 1968 on jurisdiction and the enforcement of judgements in civil and commercial matters (commonly known as 'Brussels I'). The original Convention, although formulated to include all civil and commercial matters *per se*, retreated on matters of family law because of the 'extreme divergences' between domestic systems and the perceived upheaval an attempt at harmonisation measures would create.[35] Latterly, however, it has been extended to cover all decisions concerning financial maintenance following cross-national family separation or divorce. This, like Regulation 1347/2000, has been achieved under the auspices of Title IV EC, through the March 2002 implementation of Regulation 44/2001. The Commission, however, noted that in spite of the changes and simplifications it makes to the preceding Brussels I Convention, Regulation 44/2001 'does not remove all the obstacles to the unhindered movement of judgements within the European Union and leaves intermediate measures that are still too restrictive'. It thus

[34] It remains to be seen whether the recently established European Judicial Network, which facilitates co-operation and information-exchange between Member States central authorities, will facilitate enforcement and co-ordination of cross-national financial arrangements of this nature. Council Decision 2001/470/EC of 28 May 2001 on establishing a European Judicial Network in civil and commercial matters, OJ No L 174 of 27.6.2001, p.25. See Chapter V (Articles 55-59) of the proposed amended Regulation 2002/0110.

[35] See the Jenard explanatory report on the original version of the Brussels I Convention, 1979:1.

recommended the *automatic* recognition and enforcement between Member States of all decisions taken within the scope of Regulation 44/2001.[36]

In the vast majority of cases in our sample, the custodial parent (generally the mother) received no financial support from the absent father and relied either on their own income or on family or State support (which differs vastly between countries). There were only two cases in which child maintenance payments had been formally arranged, and they highlight the difficulties inherent in co-ordinating and enforcing such arrangements cross-nationally. The following case, already referred to above, is particularly illuminating. To recap, the mother met her Dutch partner on holiday and moved to Holland to live with him. She worked full-time as a qualified nurse until they had two daughters and she then worked part-time. When the girls were aged 2 and 6 the husband left the marriage and moved in with a new partner. On leaving he paid her no maintenance and she could not afford to pay for the house she was renting. He began divorce proceedings six weeks after leaving. Unable to support the children and pay the rent on her part-time salary, she moved back to the UK into a small privately rented flat near her parents, who now support her financially. As a single parent in the UK she has found it impossible to return to work given the poor salaries and difficult hours in nursing compared to Holland. After a year or so, the father made contact with her and wanted her to send the girls to stay with him during the holidays. He agreed to pay her £250 a month provided she complied with this. At the time of the interview she was seeking a divorce in the UK on the grounds that her Dutch divorce was not recognised in England. It is interesting to note in this case how the children were used by the mother to ensure the continuity of the maintenance payments:

> I'd rather they [the children] didn't go at all. He won't pay the maintenance if they don't go and we are desperately short of cash, I need the maintenance. But I find all the empty promises – I'm going to buy you a horse ... its all emotional blackmail ... It's reached a stage where I know she [his current wife] is putting pressure on him. She's very extravagant and she wants the money he is sending here so it will stop. He is trying to blame everyone else for what he has done and when it stops they [the children] won't go and they do know that.

---

[36] Abolishing the need for a declaration of enforceability (an '*exequatur*') to render such agreements enforceable. See Proposal for a Council Regulation creating a European enforcement order for uncontested claims, Brussels, 18.04.2002, COM (2002) 159 final, 2002/0090 (CNS), Explanatory Memorandum, p.2. Plans are already in place to implement a 'Brussels III' Regulation relating to the division of matrimonial property, and a 'Brussels IV' Regulation on wills and succession.

Asked what will happen when the maintenance payments do stop, the mother answers:

> I don't know, we haven't got that far yet, I will have to get the divorce sorted out. He will stop, I know he'll stop and then I'll have to get my solicitor to write to his and try to take it off his wages. He is so mean.

It is interesting to contrast this respondent's dilemma to that of Anna Humer in the ECJ case described above. Clearly, had the respondent's ex-husband lived in Austria or another Member State offering 'substitute' financial relief for those faced with maintenance payment problems, her situation may have been very different. The joined cases of *Hoever & Zachow* both confirm that the right under domestic law to an advance on maintenance payments where a parent fails to fulfil his financial obligations applies to *all* family members, whether it be the child or the custodial parent's claim.

If such state assistance is not available under domestic law, it can have a significant impact on mobility, either precipitating or preventing migration (as it did in the above respondent's case). Among the sample of 'ecological migrants' in Portugal (referred to in chapter four), the disparity in child benefit regimes enabled many families to defraud the system. This renders recourse to legal procedures even more problematic for this 'invisible group' in the event of family breakdown. They claim to be self-sufficient but, in practice, many of them were either claiming unemployment benefits (returning regularly to their country of origin to sign on) or child benefits – which in some cases amounted to more than the Portuguese minimum wage. They were also entitled to private health care in Portugal – reimbursed by the German social security system. In order to preserve these benefits they rarely take Portuguese residency and thus live in a semi-legal situation.

For example, the mother in the following interview was ostensibly genuinely poor. Her three children were shabbily dressed and attended a poor local rural school with only nine pupils (four of which were German). She initially came to Alentejo in a bus with her partner from whom she is now estranged and from whom she subsequently received no maintenance. As a consequence, she lived with her three children in an isolated 'shack-like' home.[37] The remoteness made it impossible for her to undertake paid work and since she was not legally resident in Portugal she was not entitled to claim Portuguese child benefits. She was reluctant to give up her German residency, however, as to do so would imply relinquishing important

---

[37] Many of the respondents in this region had no electricity or telephones.

medical and other welfare-related rights to the detriment of her son who had recently undergone five operations. Accordingly, her sole income came from her parents in Germany. Asked why she did not claim German child benefit she simply replied: 'only the wealthy ones can do that – you need an address in Germany'.

In further cases, maintenance payments were agreed informally between the parents, either in the form of regular contributions, or in the form of aeroplane tickets and other costs during the child's contact visits. Some mothers emphasised the importance of other forms of contribution to the child's upbringing that they value more than financial payments. For example, in one case the father does not provide any financial assistance towards the daughter's care apart from sending her birthday and Christmas presents and contributing to the cost of visiting him in Italy. The mother works full time and she supports the daughter almost entirely on her own. She said she was happy with the efforts to accommodate them that the father and his family made when they visit Italy and this is enough for her. The mother argued that it is more important for the father to take an active interest in what the daughter is up to rather than sending money and never having any other contact with her. Similarly, another mother explained:

> And he would see the kids when ever he wanted but he said he didn't have any money so I've never bothered, you see, this is confidential. So, there was no point to go to court to get nothing. And occasionally in the beginning there wasn't really any help. Now, I have a lot more pressure ... as a lone mother I do the best I can but I can not be their father and they really need him at these ages, and I put a lot of pressure for these last 2 years for him to be more with them, but he hardly ever takes them for the weekend. Now this year for the first time he is really participating with them, he actually comes and gets them in the morning, picks them from school everyday [322].

The Impact of Divorce and Separation on Family Relationships

Previous sections have explored the limitations inherent in the formal EU definition of 'family' and the legal and practical difficulties associated with negotiating family life across geographical and jurisdictional boundaries. The aim is not, however, to present changes in relationship formation and dissolution, and in household and family diversification across the EU as a negative phenomenon with inevitable injurious consequences for children. Indeed, there is no consistent empirical or statistical data to support this perception and one is aware of conflating the disruption caused by other life events and circumstances, such as migration and poverty, with the effects of family breakdown.[38]

The interviews indicate that parents are generally very sensitive to the needs of their children to maintain their relationship with the other parent, in spite of their own relationship problems:

> This is the first time that they live far from their mother. They don't like that. They want us to be together, either in Greece or in Sweden. If they have missed home … I don't know. I think that they have missed the life they used to live with their mother in contrast to the life that they are able to have with me in Greece [410].

> I wanted my children to have a good relationship with their father even if I felt he didn't deserve it [322].

In the following case (discussed earlier in this chapter) however, the mother felt very embittered over the recent breakdown of her marriage which appeared to compromise the older child's relationship with her father in Holland. Mother and daughter were interviewed together, as they wished, so we were unable to explore this issue more deeply:

> *Mother*: The girls are going over at Easter. He has just changed beyond all recognition and we're devastated by it but what can we do. Its particularly hard for [the older daughter] because he abuses it, he phones and says, 'oh you never want to come, you never phone'. He's very selfish, desperately selfish. Its actually ripped the family apart. I'd rather they didn't go at all. He won't pay the maintenance if they don't go and we are desperately short of cash, I need the maintenance. But I find all the empty promises, 'I'm going to buy you a horse' … its all emotional blackmail. I'd rather they didn't go. I'd rather they weren't party to any more hurt than they have already been. I think [the younger daughter] remembers more than we credit her for but is more able to put it to one side. She says, 'I'd like a new daddy' and all that.

> *Daughter:* Well, I know that when we go, I don't want to upset mum. He does have a go at me over the phone sometime, he says, 'why don't you see me very much, I'm doing it for you' [003].

Most of the children interviewed showed quite a pragmatic attitude towards the breakdown of their parents' relationship, and a willingness to understand it from their parents' perspective:

---

[38] Although we would agree with the European Observatory's (1997, p.29) assertion that 'multiple changes, and disruptions are likely to produce negative outcomes'.

> I think their separation was a good thing because my mother is now very different from what she used to be when she was married to my father. My father is a decent man but I don't know if I would like to live with him. My mother she raised me and my father didn't have much to do with us [320].

One father also spoke of the pragmatic attitude his daughter had regarding his separation from her mother and linked this attitude to her decision to move to his country:

> I believe that my daughter chose to come here in order to get to know me and form her own opinion about her parents' separation: who was wrong, who acted right, if I was interested in her, how the one parent harmed the child's relationship with the other parent, etc [412].

In many of the cases, the child was very young when the parents separated and had not, therefore, had the opportunity to build up a strong emotional attachment with – typically – their father. This may be why many of the child respondents could reflect on the breakdown more objectively than perhaps their parents:

> Well, I've never really been living together with my father. When I was a child, we lived together, before my parents got divorced. So I didn't find it that difficult [320].

As expected, the emotional effect appeared to be greater on those children for whom the breakdown had occurred fairly recently, and a number were particularly concerned about the displacing impact it had had on the family unit. It is interesting to contrast some of the accounts of parents and children as to how the child has responded to the divorce. In the following case, for example, the child was quite resigned to the fact that her parents, although they were divorced, still shared the same house and were involved in relationships with other people. The adults' accounts, however, indicate that the child's positive reaction masked a more deep-rooted anxiety and unease with the situation:

> *Father*: Her teacher told me that she was a bit withdrawn lately and that she didn't express herself. But maybe it's her character not to express things in the presence of authority. She knew that we had relationships with other people. Maybe the fact that we still live together gives her the hope of her parents reunification. I don't know how she will react when I'll leave. Apart from the practical reasons, I think that it is better for her that we still live together. It's a gradual process for her and for me … I would rather live on my own. However, I am worried about [my daughters'] future, when her

> parents will reside in different countries. I'm rather worried about the effect of people's gossiping about our divorce on our daughter. In the long term, I believe that both the divorce and my repatriation will have a positive impact on our daughter.
>
> *Daughter*: I know that my parents care for each other but they can no longer be together. They have different personalities [428].

The sample identified 18 cases in which at least one of the child's biological parents had subsequently established relationships with, or had even married, a new partner. This resulted in the formation of some rather complex family networks. There were 13 cases, for instance, in which the child reported having 'step' or 'half' siblings and the response, 'we get on OK, most of the time' [004], was typical when young people were questioned about such relationships. One girl, however, felt quite excluded by the fact that her mother had had another child with her stepfather:

> My father isn't really my father, but my stepfather, and he has always ... I have always felt a bit slighted. Today, they have a child together, and he's very important ... Sometimes, I'm really bitter because of this [224].

More problematic were the relationships with their parent's new partner even if these 'new' relationships had been going on for many years, as this extract reveals:

> I don't get on with [my step father] at all. We hate each other really. We don't talk at all. It's a bit awkward for Mum. When I was younger he would sort of play with me but … I don't know when I started to not like him … I just don't like him at all … Me and Mum get on really well when he is not around. But when it was just us two we did get on but it wasn't a perfect mother-daughter relationship. A lot of people say 'well you are just jealous of him taking your mum away', but I always did want her to get married and not be lonely. I just don't like him and the person he is.

Problems experienced by children, in relation to their step-parents, is often more complex in a migration situation when linguistic and cultural differences can substantially impede communication. The following UK respondent recounts some of her experiences of visiting her father in Holland and the communication problems she has with her step-mother:

> The only place we have been by ourselves [with their father] is to wash the car, even shopping she [the stepmother] has to come … I don't really get on with her well … I don't like fighting with her but I try to avoid her, not to

> talk with her too much ... She tries to speak English but ... she doesn't really understand a word of it ... she can't talk properly really.

This can be contrasted with the experiences of other step-parents who managed to overcome the initial difficulties with their partners' children:

> The relationship with my stepdaughter became closer last year, when the child faced a serious medical problem and was in hospital for a month. She needed me and I was there for her and for her mother. It was then that she started calling me 'Dad'. I am in the process of adopting her so that she will take soon the Greek nationality [407].

> I think that my son felt the impact of his parents' divorce last year in relation to the distance from his father. Before, he was seeing his father as much as he wanted. His father had had the paternal role while he had a friendly relationship with his stepfather. Now his stepfather has a paternal role towards him as he, together with me, has a say in his everyday life [409].

> I knew my stepmother since the first time I came to Greece. She loves me and she tries to make things easier for me. She introduced me as her own daughter. She could be my mother but I know that my mother is in Germany [412].

These findings are reflected in much of the current social science and legal research on the impact of divorce and family reconstitution on children. They suggest to a large extent that the trauma commonly associated with these experiences is as much to do with children's exclusion from the legal process and negotiation over contact and residence as with the emotional upheaval involved in family transition. Particularly apparent from ours and other research conducted at national level, is the very pragmatic approach children take towards post-divorce family arrangements and their general desire to sustain a positive relationship with both parents (Rodgers and Pryor, 1998; Cantwell, Roberts and Young, 1999; Piper, 1999; Smart and Neale, 2000). The key to achieving this is through more open dialogue with children in a more positive, routine way. The extent to which EU law can accommodate such an approach will be considered in the next section.

Divorce, Parental Responsibility and the Voice of the Migrant Child

Developments in the international children's rights movement since the implementation of the UN Convention on the Rights of the Child 1989 (UNCRC) have considerably advanced the status and role of children both within the family unit and as autonomous actors. More specifically, the UNCRC, which instituted the 'best interests' principle (Article 3) and the 'agency/participatory' principle (Article 12) now serves as a universal template informing legal measures and procedures involving children. As such, concerns to promote children's rights and permit 'competent' children to have some say in decisions around parental contact and residence have arguably led to a more genuine endeavour to engage children more meaningfully in the divorce process at national level (*cf.* Article 6 The Children (Scotland) Act, 1995 and The Children Act, 1989). There is still much work to be done, however, to operationalise these provisions in favour of children even within a single country context.

The discussion so far has sought to illustrate the extent to which the greater propensity for divorce and parental separation amongst migrant families coupled with the prevalence of 'international families' in this population exacerbates the many problems ordinarily associated with family breakdown. Certainly as EU laws regulating family life evolve and the incidence of more complex cross-national parental arrangements increase, so too does the pressure on Member States to ensure that children involved in cross-national family disputes are adequately and appropriately involved in negotiations around contact and residence. Indeed, this is all the more crucial for children in migrant families since divorce may imply residence in a different country to the one in which the child was born and brought up, significant geographical distance between the non-custodial parent and relatives and lengthy but irregular periods of contact (Stalford and Donnelly, 2003).

Measures that accommodate children's interests have been notoriously inadequate at EU level, in spite of the legal developments in the family arena described in this chapter. The Charter of Fundamental Rights in the European Union[39] has provided a refreshing exception in this regard by acknowledging more explicitly the family-related rights of children. Most notably, Article 24 of the Charter (adopted in December 2000) encompasses the two tenets of contemporary children's rights discourse: the best interests principle (as embodied in Article 3 UNCRC) and the agency or self-determination principle (expressed in Article 12 UNCRC).

[39] Adopted in December 2000 [2000] OJ C364/1 of December 18, 2000.

Chapter four details the provisions in Article 24. These provisions have been heralded by McGlynn (2001, p.583) as signalling 'a new and significant change in the Union's approach to its citizens and their private and home lives' and as marking a:

> shift away from its preoccupation with economic actors and the regulation of markets, recognising for the first time the impact of the Union on families and the role which it plays in shaping, conceptualising and regulating families (McGlynn, 2001, p.583).

They are, however, only of declaratory significance with no capacity to bind individual Member States in the application of domestic family procedures.[40]

Any other references to the rights of the child in respect of the family are largely confined to EU soft law provisions. For example, Principle 8 of the Appendix to Recommendation no. R (84) 4 Social Cohesion and Quality of Life[41] states that:

> In all cases both parents should be under a duty to maintain the child. The parent with whom the child does not live should have at least the possibility of maintaining personal relationships with the child unless such relationships would be seriously harmful to the interests of the child.[42]

With regard to binding law, there is currently only very limited and fleeting reference to children's participation in decisions relating to parental responsibility, for example in Regulation 1347/2000 (Article 15). More positive developments, however, are on the horizon: the proposals to amend Regulation 1347/2000 and the aforementioned Regulation 44/2001 include a series of provisions which focus more earnestly on the rights of the child in family proceedings. A new Article 3 is thus proposed providing that 'A child shall have the right to maintain on a regular basis a personal relationship and direct contact with both parents, unless this is contrary to his or her interests', and a new Article 4 states that 'A child shall have the

---

[40] Although interestingly, the ECJ (and indeed ECHR) have already alluded to the provisions of the Charter in the interpretation and application of Community law and Article 8. See most recently the ECHR case of Goodwin v UK, Judgement of 11 July 2002, Application No. 28957/95 as well as A-G Jacobs' Opinion in *Z v EP*, Mar. 22, 2001, C-270/99 P; A-G Geelhoed's Opinion in *Baumbast,* Jul 5 2001, C-413/99; and A-G Leger's Opinion in *Wouters,* Jul 10 200, C-309/99.

[41] Recommendation Nº R (84) 4 of the Committee of Ministers on Parental Responsibilities.

[42] This was further endorsed by Recommendation Nº R (90) 2 of the Committee of Ministers concerning violence within the family.

right to be heard on matters relating to parental responsibility over him or her in accordance with his or her age and maturity'.

It is hoped, therefore, that these provisions will not only enhance the independent status of children at European level, but will also serve to inspire if not compel individual Member States to amend domestic procedures accordingly.

Conclusion

This chapter has explored the development of Community law in the context of the non-nuclear family. Taking the free movement provisions as its starting point, it has explored the limitations inherent in the ECJ's persistently conservative interpretation of the concept of 'spouse' and 'family'. The case law presented in the first part of the chapter illustrates the dilemmas facing spouses of third country nationality in particular in the event of marital breakdown. The lack of judicial certainty over the impact of divorce on their derived rights places these individuals in a highly vulnerable position with potentially far-reaching consequences for children.

Migrant family relationships raise broader issues, however, affecting EU and third country national partners and children alike. The very success of the free movement provisions has led to a greater propensity for a growing number of individuals to migrate – workers, tourists, students, retired persons, carers and the cared for. This has undoubtedly generated an increase in international relationships and family formation, necessitating the negotiation of more complex family arrangements. The EU institutions now have to address the paradox whereby its free movement formula serves to *aggravate* as much as *facilitate* family life. This is particularly apparent where such relationships break down and where difficulties associated with ensuring recognition and enforcement of divorce and parental responsibilities across Member States become increasingly apparent.

The developments brought about since the Treaty of Maastricht and the Treaty of Amsterdam clearly articulate a new extension in European competence in the private domain of family disharmony, divorce, child residence, contact and maintenance. The cluster of 'Brussels Regulations' in particular mark a decisive departure from pre-existing *ad hoc* intergovernmental negotiation and the costly, bemusing mesh of international mechanisms towards directly enforceable, uniform Community measures. Indeed, the flurry of EU activity in this respect represents not so much an attempt at super-imposing harmonised regulations on domestic family law systems as its opponents have suggested. Rather, it could be regarded more positively as an endeavour to achieve much needed co-ordination between Member States with a view to simplifying procedures and guaranteeing security and certainty to migrant families in the post-divorce period.

Such developments are, therefore, to be welcomed, not only for attempting to address the limitations and over-complexities of pre-existing international law and inconsistent domestic law, but for shifting the EU agenda towards a more realistic response to family experiences across the EU. There is a distinct anomaly in a system that discriminates against divorced and cohabiting parents and their children (under the restrictive free movement formula) while simultaneously formulating a detailed code of practice to assist families following divorce (with moves to extend this to cohabitants). It is anticipated that the ECJ will be forced to update its interpretation of 'spouse' in accordance with inevitable demographic changes in family life, relationship formation and dissolution across even the most conservative Member States. With this, however, comes greater responsibility, not least to ensure that the best interests, needs and wishes of any children involved are afforded due legal status in this emerging body of European family law.

8 The Education of EU Migrant Children

Introduction

Previous chapters have highlighted how the many diverse social needs of an increasingly mobile society and particularly the needs of migrant workers and their families have necessitated developments in Community social policy primarily under the free movement legislation. Perhaps the most significant development has taken place within the context of education. Education has emerged as a key dimension of the European migration policy agenda for a number of political and pragmatic reasons. Firstly, developments in European education policy could be viewed as symbolic of a more cohesive 'social' Union, providing a forum for developing and consolidating a sense of shared European identity. Barnard (1995, p.13) notes in this respect that education 'can be seen as a means of influencing the population at a time when the Community is conscious that the Single Market needs a human face'. Secondly, education provides an ideal forum in which to strive towards greater inter-cultural understanding, awareness and integration, as Verma (1997, p.330) explains:

> Education has an important part to play in the development of individuals – intellectually, effectively, physically, socially and morally – in the development of the wider society.

In this respect, investment in an education system which is at the same time inclusive and yet allows for a level of diversity and cultural exchange is all important for the development of the EU. Moreover, the school environment could be viewed as a microcosm of an increasingly heterogeneous society and, in the same way that domestic social policy needs to be sufficiently malleable to meet varying social, cultural and economic needs, so too should education respond to the diverse needs of children. It has been estimated, for instance, that approximately fifty per cent of all pupils of compulsory school age across the EU are in daily contact with pupils whose cultural and linguistic background is different from their own (European Commission, 2000). Certainly, as a consequence of the increasing intra-Community migration of workers and their families, education systems of nation states have been receiving a growing number of children from other EU countries. These families of diverse origins often face significant challenges adapting to a different cultural, social and linguistic environment, challenges which may be reflected in some way or another in their children's academic performance:

> To a very large extent, a child's experiences of migration will be shaped by his or her experience of the educational system of the host state and by its capacity to guarantee choices and not to foreclose options. To that extent, EC education law seems an ideal starting point for a more extensive exploration of the extent to which the children of EU migrants are 'European citizens' (Shaw, 1998, p.209).

This chapter builds on the material presented in chapter four and focuses on the educational provision available at European level for the children of EU migrant workers (as a distinct category to the children of third country national migrants). It begins with an overview of the international and European legal framework relating to children's educational rights. This includes a detailed examination of the role of the ECJ in shaping and extending the scope of EU education law in favour of migrant children. The chapter then moves on to discuss the role of the EU in shaping education policy across the Member States and it debates the merits of more active incursion into an area initially perceived as falling within the exclusive remit of domestic policy. The second half of the chapter explores how EU migrant children negotiate their education within the context of mobility.

It is important to note from the outset that the discussion aims to focus firmly on the experiences and status of *EU* migrant children, although much of the literature discussed in the chapter refers more broadly to the education of third country national migrant children. Whilst we are aware of the very distinct nature of their respective experiences (and of the relatively privileged legal status of children of highly skilled migrant workers), aspects of this literature can be usefully applied to an analysis of EU migrant children's experiences.

The 180 children interviewed for the research attended various types of schools at secondary level in Sweden, Greece, Portugal and the UK. These included mainstream,[1] private, foreign, international, supplementary schools, or, in the case of Greece, schools specifically for repatriated children. A small number of focus groups involving EU migrant children were also conducted in some international schools in Portugal and

---

[1] That is, state-funded and following a national curriculum.

a sample of educational 'experts' (that is, teachers, representatives of education authorities and embassy officials) were also contacted and, where possible, interviewed. Children were encouraged to describe their experiences of both the school they were currently attending and schools they had attended in previous Member States. In particular, they were asked about the institutional structure of the school, including the number of teachers and students who attended; how long they had been attending their current school and their experiences when they arrived there (if they migrated at school age); and what a typical day at school involved, including a description of the subjects they studied and their timetable. They were also asked to comment on any difficulties they had experienced with their studies or with the language and whether any specific assistance was made available to them. They talked about their relationships with other pupils and with their teachers, examinations undertaken in previous schools in other Member States and about exams they were preparing for in the current Member State. The children were also asked about any extra-curricular activities they were involved in and for details about their future academic plans or career aspirations. Parents were also invited to comment on these issues and to provide their perspective on how their child had adapted to the new school environment. Additionally, they were asked to fill in any factual 'gaps' in the children's account of their education of which the child was unaware or unable to recall. This was particularly useful, for example, with regard to the child's early education in the country of origin. Education experts were also interviewed more specifically about the level and quality of provision for EU migrant children. They were questioned, in particular, about their awareness of European education provision and about the extent to which implementation measures had been taken in pursuance of their legal obligations under EU law.

The Educational Rights of Migrant Children: The International and European Legal Framework

The fundamental right of children to be educated is acknowledged in a number of international instruments, most famously in Article 28 of the 1989 UNCRC, Article 26(1) of the 1948 Universal Declaration of Human Rights and Article 2, Protocol 1 of the 1950 European Convention on

Human Rights and Fundamental Freedoms.[2] More specific international instruments relating to migrants emphasise the importance of guaranteeing basic educational rights. The UN, for instance, explicitly recognises the situation of migrant children in the 1990 International Convention on the protection of the Rights of all Migrant Workers and Members of their Families.[3] Article 45 of this Convention guarantees all legally established migrants access to national educational institutions in the host state. It also provides for (but does not guarantee) reception teaching and mother-tongue teaching to facilitate integration and preserve cultural identity. Likewise, Article 14 of the European Convention on the Legal Status of Migrant Workers[4] guarantees a right of access to education and Article 15 urges inter-governmental co-operation in the provision of mother-tongue teaching for migrants' children.

In spite of positive, albeit symbolic, developments at International and European Human Rights level, the EU has been much more reluctant to endorse children's educational rights in general, reflecting a commitment to the predominantly economic impetus of the EC as well as respect for Member State sovereignty in these matters. Indeed, the founding Treaty of the EC made no provision for education as part of social policy but confined its remit to vocational training linked to labour market restructuring and mobility.[5] More general educational provision emanated both from vocational training provision and through the increasingly flexible interpretations by the ECJ of the free movement of persons provisions. This gradual and subtle extension of Community competence to the education arena has been underpinned by the non-discrimination principle as contained in Article 12 (formerly Article 6) EC Treaty to ensure that young migrants and nationals receive parity of treatment in accessing educational services in the host state.

---

[2] These rights are not exactly enforceable in individual cases before a court of law but rather express and endorse a common ideal (Shaw, 1998, p.204). For further discussion of education from a human rights perspective see Bainham, 1998.

[3] Adopted by the UN General Assembly in Resolution 45/158 on 18 December 1990 (not yet in force).

[4] Strasbourg, 24 November, 1977, Council of Europe.

[5] The former Article 128 EEC (now Article 159) provided simply for the establishment of a 'common vocational policy capable of contributing to the harmonious development both of the national economies and of the common market'.

The Development of Educational Entitlement under Regulation 1612/68

The first specific Community law reference to secondary education appeared in Regulation 1612/68 relating to the free movement of EU migrant workers and their families and is essentially based on an ethic of equal opportunity. Most significantly, Article 12 of the Regulation provides:

> The children of a national of a Member State who is or who has been employed in the territory of another Member State shall be admitted to the State's general educational apprenticeship and vocational training courses under the same conditions as the nationals of that State, if such children are residing in its territory. Member States shall encourage all efforts to enable such children to attend these courses under the best possible conditions.

Article 12 covers all types and levels of education from pre-school through compulsory courses to vocational training, higher education and special needs provision. Again, as with the free movement of persons provisions generally, the ECJ has been instrumental in opening up educational opportunities to EU migrant children through a series of innovative decisions concerning the interpretation of this Article. The first important case was that of *Casagrande*.[6] It concerned the son of a deceased worker who had been a life-long resident in Munich and sought to rely on Article 12 as the basis of a claim for a means-tested maintenance grant to continue studying beyond compulsory education. The ECJ dismissed the argument put forward by the Bavarian authorities that their actions were not contrary to Community law on the grounds that the issue was outside Community competence. The ECJ, however, while accepting that education policy itself was not a matter for the Community, asserted that:

> It does not follow from this that the exercise of powers transferred to the Community is in some way restricted if it is of such a nature as to affect the measures taken in the execution of policy such as that of education and training.[7]

In other words, policy enacted with Community objectives in mind will not be inhibited in its operation even if it overlaps with an area of national competence (Gould, 1990, p.175). Following this decision, Article

---

[6] Case 9/74 *Casagrande v. Landehauptstadt München* [1974]ECR 773, [1974] CMLR 423.

[7] [1974] ECR 773 at 779 (Consideration 12).

12 has been interpreted to encompass maintenance grants which must be awarded to nationals from other EU countries under the same conditions as nationals of the host state.

Belgium v. Humbel [8] emphasised that the benefits of Article 12 do not apply to those who travel independently of their family to another EC country for the sole purpose of pursuing their studies – migrant students, therefore, cannot rely on the Article to obtain general rights of access to education in other Member States, regardless of their nationality. Similarly, in the case of *Brown,*[9] the plaintiff sought access to education in the UK even though he was born and educated in France and his French parents had not worked in the UK since before his birth. The ECJ rejected his petition, stating that, in order to benefit from Article 12, he had to be a UK resident or at least his parents must have been resident workers in the UK during his lifetime. In this respect, the case marks a distinction between the rights attached to the status of the child of an EU migrant worker and the less privileged status of EU migrant students.[10]

In the joined cases of *Echternach* and *Moritz,*[11] Moritz differed from the plaintiff in Brown in that he wished to pursue his studies in a country in which he had previously been resident with his parents. The ECJ held that his family's subsequent migration to their country of origin did not necessarily extinguish the child's rights under Article 12 since the provision explicitly extends entitlement to the child of a migrant worker 'who is or has been employed' in the territory of another Member State. Gould (1990, p.178) notes that it could be argued that 'this phrase was intended only to apply to those workers who had lost their jobs but still remained in the host state'. In the absence of any words to the contrary, however, the ECJ held that Moritz was clearly covered by Regulation 1612/68. The decision is significant since it marks one of the few instances in which a child can exercise his Community rights (which happen to be education-related) independently of the parents' place of residence. Nevertheless, it has been argued that this decision will apply only in

---

[8] Case 263/86 [1988] ECR 5365.

[9] Case 197/86 *Steven Brown v. Secretary of State for Scotland* [1988] ECR 3205.

[10] An EU national who wishes to pursue their studies in another EC Member State and who does not qualify as either the child of an EU migrant worker or as a worker in their own right cannot rely on Regulation 1612/68, but must instead rely on Residence Directive 93/96 which allows a student to reside in another Member State, provided they have sufficient financial resources to avoid becoming a burden on the host state. For further detail on the rights of students, see Case 293/83 *Gravier v. City of Liège* [1985] ECR 593 and more generally Hervey, 1998.

[11] Cases 389 and 390/87 *Echternach and Moritz v. Netherlands Minister for Education and Science* [1989] ECR 723.

exceptional circumstances, for example, if the parents have migrated at a crucial stage in the child's education, where forcing the child to migrate would be unduly prejudicial. It does not necessarily, therefore, enable non-national children to reside in other EU Member States independently of their parents and to claim public financial assistance in the process.

The independent claim of an EU migrant child to educational rights has been reinforced very recently, however, by the case of *Baumbast*[12] which was referred to the ECJ for a preliminary ruling by the English Immigration Appeals Tribunal. The case concerned a German father and his Colombian spouse who migrated to England with their two children for the purposes of the father's work. The family's residual right to remain was called into question when the father ceased working in the UK.[13] The mother and children, however, wished to remain in the host state, primarily to enable the children to continue with their education. The ECJ was asked to consider a number of questions relating to the interpretation of Article 12 Regulation 1612/68. Firstly, it was asked to consider whether the children of an EU migrant worker, who are themselves citizens of the EU, and who have installed themselves in primary education during the exercise by their father (or parent) of rights of residence as a migrant worker, are entitled to reside in the host state in order to undergo general educational courses there. The English tribunal acknowledged that if the children were granted a right to remain in the host state, the ECJ would be required to review the right of their non-qualifying parents – an unemployed EU national and a non-Community national – to remain with the children in the host state:

> Where children have the right to reside in a host state in order to undergo general education course pursuant to Article 12 of Regulation 1612/68, is the obligation of the host state to 'encourage all efforts to enable such children to attend these courses under the best possible conditions' to be interpreted as entitling their primary carer, whether or not a citizen of the Union, to reside with them in order to facilitate such a right notwithstanding ... the father who is a citizen of the European Union ceases to be a worker within the host state? (para. 28)

---

[12] Case C 413/99, Opinion of Advocate General Geelhoed, *Baumbast and R v. Secretary of State for the Home Department*, and the Judgment of the Court of Justice of 17th September 2002, 2002/C274/03. Unfortunately, the ECJ, while it decided in favour of the claimant, was less progressive in its reasoning than the Advocate General, determining the issue instead on the basis of Union citizenship status.

[13] He had been unsuccessful in finding work following the failure of his business and had subsequently undertaken temporary contract work abroad with no immediate plans to return to the UK as a work-seeker.

Advocate General Geelhoed, delivering his Opinion on 5 July 2001, proposed that the ECJ should respond as follows:

> Children who under Article 10 of Regulation 1612/68 ... have installed themselves in a host Member State as a result of the fact that one of their parents was employed in that Member State, retain under Article 12 of that regulation the right to continue in the host Member State education already commenced there and to remain for that purpose in that Member State. (para. 23)

He acknowledged that to force a return to their country of origin (Germany) would unduly prejudice the continuity of the children's education, particularly as they do not speak German. Moreover, he recognised the 'absurdity' of granting residence rights to the children and then 'depriving them of any possibility of effectively exercising them by refusing residence to the mother' as their primary carer.[14] The Advocate General thus recommended that:

> where children have a right to remain for the purpose of continuing their education the parent carer also has a right to remain, if that is necessary for the exercise by the children of their rights. (para. 69)

This Opinion implies that the children of migrant workers retain their status as a family member regardless of whether or not their parents subsequently lose their status. This creates a situation whereby the children who derived their initial status under the free movement provisions from their parents now become the source of similar rights for their parents.[15] Significantly, Advocate General Geelhoed, in supporting the parents' right to remain with the children in the host state, relied both on the economic and social rights arising out of the free movement provisions as well as on their right to respect for family life and reunification under Article 8 of the European Convention on Human Rights.[16] As such, while the educational interests of the child were afforded greater consideration and currency in this case, it was still very much the child's place within the family unit and

---

[14] Above note 12, para. 72.

[15] This is discussed further in chapters one and four. See also para. 80 of the Advocate General's Opinion. Despite a generous interpretation of Article 12 to effectively endow the entire family with a residence right if linked to the children's education, he conceded that 'since the right to remain in favour of the parent carer is derivative in nature, that means that a Member State may under its domestic law apply a temporal limitation on that right, for example, until the education is completed or until the period of care of the children has come to an end'.

[16] *Baumbast*, above note 12, paras.' 22-27 and 60.

the need to keep the family together which underpinned the Advocate General's Opinion (Cullen, 2003).

EU migrant children's educational rights have thus developed significantly through increasingly broad interpretations of Article 12. Article 7(2) of Regulation 1612/68 has also been imaginatively applied in this respect. Article 7(2) states that an EU migrant worker 'shall enjoy the same social and tax advantages as national workers'. Initially the ECJ followed a strict interpretation of this provision applying it exclusively to the migrant worker and allowing workers' families to benefit only from Articles 10-12 of the Regulation. As chapter four has highlighted, however, the ECJ has progressively broadened its interpretation of Article 7(2) so that it has become almost a 'catch-all' provision, endowing family members with a range of direct and independent social and economic benefits. The fundamental justification for extending the definition of 'social advantage' to cover EU migrant children's education, however, remains clear: it alleviates the financial burden on the worker parent and ultimately facilitates mobility. The ECJ, reasoning in *Deak*, highlighted the correlation between the availability of such provision and the continued exercise of freedom of movement:

> A worker, anxious to ensure for his children enjoyment of the social benefits provided for by the legislation of the Member States ... would be induced not to remain in the Member State where he had established himself and found employment if that State could refuse to pay the benefits in question to his children because of their foreign nationality.[17]

This point was emphasised in *Bernini,*[18] a case in which the plaintiff was the daughter of an Italian who had migrated to the Netherlands. On leaving her job in the Netherlands she travelled to Italy to pursue her studies for which she applied for a maintenance grant. It was held that she could rely on Article 7(2) to secure a maintenance grant, but only if she could prove that she was financially dependent on the parent worker and that any financial assistance provided to her would alleviate the economic burden on the supporting parent. This provides a further example where the ECJ clearly distinguishes between the enhanced status of EU migrant family members under Regulation 1612/68 and EU migrant students. More recently, *Lubor Gaal* [19] made it clear that, in order to rely on Article 7(2) of

[17] Case 94/84 *Office National de l'Emploi v. Deak* [1985] ECR 1773.
[18] Case C-3/90 *Bernini v. Minister van Onderwijs en Wetenschappen* [1992] ECR I-1071.
[19] Case C-7/94 *Landesamt fur Ausbildungsforderung Nordrhein-Westfalen v. Lubor Gaal* [1996] ECR 1-1031, referred to also in chapter four.

the Regulation to obtain educational rights, the plaintiff must fall within the personal scope of Article 10 of the same Regulation – in other words, the child must be under the age of 21 years or be dependent upon the parent worker. Conversely, for claims made under Article 12, there is seemingly no requirement that the child be either financially dependent or under the age of 21, provided at least one of their parents is an EU migrant worker. This creates an anomaly in the Regulation in that there is a varying degree of entitlement depending on which Article the claimant relies. Furthermore, the retention of the dependence requirement for Article 7(2) claims is inconsistent with the earlier decision in *Cristini*[20] in which family members were not required to demonstrate financial dependence on the migrant worker to entitle them to benefits under this Article since the migrant worker was deceased.

Thus, following the *Lubor Gaal* decision, educational entitlement available to children under Article 12 of Regulation 1612/68 – while still limited to those who have initially moved with their migrant parents to the host Member States – is less restrictive than other free movement-related rights. *Lubor Gaal* established that for requests made under Article 12, the claimant is not necessarily subject to an age limit, a relationship of financial dependency with the migrant worker or yielding some kind of continued direct or indirect financial benefit in favour of the worker.

Nevertheless, while the Regulation refers both to rules of admission to education as well as to general measures to facilitate educational attendance, it has been criticised for its failure to address wider issues beyond securing equality of access concerned, for example, with integration, assimilation or multiculturalism (Shaw, 1998, p.205). Cullen (1996, p.111), for instance, observes that the approach of the Regulation is 'one of formal equality' that may be 'described as passive assimilation, through exposing the child only to the language and culture of the host state'. Cullen goes on to assert that this passive integrationist approach, which simply guarantees migrant children a place in a national school, has led to a high level of under-achievement by migrant children.[21] The ECJ has had limited opportunity to address this issue since the case law relating to the application of Regulation 1612/68 is almost exclusively concerned with access to third level or higher education, commonly relating to claims for state financial assistance. Consequently, Article 12 and 7(2) entitlement has evolved primarily within the context of older migrant children's

---

[20] Case 32/75 *Anita Cristini v. Société nationale des chemins de fer français* ECR 1085.

[21] We presume Cullen is referring to the educational performance of migrant children generally since our research has yielded no persuasive evidence that *EU* migrant children underachieve. This will be explored later in this chapter and in chapter nine.

education with relatively modest developments, at least until *Baumbast*, having occurred, typically, in the context of younger migrants' entitlement.

Despite these limitations, it is interesting to note that the education entitlement afforded under Regulation 1612/68 provides the only example under the free movement provisions where children have ostensibly enhanced rights compared to their parents from whom they derive their status and, indeed, compared to other categories of migrants. For example, education rights pertaining to migrant workers are largely confined to vocational training courses and exclude general educational provision.[22] Thus, while children can invoke both Articles 12 and 7(2) to enable them to study at any level, migrant workers may only invoke Article 7(2) in relation to studies which are in some way connected to either their profession, to their professional qualifications or, in limited circumstances, to retrain for another profession.[23] Ironically, therefore, in endeavouring to facilitate the mobility of migrant workers through enhancing children's corollary rights, the EU institutions have served to enhance children's entitlement (in this limited area at least) over and above that of their parents, marking a gradual departure from their derived status. The case of *Baumbast* marks a potentially decisive step in this regard.

Developments in Favour of Younger EU Migrant Children

Although not directly related to younger migrants, the early judicial developments in relation to Regulation 1612/68 in favour of migrant workers' children spawned a flurry of policy-making activities to establish and nurture a range of funding programmes with the aim of encouraging greater educational mobility and exchange as well as enhancing training and technological skills at all levels. The 1970s, in particular, marked a period of more specific advancements in relation to European secondary education policy. The action plans and initiatives developed at this time were designed to provide an appropriate context for increased communication, greater understanding, the international recognition of qualifications and, lastly, the mobility of ideas (Peck, 1997, p.17). This was in response to increasing concerns raised particularly by the institutions

---

[22] That is, unless they too qualify as the children of migrant workers in the host state in which case they do not relinquish their privileged status merely by virtue of the fact that they subsequently become employed. This was confirmed in Case 235/87 *Matteucci v. Communauté Français de Belgique* [1988] ECR 5589.

[23] See *Bernini*, above note 19; and Case C-357/89 *Raulin v. Minister van Onderwijs en Wetenschappen* [1992] ECR I-1027.

responsible for the education of migrant children (both from within the EU and from third countries), over the level of educational provision directly available to them. The Council of Europe's Committee of Ministers acknowledged these concerns in 1970 and alerted Member States to the need to eliminate the difficulties of social and academic adaptation experienced by students of migrant origin, to the advantage of maintaining cultural and linguistic ties with the country of origin and to the need to prepare them for their reintegration should those students ever decide to return home.

Subsequently, the European Commission in 1972 instructed a core group of education specialists across the EU to pinpoint essential elements of education policy which required attention at Community level. The ensuing Janne Report (European Commission, 1973) delivered a number of recommendations, which included; the provision of better facilities for the education of EU migrant workers and their children; the improvement of the teaching and learning of foreign languages; and the promotion of equality of opportunity and free access to all forms of education for all. This echoes the aspirations of the international human rights provisions alluded to at the beginning of this chapter.

Almost a decade after the introduction of Regulation 1612/68, a Resolution issued by the Council of Europe and Ministers of Education in 1976 called for the implementation of measures tailored to the needs of EU migrant children. It included:

> organising and developing a reception system which would include intensive study of the language or languages of the host country; providing more opportunities as appropriate for teaching these children their mother tongue and culture, if possible in school and in collaboration with the country of origin; and providing more information for families on the training and educational opportunities available to them.[24]

The acknowledged limitations of Regulation 1612/68, coupled with the 'soft law' measures generated by the Council of Europe's pioneering activity in the 1970s, culminated in the launch of EC Directive 77/486 on the education of the children of migrant workers. This introduced specific binding provisions addressing the distinct learning needs of child migrants by requiring Member States to implement both mother-tongue and host language tuition to facilitate the child's initial reception in the new school environment.[25]

---

[24] OJ No.C 38, 19 February 1976, pp.1-5.

[25] This will be explored in greater depth in chapter nine.

These developments indicate that, since the early 1970s, education has occupied an increasingly prominent position within the EU polity. More recent constitutional advancements bear testimony to this continuing shift by the Community from a purely economic focus towards an increasing concern to enhance social entitlement and, consequently, the substance of European citizenship. The 1992 Treaty on European Union formally acknowledged the importance of developing a Community education policy by incorporating a new Article 126 (now Article 149) into the former EEC Treaty, thereby expressing a concern, as Barnard (1995, p.17) makes clear, to:

> contribute to the development of quality education by encouraging co-operation between Member States and, if necessary, by supporting and supplementing their action, while fully respecting the responsibility of the Member States for the content of their teaching and the organisation of education systems and their cultural and linguistic diversity.

More dramatically, the Treaty of Amsterdam incorporated a new recital into the preamble of the EC Treaty which expressed the following commitment:

> Determined to promote the development of the highest possible level of knowledge for their people through a wide access to education and through its continuous updating.[26]

Most recently, the Charter of Fundamental Rights in the European Union[27] contains a specific provision enshrining the educational rights of children. Article 14(3) of the Charter announces that:

> The freedom to found educational establishments with due respect for democratic principles and the right of parents to ensure the education and teaching of their children in conformity with their religious, philosophical and pedagogical convictions shall be respected, in accordance with the national laws governing the exercise of such freedom and right.

Whilst at present this provision is only of declaratory effect, it underpins ongoing and strengthened Community action in the field of

[26] Although this is not of legally binding force, it does enhance and reaffirm the constitutional status of education at EU level (Shaw, 1998, p.203).

[27] Adopted at the Nice Summit in December 2000, O.J. of the European Communities 2000 C 364/11, 18.12.2000. For a discussion of the legal status of the Charter see de Búrca, 2001. Article 7 of the Charter which articulates Article 8 of the ECHR was referred to by Advocate General Geelhoed in his Opinion on the *Baumbast* case above note 12.

education. As Barnard (1995, p.17) points out, however, the limits of Community competence remain clear:

> The emphasis is on the importance of the role of Member States: the position of the Community is both subordinate and supplementary ... The Community may not interfere with the detailed organisation or content of education. This encapsulates the principle of subsidiarity in respect of education.

Indeed, education, like family law and policy, is informed by important cultural, economic, social, religious and political factors and, as such, has traditionally been regulated almost exclusively at national level. It is hardly surprising, therefore, that Member States have demonstrated a reluctance to allow the EU too much leeway to superimpose harmonised provisions which are inevitably less sensitive to these contextual variables. EU incursion into the domestic social policy arena thus has to be legitimised by an identifiable link with the pursuit of broader European (economic) objectives. This has, as the above case law demonstrates, been achieved primarily by means of the facilitating mobility test under the free movement provisions. While ostensibly Community action was and remains complementary to that of Member States to allow for social, cultural and linguistic diversity, the ECJ has demonstrated just how far the institutions are prepared to stretch the boundaries of competence in pursuit of these objectives. The more recent Treaty amendments coupled with the adoption of the Charter of Fundamental Rights in the European Union, however, provide a more substantial legal basis upon which to propose more direct action in the educational domain for children as independent citizens. In this respect, the presumption that Community action in the context of education and other aspects of social policy is 'subordinate and supplementary' (Barnard, 1995, p.17) is likely to be increasingly challenged.

European Education Policy and Domestic Practice

The previous section has provided an overview of the European legal framework with respect to the educational rights of EU migrant children and discussed how this is founded principally on the notion of non-discrimination and equality of access. A closer examination of educational policy and practice across the Member States, however, reveals a more complex challenge to meet the needs of children travelling between such diverse systems.

The school is an important environment in which children learn how to interact with others, develop their own individual personality and become aware of their national and cultural identity. The challenges associated with this process of integration and self-development, as far as migrant children are concerned, are compounded by the very factors which safeguard Member States' legislative sovereignty in this area – the existence of linguistic and cultural differences, as well as variations in the institutional structures and running of schools from one country to another. The experiences of many of the children we interviewed bear testimony to this – 43 of the 180 children interviewed had moved once to another Member State with their parents which was different to the one in which they were born; 37 children had undergone at least two migrations to other countries within the EC; and 36 children had returned to their country of origin having lived in another EC Member State for a period of time. Education featured prominently in both the adults' and children's accounts of their migration experiences, with 27 families asserting that the migration decision was directly influenced by considerations concerning the child's education. In 9 of these cases, the family attributed their decision not to move to either the perceived prejudicial effect this would have on the child's academic progress, to uncertainty surrounding whether or not the child's academic qualifications would be recognised in the host state, or to doubts over whether qualifications obtained abroad would be recognised in the country to which the child anticipated a future migration. In a further 7 cases, the child remained in their home country independently of their parents, often until the end of the academic year and sometimes indefinitely, to avoid any disruption which the migration might cause to their education.[28]

A brief description of the mesh of policy provision regulating different Member States' education systems provides an indication of the implications and complexities of any calls to harmonise or converge education policy at the EU level. A mosaic of provisions governs the administration, financing and organisation of education within each of the Member States creating a number of differences between them. Notable distinctions are apparent, for instance, in the length of compulsory schooling across the EU. Compulsory education begins at age 6 in nine of the Member States, but it begins earlier in Luxembourg and Northern Ireland (age 4) and in the Netherlands and England (age 5). In Denmark, Finland and Sweden, education is compulsory only from age 7. In most EU countries, education follows a broadly similar pattern until the end of lower

[28] See chapter three for a more in-depth analysis of factors motivating intra-Community migration and the involvement of children in these processes.

secondary school (age 14 or 15). A common core curriculum is followed until age 16 in Denmark, Spain, Finland and the UK. In Germany and Austria, pupils have a margin of discretion over the direction of their studies at the beginning of lower secondary education (at age 10) and in Luxembourg at age 12 (EUROSTAT, 1996, p.13). Full-time compulsory education lasts until age 16 in most nation states apart from Greece, Ireland, Luxembourg, Austria and Portugal where it finishes at age 15 and, in Italy, at 14. Generally, full-time compulsory education lasts 9 or 10 years, but there are exceptions – Italy's compulsory education lasts for only 8 years, Luxembourg's and England's lasts 11 years and in the Netherlands and Northern Ireland, compulsory education lasts for as much as 12 years (Ruxton, 1996, pp.200-207). The organisation of *secondary* education differs from one Member State to another, but usually includes a first and a second stage of varying lengths. The age at which pupils begin secondary education also varies. It is generally set at age 11 or 12 across the EU apart from Germany and Austria when it begins at age 10. In the majority of Member States, the first stage lasts for either three or four years, apart from in Germany where it lasts for five or six, and in Belgium where it lasts for only two years. In Denmark, Portugal, Finland and Sweden, there is no lower secondary education as such, but instead 'basic education', organised in one single structure over nine years.

Important differences are also evident in the content of educational curricula across the EU, and particularly in relation to the learning of foreign languages. Nearly all pupils begin learning a second language at primary school – English language is compulsory in Denmark, Greece, Spain, Italy, Luxembourg, the Netherlands, Austria, Finland, Sweden and Belgium (at least in Brussels). In England, Wales and Northern Ireland, foreign language teaching is offered in some but not all schools depending on resources. Finland offers the highest proportion of English language pupils at primary level (60 per cent), followed by Sweden (49 per cent), Austria (48 per cent), Greece (41 per cent) and Denmark (35 per cent). French is the second most widely taught language at primary level, although to a much lesser extent than English (apart from in the Flemish Community of Belgium and Luxembourg where French is compulsory from the second year of primary school) (EUROSTAT, 1996).

From the age of 13 all pupils in the EU are taught broadly the same compulsory subjects although the amount of time allocated to these subjects can vary considerably from one Member State to another. The time devoted to mother-tongue teaching is set at 30 hours a year in Luxembourg, compared to 200 hours a year in Italy. The minimum amount of time allocated to mathematics is found in Finland (approximately 86 hours per year) and the maximum is found in Austria (165 hours a year). While Finland devotes 257 hours per year to artistic activities, Germany allocates only 26 hours. In relation to science subjects, Luxembourg pupils receive on average 30 hours of teaching a year, while Danish and Austrian pupils benefit from as much as 180 hours. Teaching of the human sciences also varies widely, from a minimum of 57 hours per year in Finland, to a maximum of 210 hours in Portugal. Pupils in Luxembourg spend most of their time learning foreign languages (270 hours a year) (EUROSTAT, 1996, p.52).

These figures indicate that while subjects studied at secondary level are broadly similar across the EU, there are huge differences in the way that some subjects are prioritised over others, as evidenced in the number of hours allotted to them in the school timetable. More marked differences relating to subjects studied emerge when students reach the age of 16 and have greater choice over the studies they wish to pursue. In general, EUROSTAT (2000) data indicates that somewhat more time is allocated to foreign languages at this age, apart from in Spain, Italy and Portugal.

Modes of assessment and the award of diplomas also differ considerably between the nation states, as do access requirements for entry into higher education. The European Commission, in its 1996 report on education in the EU, identified three main approaches to assessment. The first approach consists of certification based on external, standardised (public) examinations (evident in Denmark, Germany, France, Ireland, Italy, Luxembourg, the Netherlands, Austria, Finland and the United Kingdom). The second approach is certification based on internal final examinations (evident in Belgium and Greece), and the third is that of certification with no final examinations (as is the case in Spain, Portugal and Sweden) (EUROSTAT, 1996, p.56).

Whilst existing supra-national provision caters more for the transferability of qualifications and skills of those at vocational training and professional level,[29] the respondents' experiences demonstrate that issues of transferability and progression between Member States are of significant concern at primary and secondary school level. Current EU provision, for instance, does not address the situation in which nationals are required to have specific academic credentials to gain access to certain systems of education and how qualifications obtained from other Member States will be regarded. This problem is most likely to arise in relation to access to university places in other EU countries as there are no enforceable

---

[29] For a detailed analysis of the law underpinning mutual recognition of qualifications in a migration context, see Stalford, 2000 and the Council of Europe website, www.coe.int, for details of relevant international, bilateral and EU law regulating this issue.

mechanisms in place either at EU level or in every Member State to ensure that comparable national secondary qualifications are recognised by the host state for initial access. Instead, this is determined by agreements between countries and 'mutual trust' (Dalichow, 1987; Verma, 1997).[30] Forty-two of the parents and children interviewed for this research, for instance, commented that they were unsure whether or not their final year school qualifications would be valid in other Member States to which they had migrated or to which they anticipated migrating in the future.

Problems relating to transferability were particularly acute in cases where the young migrant wished to attend university in Greece where access is normally subject to passing a special national examination. In two illustrative examples, both respondents (who had migrated from France some years earlier) had already obtained their Baccalaureate[31] from a French private school in Greece which would have entitled them – and the nationals of any other Member State who had concluded a reciprocal agreement with France – to attend university in France. In order to attend a Greek university, however, they were required to sit the national examination under the same conditions as nationals, despite the fact that most nationals received preparatory training for the examination throughout their schooling and were, therefore, in a highly advantageous position. The following parent explained the procedure:

> Graduating from high school, thus obtaining the Baccalaureate, the children will have already taken the grades for their admission to the university [in France]. However, Baccalaureate is recognised in Greece only as a high school qualification. If they want to study in Greece, they have to participate in the National examinations otherwise they will go for studies in France [431].

A case brought before the ECJ illustrates that this issue continues to present difficulties to young migrants who wish to make the transition from education to the world of work in another Member State. In November 1999, the University of Northumbria welcomed an ECJ decision to support one of its postgraduates in her campaign to force Madrid's Prado art gallery to consider her application for a post there. The student had obtained a Masters degree in fine arts restoration from the English university in 1999,

---

[30] The Council of Europe and UNESCO have, however, adopted a Convention on the Recognition of Qualifications Concerning Higher Education in the European Region (commonly known as the Lisbon Recognition Convention). This entered into force on 1 February 1999 and will gradually supplant earlier Council of Europe Conventions between signatory states.

[31] The French High School leaving certificate.

ironically with the support of a grant awarded by the Prado gallery. She pursued legal action in 1992 after the gallery refused to acknowledge her qualification, claiming it was not officially equivalent to a similar Spanish qualification. Spanish officials informed her that she would have to take two further examinations to prove that she had sufficient knowledge of the subjects covered by the formal Spanish degree. The ECJ accepted that this was in breach of Community law, in particular the free movement of persons provisions, and that the onus was on the Spanish authorities to re-examine whether:

> ... the knowledge and qualifications certified by the diploma ... correspond to the knowledge and qualifications required by the host Member State's legislation (Nuthall, 1999).

Furthermore, the Prado were obliged to consider the student's application regardless of whether her English degree was granted recognition or not.[32]

One could argue that the same principle can be applied analogously to secondary education. If so, local authorities would be precluded from requiring young migrants to take additional exams or re-sits a year before they are granted access to education at the same level as that which they had attained in their country of origin, particularly if they are sufficiently competent in the language of the host state.

Problems of transferability and mutual recognition also arise at a lower level. Northern Ireland, for example, operates a selective system of state education at secondary level whereby pupils are prepared for approximately two years prior to undertaking an examination in their final year of primary school to determine which type of secondary school they can attend.[33] This presents significant problems to migrant children who have not had the opportunity to prepare for and sit this qualifying examination. In many cases, the local authorities allow them to undergo an alternative assessment in order to determine whether they are of a sufficiently high academic standard to attend grammar school. This assessment, which is generally composed of English language, verbal reasoning, grammar and arithmetic (in Northern Ireland at least), clearly prejudices those children who, while perhaps of sufficient academic ability to cope with a grammar school education, lack confidence in speaking or

---

[32] Case C-234/97, *Maria Teresa Fernández de Bobadilla v Museo Nacional del Prado and Others*, OJ 1999/C 366/01.

[33] The 'Eleven Plus' Examination. This selection procedure also operates in 5 per cent of schools (totalling 169) throughout England.

writing the host language or are unfamiliar with this form of assessment and curriculum. The experiences of one respondent, who transferred from the Dutch to the Northern Ireland education system at the age of fourteen, highlights this problem:

> When I came here I had this big exam to do and out of those results they see if you can go to Grammar school or not … All the other people there were actually English [055].

In some cases, it seems that the requirement to sit any such test will be waived and an alternative form of assessment adopted to minimise the stress of adapting to another school. This, however, seems to depend very much on the discretion of the schools and teachers involved. One young Irish migrant remembers her experiences five years previously when she migrated to the North of Ireland where the education system is more akin to that of England:

> So when I was ten, and about to do the eleven plus we came to Belfast and I was so far behind it was unbelievable ... I was so far behind that I worried about what was going to happen with my eleven plus but the Headmaster eventually told my mum that I didn't have to sit the test because I'd moved over here and that I could just be assessed on my course work ... I could go to grammar school then … but I had some tuition beforehand to help me catch up on the basics, otherwise there was no way I could have gone onto a higher level [057].

Of course, one might argue that many problems associated with gaining access to educational institutions in other Member States is as much if not more attributable to linguistic incompetence as it is to recognition of foreign qualifications. In that sense, the debate shifts from mutual recognition of qualifications into issues of progression and the level of European provision in place to aid progression following transition to another country's education system. The case law of the ECJ concerning implementation of Article 12 Regulation 1612/68 (as described in the first section of this chapter) confirms that gaining formal access to state schools is generally not an obstacle for migrant children. Indeed, initial access was problematic for only one child interviewed who had moved some years earlier from France to the south of England. He was refused admission to the local primary school on the basis that his language skills were insufficient. Consequently, his parents had little option but to pay for him to attend an expensive private school further away. His mother commented:

> We did have a problem with schools at first because none of the schools would take him because he couldn't speak English – they said the only school was [a local private school] which cost a lot but his father managed to pay [081].

In most cases, however, it was other, more subtle factors once the child had actually gained access to the school, which were in fact prohibitive. These included the level of language support available to the child to enable him or her to progress at the same rate as national students in curricular subjects and the lack of familiarity with methods and programmes of learning as well as with methods of assessment. Furthermore, since many subjects are continually assessed on a modular basis, commonly over a period of two years, a child who moves to a new school in the host state mid-module may be significantly behind other students in the class with no other option than to start at the beginning of a new cycle of assessments.

These factors were perceived in a number of cases as having directly impeded the child's academic progress, as this respondent, who migrated from Germany three years ago with his family recalled:

> It was difficult at school in the beginning. The lessons, the system, the way of studying were very different from the corresponding German. This is the reason why I failed the first year. I hated that [420].

It is interesting to note that respondents encountered difficulties with some curricular subjects more than others. Mathematics, science, history and geography presented problems most commonly, probably because maths and science-based subjects are often approached using different methods which is further compounded by the technical language involved, as one UK respondent explains:

> I'm not that good at maths – they do the sums differently than in Holland – so when I first started they did all these sums that I didn't understand – but I understand it now [003].

Furthermore, the content of geography and history are usually specific to the cultural context in which they are being taught as this quote from one respondent, who returned to Sweden following a period in Germany, demonstrates:

> In history, I was a bit behind the others because I've never studied Swedish history. And I found social studies rather hard as well, since I've never

> really been part of Swedish society. But I was doing quite well anyway. In the beginning I was studying all the time to catch up with the rest of the class. Now I'm as good as the others [230].

More positive accounts described how the child had already had the opportunity to study the subjects in a previous country and some referred to the advantage they had over the other students when it came to studying those topics in the host country. This was especially the case for one Swedish respondent who moved to Austria for two years where her father was working, before returning to Sweden:

> My mother thought that it would be really difficult because they use another way of teaching ... in Austria we had science and we studied different kinds of trees and we're doing the same thing right now, in biology, and I'm in the eighth grade!! I did it in Austria five years ago so there's a huge difference [215].

Conversely, this can also have the negative effect of de-motivating a child. The following Swedish respondent, having already covered the subject area in Italy, became very complacent when she returned to Sweden, admitting that she had lost all enthusiasm for studying:

> In Italy, it was much harder, but at the same time funnier since I learnt a lot. When I got back to Sweden I was way ahead of my classmates so I didn't care that much. I had a feeling that I didn't have to care at all and because of this I got behind the rest of the class [219].

These examples reinforce the need for individual Member States' education policy to account for inter-state diversity in the organisation and provision of education. They also reflect the specific difficulties disparities between educational provision can create, not least in terms of shifting access criteria and the nature and extent of children's entitlement from one system to another. This raises the question of whether or not there is a need for greater convergence, or at least an enhanced level of mutual understanding of education policy across the Member States in order to facilitate children's adaptation to the new school environment in the host state.

Promoting Harmonisation and Mutual Understanding in the Provision of Migrant Children's Education Across Member States

The implications of promoting greater convergence are huge given the vast differences between existing domestic set-ups, not to mention the varying cultural, social and economic contexts within which education policy is framed. Acknowledging this, the Treaty of Maastricht simultaneously called for harmonisation of Member States' educational policies but, as already commented, preserved the Member State's right to determine the content and form of teaching and assessment. Certainly, arguments against further convergence between Member States' forms of teaching and assessment are as much practical as ideological. McClean (1995, p.29) outlines some of the practical implications:

> Despite conventions of mutual recognition, diplomas of differing states retain varying informal levels of status which determine in practice the treatment that nationals from different states will receive in other countries. Content is the final impediment to the comparability of educational qualifications necessary to the mobility of the peoples of Europe.

McClean goes on to comment on the fact that there is now more diversity in certification in EU countries with the consequence that equivalences across EU countries are now more difficult to achieve than in previous decades. The specialised English A-level[34] is matched only by the Irish and Scottish Highers, French Baccalaureat or German Arbitur, while the equivalent Spanish Bachillerato has not retained as elevated a status. In this respect, additional university entrance tests become more important in some countries (including Greece) than others. The same disparity is apparent at a lower level in that intermediate exams are less important in other EU countries than in the UK. The English GCSE, for instance, has no equivalent as a universal and crucial stepping stone to advanced level learning. Other Member States' intermediate qualifications, such as the Hauptschule or Realschule, in reality survive only because employers may require evidence of general educational achievements of those entering vocational training (McClean, 1995, p.38).

Added to these practical considerations is the simple fact that maintaining a rich diversity between Member States' education systems is arguably more desirable than achieving uniformity to enable cultural,

[34] Which itself has undergone dramatic changes since the introduction of Curriculum 2000 to replace the pre-existing A-level system. This will encompass a broader range of subjects, bringing it in line with some other European systems.

linguistic and social traditions to be effectively preserved, explored, nurtured and valued, as McClean (1995, p.45) argues:

> [Europe] has a richness in its educational diversity. The advantage needs to be encouraged. The major challenge in Europe is not the negative differences between the national systems, but the positive stimulus to make the wealth of this diversity accessible to all citizens of the continent.

This has prompted some authors to advocate co-operation, transparency and understanding as a more effective and appropriate approach than harmonisation. Again, McClean (1995, p.31) highlights some of the implications of this:

> More important than the will to harmonise is the need to disseminate understanding of the nature of differences between countries. Curriculum involves much more than lists of subjects and the topics to be covered within each. Underlying these formal elements are widely held conceptions of the purpose of teaching and learning; the ways in which knowledge and skills are acquired, the kinds of assessment of students that should be applied; rights of access to various kinds of learning of different social groups and structures of control and participation. Mobile students need to be able to understand these differences ... The immediate difficulties are not so much about how to harmonise differing systems, but are much more elementary. They are about how to describe differences in a simple, coherent, meaningful way.

What is central to the case law outlined above concerning the scope of Regulation 1612/68, is that EU migrant workers' children have the same rights of *access* to education as nationals, whether it be in the form of maintenance grants or enrolment rights. Indeed, the Regulation has achieved much in the way of ensuring that EU workers will not be dissuaded from migrating due to a lack of basic formal educational rights available to their children. What the Regulation and the accompanying case law fail to acknowledge, however, is the fact that simple rights of access are insufficient in themselves to ensure the effective integration of a migrant child within the education system of another Member State. As already noted, Cullen (1996, p.114) comments that 'the view of integration promoted by the Regulation is a very basic one, which leans towards assimilation of migrants'. Its inadequacy, therefore, lies more in what it does *not* say rather than what it does say in relation to EU migrant children's education – the presumption seems to be that integration can be achieved simply through immersing the child in the language, culture and educational system of the host state. It fails, however, to account for the fact that a basic assimilationist approach prompts the majority of EU migrant families to resort to international and private foreign schooling as a more appropriate and substantial educational alternative to state schooling. In itself, this may achieve a smooth transition in the child's academic progress, but it has implications for their integration with nationals and familiarisation with the culture of the host state. Moreover, it fails to address the status of migrant children from families which simply do not have access to sufficient financial resources to fund an exclusive education of this nature.

The following section considers our child respondents' integration in the school environment following migration and aims to illustrate some of the issues described above.

The Impact of European Education Provision on EU Migrant Children's Lives: Integration in the School Environment

The children interviewed were asked to recall how they had found settling into the new school environment, how they related to other pupils, and about measures which had been taken by the school, parents or peers to facilitate their adjustment. The responses indicate that a number of variables have an impact upon the level of integration achieved by an EU migrant child following arrival at the new school.[35] Firstly, it is significantly influenced by the age of the child at the time of migration and their length of residence in the host state since this impacts upon the child's familiarity with the culture and language of the host state which are important factors aiding the integration process. Secondly, the role of teachers in facilitating the child's integration is a significant factor in easing the child's adaptation to the new school environment. Thirdly, integration can depend on the type of school which the child attends, whether it be international, private, mainstream or supplementary, and the methods of induction which are in place for these children. A fourth variable relates to the number of times a child has had to move schools and the extent to which they have developed coping mechanisms to enable them to adjust quickly to a variety of different surroundings or, indeed, whether serial migration hinders their ability or desire to adapt to new schools.

It is worth noting that many of the problems identified, particularly in relation to integration, are not necessarily specific to EU migrant children but are shared by many children who move even within a single

---

[35] This is apart from obvious factors such as the child's home environment and family situation.

country to a different school. Furthermore, given the age group of the sample of children interviewed, there is a temptation to conflate difficulties associated with migration with attitudes and problems accompanying adolescence and simply 'growing up'. This is a particular hazard of conducting research with the 11-19 age group when conflict with parents and peers is commonplace and when a young person may be more susceptible to trauma and difficulties in adapting to new surroundings. Equally hazardous, however, is the tendency to dismiss any difficulties experienced as merely a symptom of teenage angst, since the challenges associated with migration may be compounded by cultural and linguistic boundaries and a heightened sense of social and cultural dislocation.

The respondents generally acknowledged the significance of the school environment as a crucial medium for integration. Attendance at school forms such a substantial part of young people's everyday lives that a smooth transition is vitally important to the post-migration experience. Indeed, when reflecting on their migration, many of the respondents viewed their progress at school as an appropriate indicator of the extent to which they had adapted generally to the new environment. This highlights the emphasis children place upon education, not simply as an arena for learning, but much more generally, for social adaptation and for developing a sense of personal and shared identity. One respondent, who had migrated several times as a result of her father's job as a diplomat, described how she felt following her latest move from Belgium to a French school in Greece:

> It was very difficult for me ... the school was big with many children and teachers. It was the first time I had to be adjusted in such crowded conditions [447].

Another child, who transferred from an expensive private French school in Greece to a Greek state school (owing to his parents' financial difficulties), made similar comments:

> I remember my transition to the Greek school. I had a very difficult time in the beginning. I hated going there. I didn't like it at all. I didn't like the teachers [404].

One respondent, an EU migrant child with cerebral palsy whose parents were interviewed, reacted particularly adversely to going to school initially:

> It was dreadful when we first came here and we went to the school for the first time. She didn't like the car and she didn't like to travel and when we

arrived here, to get her to school we had to order a taxi and she would scream. There was obviously something within her, even though she is a very handicapped child [051].[36]

Age as a Factor Influencing Integration

Many of the respondents attributed the ease or difficulty with which they adapted to the new environment to the age at which the migration took place or, indeed, to the fact that no migration took place at all during the child's lifetime (that is, they were born in the host state following their parents' migration). Thirty-five per cent – 63 out of the 180 children interviewed – were born in the host state to 'international' parents[37] and the prevailing view seems to be that they did not experience problems in integrating in school to any greater extent than national children. The same could be said of those who had been living in the host country for at least eleven years prior to the interview (a further 33 children). This supports the common presumption that adaptability to new environments is easier for younger children than it is for teenagers or adults. The parents interviewed were certainly very aware of this, with some asserting that this influenced the timing of their migration or, indeed, their decision not to migrate at all. The following parent, referring to her decision not to return to France with her twelve year old daughter revealed:

> We thought that would be a lot to take on – making new friends, a new culture, learning the language and then picking up the schooling – well it was a lot at an age when she was so conscious. I talked a lot about it to other people who seemed to say that when they moved themselves, the children who were very young were OK – the children whose ages were in the middle, on personal grounds as much as academic, suffered [001].

Other parents made a very direct link between age and integration:

> As far as it concerns the children's education, it's OK as long as they are small. When the schooling starts to be associated with their further education then the appropriate knowledge is not provided ... I believe that if

---

[36] This couple from Northern Ireland had adopted their daughter while they were living in Portugal and moved back to Northern Ireland with her seven years previously when their daughter was six years old. It is telling that the child only reacted badly to going to school and otherwise did not object to travelling alone in taxis or in her parents' car.

[37] That is, where at least one of the child's parents is of a different EU nationality to that of the host state.

> my son goes to Sweden early, before graduating [primary] school, he will have less difficulties in adjusting to the Swedish education system [444].

One of the children, a migrant living in Northern Ireland, compared her experience adapting to school following a migration from Holland to that of her sister, attributing the difference to their ages:

> It was sort of a harder time for her [referring to her older sister] as she's doing her GCSEs now but I started in first year so it was easier for me. [She] was at a more difficult age [055].

There were, however, some exceptional cases where children, regardless of having migrated at a young age, failed to adapt to the new school environment. In one extreme case, the difficulties an English child experienced adapting to his new school in Germany actually precipitated the family's return to the UK, as his mother recalls:

> I think the main reason for coming back was really because he wasn't very happy in the kindergarten at all and there was no possibility of changing it and also the big school didn't start until they were seven. He seemed to me so unhappy that I thought, "I can't continue this". I mean I look back on it and wonder whether it was the right decision – whether we should have persisted or whether it was right to upheave him again and bring him back for another change [074].[38]

Whilst in many cases the children felt that the migration had had a negative impact upon their ability to progress at the rate of national children at the initial stages following the migration, most of them asserted that these difficulties generally subsided after a matter of months or a year when the family as a whole was more settled into their new life. One child, who had returned to the UK after living for one year in Italy, talked about his adaptation to school in this way:

> I had my first year of school when I was over there [in Italy] and that's how I picked up the language really. I found it hard, I didn't like it at all because I couldn't speak a word of the language and I just got put in that school with a load of people I couldn't understand at all. I had a bit of a bad time actually but after a couple of months I got used to it and it was fine [069].[39]

---

[38] It is worth noting that in this case, the child's father had recently died which may have had a significant impact on the child's ability to adapt to any environment at the time.

[39] This boy moved to Italy from the UK nine years previously so that his Italian father could find work. The family returned to the UK after a year.

A mother also talked about her children's experience in these terms:

> The children had some difficulties in the beginning, not language problems but rather adjustment problems in the Greek education system. It was over soon with some effort and support though [429].

Initial teething problems were sometimes exacerbated by a failure to integrate fully with classmates and a number of children recounted experiences of being teased. This is somewhat common among children of all ages, regardless of nationality, but does potentially affect migrant children to a greater extent since they often have a distinctively 'foreign' appearance or accent to distinguish them. Most of those interviewed could dismiss this as a joke and as part and parcel of peer-group relationships. One child, for instance, talked about his school friends in Portugal teasing him about his Italian name and accent:

> They may find my accent funny but that's all ... my school friends found it a bit weird [311].

Another interviewee in Northern Ireland was very aware of the fact that she was distinguished by her classmates as being 'foreign' and had tried to perfect her Northern Irish accent in an attempt to integrate better:

> I get really annoyed with my accent sometimes – people hear that and they repeat words and call me 'import' [052].

Comparable experiences have been recorded in previous research examining the impact of intra-Community migration on women (Ackers, 1998). Since most of the difficulties in this regard were encountered when the women interviewed were much younger, their accounts provide an interesting retrospective reflection which, reassuringly, does not seem to have affected them in the long run. The following account by a migrant woman who had moved from the Netherlands to Sweden as a child, provides an example of common experience:

> During this period I didn't feel that I was accepted by my schoolmates. I didn't understand what the teacher said and I didn't understand when my friends in school spoke to each other, so I felt a bit alone ... I felt that I wasn't really welcome, even though I never really met any real racist abuse or comments or anything of the kind. It was more in my head I think actually ... But ... after 6 months I started speaking and understanding Swedish and then I also started to make some friends. But the whole situation was very difficult for me. I mean coming to another country when you are supposed to start forming your own independence. It was really

> tough at the time and I became very shy and quiet since I felt very insecure. I really feel that my personality changed due to the migration. Before we moved I felt quite self-confident, talked a lot and was rather pushy, but then I became much more insecure and shy at the time of the migration. Everything got turned upside down ... But today I have several very close Swedish friends and I don't find it difficult to get to know Swedish people at all any more [D235].

In a minority of cases, some children and their parents recounted fairly traumatic instances of prejudice and abuse from other pupils. One mother describes an experience her son had in his last school year in Sweden:

> A team of Swedish boys called him 'Greek black head' and the boy felt harassed. He didn't want to go to school ... He was crying every morning before going to school. However, this was the first time that we faced any discrimination in Sweden. It was not only mine, but other Greek families felt harassed by similar incidents [419].

These xenophobic incidents actually prompted the family's decision to return to Greece:

> The recently developing racism against Greeks was the reason that hastened us to make our decision to come back to Greece the second time. We didn't want our children to live in a hostile environment [419].

German children interviewed in Greece seemed to experience more radical forms of discrimination, as one young girl's account of her experience in a Greek state school reveals:

> The children at school didn't like the fact that a German girl can have better marks than they have. Last year I held the Greek flag in the parade on Greek Independence Day and a lot of children were bitter towards me. I heard them saying, "How can a German hold our flag?" I don't like having enemies but I face a lot of hostility from a lot of my school mates [426].

One mother talked the physical assault her daughter experienced:

> My first daughter mentioned incidents of prejudice against her on the part of her schoolmates. One was really serious. Two children battered her at the end of the national celebration at school [to commemorate the end of the German occupation] [424].

While reports of such incidents were rare they do serve to illustrate that EU as much as third country migrant children can be the targets of racial prejudice.

Integration in Different Types of School

One could argue that by attending an international or 'foreign' school, as opposed to a national school in the host country, a migrant child is likely to settle in more quickly. This may be due largely to the fact that the child is amidst children of similar backgrounds and experiences and, more significantly, amongst those who speak the same language and understand the culture of the child's country of origin.[40] Attending a school which caters for those from the country of origin or an international school would appear to be the ideal solution to cushion the impact of changing schools, at least insofar as it ensures continuity in learning in terms of curriculum and language. Of the 180 interviewed, 45 children (25 per cent) were attending or had attended an international school and 26 per cent (47 children) had attended or were attending private foreign schools at the time of the interview.

Whilst foreign or international schools may have more appropriate resources to deal with migrant children's educational needs, there does not, however, appear to be any distinct correlation between the likelihood of experiencing problems integrating socially in the new school and the type of school attended. The international school system in particular is not necessarily conducive to integration, partly because of the high turnover of pupils. The system attracts many children of contract workers or diplomats who remain in the host country for only short periods of time before moving on.[41] This is both unsettling for the children themselves and for those with whom they make friends with during that period. A number of interviewees commented somewhat regretfully on the often transient nature of friendships. One child who had migrated from Spain, compared his experiences in an international school there to the state school he currently attends in the UK:

---

[40] Discussed further in chapter nine.

[41] Since attendance at international schools is generally expensive, it attracts mainly high-income families. In many cases, the parent's employer met all of the children's educational costs. There were other children whose parents worked as teachers in the school, thereby benefiting from a significant reduction in school fees as one of their employment perks.

> A lot of children were coming and going [in the international school], so there was a different attitude in that sense, because at this school [his current state school] all the children are here all the time. I mean one or two do leave but they are nearly always the same; but at that school, you had to learn to make a friend and lose a friend quite quickly because they were coming and going ... And because all these children were coming and going, and all these different nationalities there wasn't a good atmosphere [086].

A parent who had migrated to Portugal with his family made a similar observation:

> Even if I could have afforded it I would never have chosen the international schools. I felt we live in Portugal, they [the children] can go to a Portuguese school. The international school is full of children in transit [322].

Furthermore, many children had only managed to form friendships with other foreign children and a number had failed to integrate with nationals at all, as if existing in a kind of migrant cultural bubble. This situation is best reflected in the comments from a Finnish woman interviewed for previous research on women and intra-Community migration (Ackers, 1998):

> Well in the beginning I went to a Finnish speaking class so language was not a problem in school. I made several friends very soon, but they were all Finnish. It wasn't that I didn't understand Swedish but I was very insecure and felt very uncomfortable having to speak Swedish so I chose not to speak any Swedish for the first couple of years. I became very shy and quiet, totally different from who I was when I could speak Finnish. But when I started working I had to start speaking Swedish, but it was thanks to the work that I started to do that. I don't think that I would have done it otherwise, since I got along just fine speaking Finnish [239].

On the whole, however, this environment was generally seen in a very positive light by the children interviewed who valued mixing with a variety of different nationalities to a greater extent than integrating with nationals of the host state. One child, whose mother is Dutch and who had transferred from a Greek state school to an international school, makes a fairly typical comment in this respect:

> I like this school [the international school]. It is more interesting and less stressful than the Greek one. I enjoy especially the fact that my school mates come from various countries [439].

A French teenager who migrated to Sweden made a similar observation:

> I like going to an international class. It's much easier for a French kid to meet Russian and Chinese kids and get along compared to in a state school where everyone is of the same nationality and everything is much more standardised [202].

Most children valued having made friends who shared a common migration experience to their own but, like the French teenager quoted above, had virtually no friends of host state nationality and limited knowledge of the host language.

The socio-economic and cultural background of children attending private foreign schools (for example, the German school in Greece, or the Spanish school in Lisbon) were, for obvious reasons, more culturally homogenous. These schools benefited, however, from some interesting bilateral funding agreements between Member States. For instance, the learning resources and accommodation of a Swedish primary school in Portugal were funded by the Portuguese state whilst the Swedish state funded the teachers' salaries. Interestingly, there was evidence of greater host state financial support for foreign schools of this type than for special learning measures for migrant children in mainstream state schools.[42]

Schools for Repatriated Children

In Greece, the existence of 'Schools for Repatriated Children' provide perhaps one of the best examples of a system which caters specifically for the educational needs of its young migrant population without the hefty price tag attached to other international schools. These schools, which cater specifically for migrant children at both primary and secondary level who have been residing in another country for at least two years, were established in 1982 and are funded by the Greek Ministry of Education. They follow the Greek national curriculum and students who graduate from them receive an identical qualification to that awarded by state schools. Seven children interviewed for this research attended these schools in Greece and all appeared to have had very positive experiences of the system. The following parent, for example, reflects on her Portuguese daughter's attendance at the school:

---

[42] This is explored further in chapter nine.

> I think the fact that she met children with the same experiences and difficulties was a very supportive and helpful factor [407].

Similarly, a 17 year old girl who had migrated to Greece eighteen months previously after sixteen years in the UK, commented:

> I have no problem with the other children at school. On the contrary, they are very supportive. We have the same experiences [408].

The motivation behind such schools should be applauded for explicitly addressing and accommodating the learning needs of Greece's migrant population and for dealing with the educational needs of its growing number of return migrants. They could be equally criticised, however, for serving to further marginalise the children of migrants by effectively ghettoising them in a separate institution as opposed to integrating them into mainstream education. Furthermore, these schools cater primarily for returning Greek children rather than for migrant children generally and, as such, the curriculum and teaching content is still very Greek-based presuming a prior knowledge of the Greek system, language and culture.

Conclusion

Without exception, education features prominently in children's accounts of their experiences of migration and this chapter has highlighted the respondents' own recognition of the school as an important forum for integration and socialisation. The age at which the child migrated to the host country coupled with the type of school attended were identified as just two of the many variables aiding the child's integration in the host state.

This chapter has charted the gradual evolution of substantive European education policy through the interpretative practices of the ECJ. It moved on to consider more specific policy that targets the children of EU migrant workers as germinated by the activities of the Council of Europe. Consequently, it seems a fair assumption to suggest that education now stands out as the most developed set of formal social rights available specifically to children under EU law. A closer analysis of the ECJ case law indicates, however, that beyond the veneer of substantial formal entitlement whereby children in fact enjoy a privileged status compared to other categories of EU migrants and indeed even workers themselves, in practice, Regulation 1612/68 has been most effectively (and almost exclusively) deployed at third level to ensure access to higher education courses in other Member States. Aside from the *Baumbast* and *Echternach and Moritz* cases, its application has so far been much less effective, or indeed less relevant, in the context of secondary or primary level education. This reflects two main issues. First, it reveals a steadfast reluctance by the ECJ to intervene in domestic policy matters without the ubiquitous justification of doing so in the long-term interests of the European labour market. Second, it shows an apparent lack of demand for such measures since most problems of access and entitlement at below third level are dealt with effectively on a private case-by-case basis by the schools and families concerned. Those children who may be adversely affected are regarded as being sufficiently catered for by international or private foreign schools.

An analysis of European statistics highlighting difference between Member States' education systems, juxtaposed with first hand accounts of the children and parents interviewed demonstrates, however, the need for a more substantive entitlement which extends beyond ensuring equality of access and which gets to the root of the educational obstacles facing EU migrant children.

9 Language, Learning and EU Migrant Children

Introduction

Issues relating to language are an inevitable feature of cross-national migration within the EU. Language was a prominent concern raised by many of our respondents in their accounts of their migration experiences. Chapter six has already explored the extent to which language proficiency impacted upon transnational kinship and the additional challenges it posed to communicating with separated relatives or parents. Language provides a key resource not only in the short term, for aiding social adaptation and integration, but also in the long term, for enhancing interpersonal development, intercultural understanding and, ultimately, for enhancing mobility.

This chapter thus considers the implications of adapting to a new linguistic environment upon children's formal learning experiences. It focuses on the school as a crucial site for enhancing social and intellectual development and explores the added challenges that this process creates for young migrants. This demands a consideration. first of all, of the legal framework at EU level underpinning Member States' responsibility to provide, where necessary, additional linguistic support to migrant children. Clearly this differs according to their status as an EU citizen, a third country national, or as a member of another 'minority group' (such as a refugee or asylum seeker). The very distinct status and experiences of these communities of children and the relatively privileged status of EU migrant children who may typically, but not exclusively, have access to a greater range of educational alternatives, is recognised. The previous chapter has already highlighted, however, how basic access to and equal treatment rights within education, as guaranteed by the free movement provisions, are insufficient in themselves to significantly enhance the status and experiences of migrant children and that certain accompanying measures are necessary to transform them into a practical reality.

The following discussion, therefore, will assess the nature and extent of language-related challenges facing EU migrant children within the context of education. In doing so, this chapter will consider the role of teachers in aiding this process and the special measures taken by children and parents to enhance language learning or to cushion the impact of the transition to a new linguistic environment.

The EU Legal Framework Governing Language-related Rights of EU Migrant Children

Chapter eight considered the main legal and policy context underpinning the educational rights of migrant children under the Community legal order and it also highlighted some preliminary findings as to EU migrant children's experiences of education in the host state. It illustrated how the limited scope of European legislation relating to the education of migrant children (and particularly Regulation 1612/68) prompted a surge in activity by the European institutions and, particularly, the Council of Europe throughout the 1970s to enhance their status. This initially yielded predominantly 'soft law' provisions but sowed the seeds for the introduction of enforceable measures tailored to the specific learning needs of Europe's young migrant community. This culminated in the implementation of Directive 77/486 on the education of the children of migrant workers. Although it has a much narrower scope than Regulation 1612/68, in the sense that it applies only to compulsory education (Article 1), Directive 77/486 is innovative in its formal recognition of EU migrant children's educational experiences as distinct from those of national children. Indeed, it is one of the few pieces of European secondary legislation explicitly and exclusively targeting children.

There are three main strands to Directive 77/486, all of which are aimed at facilitating the child's adaptation to the new learning environment. First, Article 2 obliges Member States to ensure the provision of free supplementary tuition to assist them with learning the language of the host state. Second, Article 3 requires the Member States to take all appropriate measures to promote and preserve the culture and native language of the child's country of origin. Third, consistent with Article 2(2), the directive was reinforced and complemented by a programme focusing on methods of teacher-training which would be sensitive to the needs of an intercultural learning environment. Theoretically, therefore, the directive goes beyond reliance upon the principle of non-discrimination which underpins the application of Regulation 1612/68 and, instead, advocates more positive action – as opposed to passive assimilation measures – on behalf of EU (and, arguably, also on behalf of third country national) migrant children.[1]

[1] The scope of the Directive is confined to the dependant children of a worker who is the national of another Member State although a Council declaration published at the same

The following sections will consider, firstly, the Directive provisions relating to teachers in the context of a more general discussion, drawing upon the empirical data, of the role of teachers in facilitating the migrant child's integration in the new school environment. The second section focuses more specifically on issues relating to the language provisions of the directive. The third and final section will evaluate the extent to which language proficiency impacts upon the educational attainment of the migrant child as a means of illustrating or challenging the importance of the directive provisions.

The Specialist Role of Teachers

Having identified education as a necessary and important forum for European integration in chapter eight, the role of teachers becomes all the more significant. Increased awareness and openness on the part of teachers towards Europe undoubtedly impacts upon their attitudes towards pupils and the steps they take to bring this to life in the classroom. Indeed, this is the very purpose of the second paragraph of Article 2(2), Directive 77/486 which states that 'Member States shall take the measures necessary for the training and further training of the teachers to provide this tuition'. This places an unequivocal obligation on Nation States to provide initial and further training for teachers who are responsible for the children of migrant workers.

The 1988 Commission report on the implementation of the directive (European Commission, 1988) identified various models of training developed in compliance with this Article. These models included: optional or compulsory training modules designed as an introduction to the problems of foreign children and teaching methods; additional specialist training such as specialisation in teaching the host language as a second language or in intercultural education; in-service training to make staff more aware of the problems of immigration; or further training in teaching methods suited to the needs of the children of immigrants (European Commission, 1988, p.6).

Concern to raise the profile of teachers at European level is reflected in the establishment of new cross-national teacher associations, such as The European Association of Teachers (AEDE), The Association for Teacher Education in Europe (ATEE) and the European Secondary Heads Association (ESHA). These associations, however, were established more

---

time suggests that the Directive should also be implemented in relation to non-EC migrant workers' children (European Commission, 1988, p.4).

to draw attention to the needs of and opportunities for teachers as mobile professionals themselves, rather than enhancing awareness of the educational needs of migrant children in their care or facilitating their adjustment to the new school.

Other European and national measures designed to enhance teaching skills in favour of migrant children target predominantly minority ethnic groups but provide a valuable example of how such education programmes can be adapted to EU migrant children's learning. The activities of the European Jewish Information Centre (EJIC), a Brussels NGO, provide an illustration of how this can be achieved by adapting a US-pioneered schools-based programme, 'A Classroom of Difference', to a European context. Recognising the role that the educational environment plays in combating racial prejudice and promoting tolerance, it has implemented a similar teacher training programme in Belgium, France, Italy and the Netherlands. This seeks to provide teachers with educational tools and methods designed to help create a learning environment which is respectful of cultural diversity and which challenges prejudice, discrimination and racism (European Union Migrants Forum, 2000, p.8).

The Irish Department of Education, for its part, has no statistics available regarding the presence of migrant children in Irish state schools. Indeed, the European Union Migrants Forum (EUMF) (2000) observes that the arrival of migrant families is still somewhat of a paradox for an island that for hundreds of years has seen its nationals leaving to make their living elsewhere. Nonetheless, this country provides a further example of measures which have been introduced to better equip schools for the increasing number of minority ethnic children in their classes and, in very recent years, to respond to the huge influx of refugee children and asylum seekers. 1999 saw the launch in Ireland of a new service called 'Support Teachers for Non-Nationals'. This has been expanded by the Department of Education so that any school with more than 15 pupils whose first language is not English is entitled to a support language teacher. Schools with less than 15 such pupils receive financial support to enable them to employ a teacher for assistance for an appropriate number of hours. This programme, while providing an explicit acknowledgement of the need to implement additional measures to facilitate migrant children's learning, has been criticised for focusing exclusively on the issue of language support while ignoring more basic concerns relating to the impact of migration on children's education more generally. EUMF (2000, P.8) proposes that:

> Areas which need to be addressed include: ensuring that both parents and children understand how the Irish education system works; providing specific support and counselling; and finally introducing changes to the

curriculum to bring about Multiculturalism in the classroom and the education system.

The following section, through drawing on interview data, explores the extent to which teachers and students could potentially benefit from similar measures across the EU.

Teaching EU Migrant Children

In general, most children seemed satisfied with the treatment they had received from teachers in school. A small proportion of the interviews, however, exposed some instances in which teachers' behaviour served to hinder the integration process both in their initial reception of the migrant child and in their subsequent lack of sensitivity or attention to children's specific needs and difficulties. One Swedish child, attending a state school in Italy:

> I don't think they wanted me to go to that school. This is how I felt anyway. The principal and the staff and ... they didn't seem to be too pleased about it.

She went on to consider why this was the case:

> It was a small city [in Italy] I don't think it was a matter of racism, but rather, they weren't used to it ... Therefore they just weren't too happy about it [219].

In another case a parent residing with her children in Portugal complained that:

> The younger one had a big problem with this school [a local Church-funded school]. It seems he had a total mental block against his teacher – she was an older teacher and she used to call him stupid and I found out that in fact he had just blocked learning for a year or maybe longer. I was sad I didn't notice it before but I realised on time and I immediately moved him from that school [322].

Similarly, a Swedish boy responding to a question about whether or not he enjoyed school in Italy, commented:

> Yes, but in the beginning I didn't. I didn't like it at all because I didn't get along with the teacher [who was Italian]. I really don't know the reason ... I

> didn't understand what she was saying and I made some mistakes and had to stay after school and ... we had some arguments [222].[2]

A less positive attitude on the part of teachers seems prevalent in more culturally homogeneous areas with a low immigration rate and, accordingly, where teachers have limited exposure to children with these types of needs. Consequently, they are ill-equipped and poorly-trained to accommodate migrant children. Costa (1997, p.184-185) makes the following observation:

> They [some teachers] consider the minority culture to be a negative factor which distorts the educational process ... In terms of training teachers are conscious of their lack of preparation in intercultural education and ... this is not considered as one of their high priorities. Thus, although it is recognised that the training received is practically zero, this reflects the actual demands of the teachers themselves which are scant and limited. [3]

Given the increasing constraints placed on teachers' time, as they struggle to meet the ever-demanding targets imposed by continuous curriculum changes, coupled with the burden of growing administrative duties and the lack of financial resources generally, it is hardly surprising that there is limited disposable energy to invest in training adapted to the specific requirements of migrant children. Furthermore, it would be unrealistic and unreasonable to expect teachers to have an exhaustive knowledge of every individual existing culture that is introduced into their classroom and for them to adapt their teaching approach or programme accordingly (Camilleri, 1986).

Rather, they should be encouraged to actively assist in creating an environment which is conducive to more open communication, interaction and cultural exchange. It is through this increased awareness that a common basis for learning can be established. Returning to Costa's (1997, p.193-194) analysis:

> Teaching methods and curricula can no longer be based upon the false assumption of the homogeneity of pupils. Rather, it must relate to the

---

[2] In fact, this boy had become involved in a fight with a Swedish boy in his class and had sworn at him resulting in his detention. He goes on to describe how this conflict with his teacher subsequently subsided and that six months later, by his own admission, they were 'really good friends'.

[3] This view is reinforced within the context of language in that there is some evidence of a conflation of migrant children's language problems with special educational needs generally (see below).

heterogeneity of the classroom and be responsive to that diversity ... maintain social cohesion whilst recognising individual identities.

Many parent respondents who expressed dissatisfaction with teachers conceded that this required a concerted effort between both the teacher and the parents to assist the child's integration in and progress at school. This, however, is more problematic when the parents are unfamiliar with the system in the host state or, worse still, unable to speak the language of the host country, as the following Irish mother in England commented:

> I think a lot of it has to do with the home and if you encourage them [the children]. Especially if you come into the country and you haven't grown up there and don't understand the system, you leave it to the teachers [067].

A parent who had migrated from Germany to Greece described her dilemma regarding her inability to assist her son in his learning because of the language barrier:

> We had many difficulties at school as I couldn't help him effectively due to the language. In the beginning it was easier because I was learning through his homework together with him. Now it is extremely difficult for both of us: He is at a new school level and he needs help and guidance. Therefore I need to know more than him in order to help him ... I always had co-operated closely with the teacher as long as he was in primary school. Now there are more teachers and they are not always accessible. Sometimes they tell me things that I cannot understand due to the language. Sometimes I find them insensitive to the children's needs and unwilling to support the children [423].

This mother's account provides the only example of such a sense of helplessness but it serves to highlight the importance of teachers' expertise in assisting the migrant child at school and involving parents in this process.

More commonly, respondents alluded to the invaluable role played by teachers in easing the child's transition to the new system, as this comment from one child who migrated to Italy for one year where he had attended a state school, illustrates:

> I remember spending the first day just crying my eyes out actually. The teachers were fine – one teacher I had was really helpful and she'd help me out a lot – she'd sit me down and give me personal attention, things like that [069].

Adapting to Education in a New Linguistic Environment

A significant challenge identified by the EU migrant children interviewed concerns adapting to a new language both in a social and academic context. This section documents the endeavours of EU migrant children to overcome linguistic barriers or, indeed, to perfect additional language skills (in cases where they are already fluent in the language of the host state). The enormity of the challenge is evidenced in the vast number of EU migrant children attending supplementary language classes in the host state. 42 per cent of the young people interviewed were attending or had at some point attended supplementary classes in either the language of the host state or that of the country of origin.[4] A variety of reasons were given for this, the most common being that state provision in this regard was either inadequate or non-existent. This suggests that the terms of Directive 77/486 have not been properly implemented in most Member States both in terms of mother-tongue teaching requirements and in the provision of extra tuition in the language of the host state. Secondly, a number of the migrant children questioned felt that proficiency in more than one European language was necessary to enhance their future prospects in terms of access to university, their career development and possible future migration. Certainly, both parents and children interviewed placed a high premium on additional language acquisition for this reason. A third reason offered by respondents was that supplementary classes – and particularly those organised by migrant organisations – provide both an opportunity to improve language skills as well as a social opportunity to meet other ex-patriots and to participate in cultural events with those from a similar background. This provided an invaluable means of tapping into their own cultural heritage or sharing in their parents' or grandparents' sense of cultural identity. Indeed, the children were often attending supplementary schools simply to satisfy their parents' or grandparents' desire for them to further appreciate and familiarise themselves with their cultural birthright.

The need and desire to obtain extra language tuition on arrival in the host country is largely dependent on the level of tuition already received in the country of previous residence. As the previous chapter has highlighted, all pupils in the EU are taught broadly similar compulsory subjects from the age of 13. However, a closer inspection of the amount of time allocated to these subjects reveals significant inconsistencies from one Member State to another. In most EU countries, the teaching of foreign languages begins

[4] This high percentage is largely due to the fact that many of the interviewees were contacted through organisations and schools that provide such services. The figure may not, therefore, be representative of all EU migrant children in the countries involved.

in earnest in the early years of primary education and is generally compulsory from the third or fourth year of primary school.[5] In Belgium, France, Germany and the UK (excluding Scotland), modern language classes are not compulsory until the first year of secondary education. A second foreign language is compulsory in Sweden before the end of primary schooling but not until secondary education in Belgium, Greece, the Netherlands and Finland. Ireland provides a notable exception in that foreign languages are not a compulsory component of the curriculum at any level even though students learn English and Irish throughout the course of their compulsory education. English remains the most taught foreign language at secondary level with an average of 91 per cent of pupils in general secondary education learning English across the EU. The other official languages of the EU are taught to a much lesser extent, namely French (34 per cent), German (15 per cent) and Spanish (10 per cent) (EUROSTAT, 2000, p.159). This would suggest that EU migrants entering the UK or Ireland are likely to have a significantly better grasp of the host language (that is, English) and would generally require much less supplementary host language support than those of UK origin who migrate to another EU country.

The following section will explore more fully some of these issues by reference to the interviews and provide illuminating examples of 'good' and 'bad' practice in different education systems across the EU in both the public and private domain. First, it will assess the extent to which individual Member State systems have adhered to the recommendations set out in Directive 77/486 in terms of providing supplementary tuition in the host country language. Second, it will include a consideration of individual state efforts to implement mother-tongue tuition both in their own country and in other EU Member States. Third, the section will consider alternative supplementary tuition such as that provided by foreign and international schools, private tutors and by the parents themselves.

Supplementary Tuition in the Host Language

Supplementary tuition is available from various sources in each Member State – some parents pay for private tuition or, alternatively, language classes may be provided and funded by mainstream schools, migrant

---

[5] Luxembourg, however, introduces compulsory foreign language classes from the start of the first year of primary school. A second foreign language is taught from the second year of primary school.

organisations, church groups and Member States' embassies. Article 2 of Directive 77/486 provides that:

> Member States shall, in accordance with their national circumstances and legal systems, take all appropriate measures to ensure that free tuition to facilitate initial reception is offered [to the children of EU migrant workers] including, in particular, the teaching – adapted to the specific needs of such children – of the official language of the host state.

The accounts given by the interviewees suggest that the availability of supplementary tuition in the language of the host country in compliance with Article 2 varies nationally across the EU as well as regionally within each individual Member State.

In the UK, a Circular issued in 1981 by what was then the Department for Education and Employment (DfEE)[6] provides the most recent (and indeed only) guidance document as regards implementation of Directive 77/486. Concerning teaching in the host language, Article 6 of the Circular states:

> The provision of suitable education for a child who speaks little or no English must entail the provision of English language tuition appropriate to the child's needs (Circular No 5/81).

Thus, specialist support is available to schools with children whose mother-tongue is not English to help them acquire the language and access the national curriculum (although the target of these measures are predominantly minority ethnic children rather than EU migrants as such). This is financed by means of a specific grant administered by the DfEE which is available to all local education authorities.[7] The interviews, however, painted a rather less positive picture, with strong evidence of a 'sink or swim' approach adopted by most mainstream schools. This was certainly the case for one child, who migrated from France to the UK with her parents two years previously:

> There has been a lot of avoiding issues here between the home and foreign students. I did not notice it before. This year it has started to grate a bit more and I have got annoyed about it. It is not easy for foreign students to adapt

---

[6] In June 2001, the DfEE was reorganised as the Department for Education and Skills (DfES).

[7] Research Community from Keith Dawes, Ethnic Minorities Pupils Team, DfEE, 5 July 1999.

> to being taught in English and they need a lot more help but they are not getting it [088].

None of the respondents attending state schools could say that such specific assistance was available to them although an education authority in Northern Ireland had made some limited efforts to provide tuition of one hour a week for foreign students to assist them with their English spelling and grammar. A young beneficiary of these lessons drew some interesting comparisons between the Northern Ireland system and the Dutch system from which she had migrated:

> They didn't give me any help with my spelling problems [in Northern Ireland] ... we haven't been approached by anybody at all about extra help ... they were more socially aware about things like that in Holland [052].

Another boy in England made a similar comment with reference to the Dutch system:

> [In Holland] if I didn't understand it there was this lady in there ... who came to help because I wasn't Dutch. Whenever I didn't know what something meant, I asked the lady [081].

Part of the reason for the UK's complacency in this area may be linked to the lack of demand for extra tuition given the predominance of English as a spoken language across Europe. Most children migrating to the UK at least have some knowledge of English and those that do not tend to be absorbed by the private foreign or international school system.

In Sweden, whilst again the interviews suggest that the private and international schools sector accommodate most of those students for whom language may pose a problem, all migrant children (both from within the EU and outside) who attend state schools and whose first language is not Swedish are entitled to study Swedish as a second language subject in its own right. Migrant children are also given the option to attend alternative classes (to those provided for national children) in certain subjects in which their learning might have been impeded due to insufficient language skills (such as mathematics, and natural sciences). These classes provide individual support, adapted to the specific academic needs and capabilities of the student, enabling the vast majority of them to progress to upper secondary school along with their Swedish counterparts. It is also interesting to note that the Swedish state funds extra Swedish teachers to tutor national children within international schools (although migrant children also have the option to attend these classes), as one child, who migrated from France to Sweden in 1994, explained:

> At the international school there's a Swedish teacher employed and that's the reason why Swedish people tend to choose this school. I had lessons in Swedish twice a week. I don't think it was compulsory, but I think all the Swedish children chose to attend it. The teacher was paid for by the Swedish state [229].

Such children, therefore, have the best of both worlds in that they receive a similar level and type of teaching support they would have had had they attended a state school, but they also enjoy the benefits and facilities offered by exclusive international schooling.

By contrast, respondents in Portugal expressed dissatisfaction with the level of state language provision for migrant children and were critical of the burden placed on parents to pay for private lessons should their child require additional help:

> In general she's happy with the school. But the way Portuguese is taught is not the best and this may cause some problems for the children who do not get enough support at home [304].[8]

Another child who moved from Holland to Portugal in 1990 echoes this sentiment:

> I would like very much for the school to change [for example to have] different levels [of language tuition] for the child to feel happier on his own level to avoid unsatisfactory results. [As it is] parents spend money on private lessons. Only rich children can afford to have these lessons [316].

Again, foreign and international schools in Portugal appear to offer more in the way of host language teaching, although again this appears to be reserved predominantly for pupils attending foreign and international schools, as one child who attended a German school in Lisbon observed:

> The school has a special concern in the last years giving supplementary classes to the students according to their choices. This is a bilingual school – they have always had a great concern with the Portuguese language and its teaching [336].

---

[8] This was an interview with a family whose daughter was born in Portugal although her mother is French and she has regular contact with her French relatives.

A parent, referring to her son who was attending the German school in Lisbon, makes a similar comment:

> Today my children have a great aptitude for languages and that was because of the teaching I have no doubts. In comparison with the eldest one who has studied in a Portuguese public school, I can see that the other two have a much better domain of the languages ... My oldest son ... he's behind his brothers because he's not so consistent when it concerns written language [346].

The Greek system is marginally better due to the presence of 'schools for repatriated children'[9] since they provide language assistance adapted to the specific needs of (mainly returning) EU migrant children. Criticism, however, was levelled at mainstream schools' scant provision for foreign children. The following father's reflection on his son's difficulties represents a common experience of migrants in Greek in this respect:

> The youngest one still has problems in the spelling of words. These learning difficulties were not handled by the school. There are no such provisions [444].[10]

Supplementary Tuition in the Mother-Tongue

If state school provision of host language teaching in some EU countries may seem at best inadequate, the availability of mother-tongue teaching in the public system can be similarly criticised. This is in spite of explicit provision within the directive obliging Member States to adopt a more positive approach to linguistic and cultural diversity in the classroom. Article 3 of Directive 77/486 states that:

> Member States shall ... in co-operation with States of origin, take appropriate measures to promote, in co-ordination with normal education, teaching of the mother tongue and culture of the country of origin for the children [of EU migrant workers].

In the UK, however, evidence is emerging of an increased openness to the merits of bilingualism. This is despite (and perhaps a response to) criticism of the British education system having a deep mono-cultural and

---

[9] Described in chapter eight.

[10] The mother is Swedish and the youngest child was born in Sweden and was brought up as bilingual following a subsequent migration to Greece.

monolingual orientation resulting in a distinct lack of proficiency in additional European languages on the part of British children. As such, the UK government asserted in its document on English and the national curriculum (Department of Education and Science Report: The Welsh Office, 1988, p.5) that:

> Bilingual children should be considered an advantage in the classroom rather than a problem. The evidence shows that such children will make greater progress in English if they know that their knowledge of their mother-tongue is valued.

Furthermore, Circular 5/81 states that:

> Local education authorities ... should explore ways in which mother tongue teaching might be provided, whether during or outside school hours...In some areas, provision is already made by the minority communities, either through voluntary self-help schemes, or through teachers employed by foreign embassies and, in some instances, such initiatives receive support from local education authorities. There may be further scope for local education authorities to encourage co-operation between mother tongue teachers and the teachers responsible for the same children in ordinary schools, and to provide material help, such as accommodation for classes (Article 7).

Referring to this provision, the DfEE reiterated the government's recognition of the value of maintaining linguistic and cultural traditions, but emphasised that:

> given the large number of different languages spoken by pupils attending schools there are great practical difficulties for teaching in the mother tongue.[11]

The onus is, instead, placed on the respective migrant communities to provide the necessary mother-tongue teaching in the form of supplementary classes. Almost as an irresolute compromise, the DfEE asserted that:

> there is no impediment to local education authorities continuing to support existing or new activities, although they may of course be constrained to a certain extent by other demands on available resources.[12]

---

[11] Above note 7.

[12] Above note 7.

The prevailing attitude throughout the EU appears to be that mother tongue teaching is not a priority for the child's educational development in the host country. Indeed, the promulgation and co-existence of many languages are considered by many educationalists as obstacles to learning, not to mention inconvenient and expensive to accommodate. It is, therefore, viewed as the responsibility of the parents to seek private home language tuition if so desired, as the following parent acknowledged:

> [In Holland] we started to speak to them in English at home because when they started going to school the teacher told us that they would teach them Dutch and we would teach them English. We would teach them the right way to speak English and they would teach them the right way to speak Dutch [052].[13]

Interestingly, some respondents felt that mother tongue teaching should not be part of the main education curriculum at all and that incorporating it into the curriculum would serve only to further marginalise EU migrant children from nationals and detract from more important subjects. A German mother residing in the UK with her three children commented:

> In a way I think that it is ridiculous. If they move permanently then it should be up to the parents to keep up with them in their home language. If they plan to stay in the new country then what is the point? ... as a parent I feel strongly that the child should speak the mother tongue but at the same time they need to adjust and the sooner they do it the better. Children don't want to stick out. David [her son] ... said to me this morning ... that it gets on his nerves [when they ask him to speak German] and it is because he doesn't want to be different [083].

Indeed, it has been argued that to introduce the teaching of languages other than that of the host country in the context of intercultural education involves major changes within the education system, requiring substantial resources, not to mention the re-training of teachers and employment of more suitably qualified teachers (Mallick, 1999, p.106). It also assumes that the families and children themselves *wish* to be taught in their mother tongue while indeed a number of the young people interviewed in our research did not express any particular desire to receive such provision.

Conversely, some Portuguese respondents felt that mother-tongue teaching was an important aspect of their learning and that the EU should

---

[13] Northern Irish parents who returned from Holland with their two daughters one year previously.

make greater efforts to ensure implementation of the requirements and objectives set down in the directive. This was particularly so for the sample of migrant children interviewed in rural Alentejo, Portugal:

> I have talked with the teacher here in the small village and told him we need somebody [to help with German lessons] ... The EU should provide some help [330].

Five families were interviewed in rural Alentejo. These families represented an interesting category of 'ecological' migrants, distinct from other migrants, since their primary motivation for moving was to eschew many of the trappings of western materialism and attain a more peaceful, simple life in the Portuguese countryside. Their children attended very small schools of about nine children. Despite the fact that in many cases over 50 percent of pupils in these small schools were not Portuguese (many were German or Dutch), there was no additional language support in either the host or home language, particularly in the more remote areas.[14] The German children interviewed and observed were unable to benefit from this type of support in contrast with German children living in the Lisbon area who are entitled to free private language tuition paid for by the German education authorities. This kind of territorial injustice is partly due to the fact that the cost of providing educational support for dispersed families in such a remote and vast area is no doubt seen as an impractical use of resources. It is also attributable to the irregular status of Alentejo migrants since most of them had not registered as legal residents in Portugal and were, therefore, 'invisible' to the Portuguese authorities. This enables them to continue claiming unemployment and other benefits from their country of origin which places them in a much more favourable financial position than they would otherwise be if they were to claim unemployment benefits or work (and have to pay tax) in Portugal.[15]

This begs the question as to whether these 'shirkers' should be entitled to claim support from countries like Portugal given their refusal to pay taxes or take on formal employment. Indeed, the scenario provides an interesting example of migrants negotiating the terms of their European citizenship entitlement – by claiming both educational support for their children from Portugal, as well as social security or other unemployment

---

[14] One Dutch child living in a less remote area received three hours tuition in the Dutch language per week. This was provided after school by a Dutch teacher, jointly funded by the Portuguese education department (which paid her salary) and Holland (who paid for teaching materials).

[15] The implications of the legal 'invisibility' of this community is explored further in the context of divorce and child maintenance in chapter seven.

benefits from their country of origin, they are effectively licking the cream of citizenship entitlement in the respective Member States between which they have moved. As it stands, the interviews suggest that by prioritising continued access to social security benefits available in their more wealthy country of emigration they are effectively relinquishing any claim their children may have to state educational and linguistic support. In other words, the parents' choice and negotiation of their citizenship entitlement is prioritised over that of their children who have no claims to social entitlement in their own right.

Sweden has taken some important steps in implementing the mother tongue teaching requirement of the directive by incorporating it into the main teaching curriculum for EU migrant children. Firstly, language tuition is organised variously according to local education authorities and may be scheduled during main school hours as an optional subject or as a further language to be studied in addition to Swedish and English. Alternatively, it can be studied outside school hours as a supplementary course. There are more than 100 foreign languages available for study on this programme throughout Sweden. In 1997/98, a total of 115,846 children were entitled to attend classes in their mother tongue, that is 11.8 per cent of the total population of pupils in mainstream education (Swedish research partners' national report). During that same period, 53.6 per cent of these qualified students had opted for this mother-tongue tuition. The young people interviewed, for example, mentioned a Finnish teacher as well as a Greek and English teacher employed to teach some classes in state schools. Whilst in theory this is impressive, in practice the children interviewed felt that attendance at these classes was more of a burden than a benefit. To this end, these classes simply presented children with additional work which would be readily sacrificed by the majority in favour of extra recreational time:

> I used to take classes in Finnish until earlier this year. Our Finnish teacher got extremely unhappy because almost all her students left the class at the same time. I didn't quit because I didn't like it, I just didn't have enough time to continue [201].

This can be contrasted with the views of the following respondent who objected to the Swedish authorities' plans to cut back on home language instruction:

> I think it's very sad that they have all these cut-backs for home language because it's really such an advantage to have a culture where people are bilingual. The rest of Europe they have bilingual and trilingual so I can't

understand why they don't promote it here and invest more in it. It's just one hour a week and that's it [211].

The conflicting opinions and experiences of EU migrant children is very evident here. The fact that a number of children interviewed did not express a specific desire or need to receive any additional support or special treatment partly reflects the breadth of the sample since this attitude was predominant amongst those children who were born or brought up in the host state by migrant parents. Other children who migrated with their parents often adopted a very pragmatic approach to any educational problems they initially experienced, in other words, they 'just got on with it'. The impetus and enthusiasm was not, therefore, always lacking on the part of Member States, but often on the part of the migrant communities themselves. At the other end of the spectrum were cases where the child's academic progress had clearly suffered in some respects as a result of insufficient or inappropriate educational support.

The interviews conducted in Greece indicate that the country has cultivated a definite 'supplementary classes' culture with national and migrant children taking additional lessons in a range of subjects to supplement those provided during official school hours which are viewed by many as insufficient in themselves. It is hardly surprising, therefore, that the state system does not incorporate language assistance for EU migrant children into its curriculum given that it is ill-equipped to sufficiently cover the core subjects for its nationals. The only means, therefore, of obtaining additional language support in Greece is by attending a school for repatriated children, a supplementary school[16] or paying for private language tuition.

'Looking After Your Own': Supplementary Mother-Tongue Classes

There is evidence that some Member States are funding supplementary mother-tongue classes for their nationals who have migrated to other EU Member States. Interviews conducted with Italian families in the UK provide an example of this. The Italian Ministry of Foreign Affairs currently runs 309 supplementary classes throughout the UK which are attended by approximately 5,500 children of Italian origin.[17] Other migrant organisations also run some classes and receive funding from the Italian

---

[16] One respondent, for instance, attended the Swedish school in Athens every Saturday.

[17] This data was obtained in the course of an interview with a representative from the Italian consulate.

government. These classes not only provide an opportunity for children to improve or sustain their proficiency in Italian, but they also offer the opportunity to make social and cultural links with others from a similar background. As commented earlier, supplementary classes, therefore, are as much about language learning as about sustaining cultural identity and establishing social links. This is reflected in the structure of the courses offered by these classes, as one child and her mother explained:

> We learn grammar and history and a bit of geography and we learn about carnivals and things and we do a lot of ... plays which involve carnival characters.
>
> *Mother:* It used to be free up until about two or three years ago and now it's £25 per head for the year and it's twice a week and they do two hours. The teachers are from Italy and they are qualified primary school teachers [061].

Children attending these classes also have the opportunity to obtain formal qualifications in Italian at both GCSE and A-level and all four of the sample who had taken this option had achieved very high grades at both levels:

> I did my GCSE [through the external classes] and got an 'A' when I was fifteen and then I had a year's rest and went to finish my other GCSEs. Then after that I started up the Italian again and did it at A-level with French. I did about two hours a week [069].

Similarly, the Greek government started funding supplementary classes in Sweden for Greek children in the 1970s in response to the increase at that time in migration from Greece to Northern Europe. This arose out of a concern on the part of the Greek authorities to facilitate Greek migrants' eventual return and subsequent re-integration. Indeed, as chapter four has highlighted, this was initially the main thrust behind the Directive 77/486 provision on mother-tongue teaching (as opposed to aiming to simultaneously promote integration and sustain cultural diversity in favour of migrants generally). The classes are offered free of charge although children may be required to pay for materials such as books and are generally offered in Sweden's main cities where there is a higher concentration of Greek migrants. The courses do not teach the Greek syllabus but focus rather on language and history. Interestingly, they are available mainly to younger children (of primary level), which is justified on the basis that older children are unwilling to attend them due to other academic commitments. In addition to provision for Greek migrant children in Sweden, a number of independent schools provide mother-tongue teaching for Finnish migrant children, the largest migrant community in Sweden although this is offered in accordance with the Swedish rather than the Finnish national curriculum (Swedish National Agency for Education, 1998).

Similarly in Portugal there were some examples of Dutch respondents attending supplementary classes funded jointly by the Dutch Embassy and the Portuguese state:

> Our elder daughter has Dutch lessons officially one afternoon a week [funded by the State] – the Portuguese State – it's officially recognised they have three hours a week for the children who don't go to private school ... the parents pay every year for the books and things. The Portuguese Ministry of Education pays for the teacher and the Dutch government pays the materials [333].

This practice could be seen as hampering effective European integration and the values underpinning European citizenship – essentially, each Member State is 'looking after its own' by confining funding of supplementary classes to their own nationals living abroad while neglecting the needs of the migrant community already resident in its own territory.

The Impact of Language Acquisition on the Educational Attainment of EU Migrant Children

Aside from the provision of supplementary language classes, it is interesting to consider whether acquiring another language either augments or diminishes academic performance. This necessarily requires a consideration of the educational value of bilingualism.

Attitudes towards bilingualism have oscillated between dismissal of it as an academic liability and, in more recent years, esteem for it as a distinct educational and social advantage, as enhancing academic progress and as a gateway to a multitude of opportunities. As mentioned previously, the type of school attended is a significant factor. If a child attends a school which offers the same curriculum and teaches in the same language to that of the previous school attended, there is less likelihood of any major disruption to his or her education, not least because of the level of awareness of and provision for language assistance. In this respect, there is a very definite and understandable justification influencing EU migrant families' decision to avoid state schooling in the host country. The following Greek girl had lived in England for 16 years before returning to live in Greece with her family:

> I still have difficulties at school with the language mainly. The teachers expect us to speak and understand everything in Greek. Some of my schoolmates are Greek and their first language is Greek, It's not the same with me. I don't think that I could cope in a Greek school [408].

Most children, despite initial difficulties, did not attribute any underachievement at school to their migration, even in cases of multiple moves. In fact, only two out of 180 respondents made this explicit link, both of whom were residing in Greece. The first of these remarks on her daughter's progress in the state school:

> She has been discouraged and disappointed because she was a good student in Germany. She feels that despite the fact that she tries harder than she did in Germany, the results are unequal [420].

The second respondent, who had migrated from Germany, was also attending a state school and notes:

> This year, I am now in my third grade of high school – I have unequal conditions with everyone else in my classroom. I still have difficulties following the pace. This is very hard and discouraging to me because I used to be a good student with very good performances [422].

More common were instances in which interviewees felt that the move had had an effect on their level of *interest* in school and education rather than on their actual academic attainment. Additional difficulties and challenges of adapting to a new school often had the effect of discouraging and demotivating them. This is illustrated by one child's account of her experience at school in Ireland after moving from the UK:

> I think I was doing really well at the grammar school [in the UK] and there was so much competition to do well and I did really well – everything was based around education and doing well – and I came to Ireland and it was a mixed school and there were boys and it wasn't really centred on education and I let my standards drop which hasn't been a good thing because I never got them back up, I can't be bothered. I don't like school any more, not the working part of it [004].[18]

[18] The girl subsequently returned to the UK and has never regained her initial enthusiasm for school.

For many respondents, concern over the impact of language on learning was levelled, not necessarily at their present educational attainment, but at their future university and career prospects. This was the case for one interviewee who remarked generally on the value of possessing more than one European language in terms of access to university:

> If you have a language at A-level then the universities look at that and see that you can speak another language fluently. I've heard people say that if you have a language then you might be chosen in front of somebody else, that the university might think better of you and let you in. It's the same with computers nowadays [054].[19]

Twelve young people expressed the view that unfamiliarity with the language presented a definite obstacle to their access to higher education in the host country. Many resolved, therefore, to move back to their country of origin or somewhere where language would not present a problem in order to pursue their university studies, as this quotation from a French boy living in Greece indicates:

> I don't know yet what I'm going to study. What I know is that I won't study in Greece. It would be very difficult for me as I don't know the language [442].[20]

Those for whom language did present a problem in their education expressed some difficulties adapting to their new learning environment and meeting the needs of the 'foreign' curriculum.[21] Some respondents, while sympathising with the needs of EU migrant children in this respect, felt that the provision of additional educational assistance would potentially impede the learning of the remainder of (national) pupils in the class. The following parent's comment illustrates this point and his sentiments are undoubtedly shared by many educationalists and national policy-makers:

> If an English school allows the attendance of children who do not have English as their first language this will inevitably pull back the standards at an educational level because of the language constraints [309].

---

[19] This respondent was born and lives in Northern Ireland although his mother is French.

[20] This boy had lived in Greece most of his life although his main language is Spanish since his mother is from Spain.

[21] Such problems were experienced mainly by those who had been abruptly inserted into the new school environment and in, time they managed to overcome these problems.

When asked about any specific problems they were having with language, many respondents talked about their difficulties with the grammatical and technical intricacies of the language rather than with the oral aspect:

> I don't mind a lot about the language. I can understand everything but I make many mistakes when I write [421].[22]

> I found some subjects a bit difficult ... like Italian. I knew how to speak but I didn't know any grammar. It was a bit hard in the beginning ... like when we were supposed to write an essay, then I felt really inferior ... And they [the teachers] took it for granted that I would manage it as well [219].[23]

Thirty-two respondents referred to the benefits of bilingualism, viewing it as having enhanced their education performance generally, with particular benefit when it came to learning third or fourth languages as part of the school curriculum. This is particularly the case with children who have either grown up in the host state and who have always been exposed to two languages, or those who had migrated many years previously and were fully adapted to the education system of the host State. Many interviewees also had the opportunity to pursue studies in their second language on a more formal basis and obtain qualifications in them. They saw this as providing them with a head-start in school, enabling them to accumulate additional qualifications with relative ease and at a faster rate than their peers. Problems were experienced most commonly therefore by those who had undergone an abrupt insertion into the new learning and linguistic environment during their teenage years.[24]

The International and Private Foreign School System

In spite of the many language-related issues raised, the majority of migrant children interviewed for this research had not experienced any significant ongoing problems in adapting to the new learning environment to any greater extent than children who move within a single country. This, however, is not necessarily because such barriers do not exist, but may be

---

[22] This comment was made by a girl who had migrated from Holland to Greece only one year prior to the interview.

[23] This girl was born in Sweden and migrated to Italy for one year before returning to Sweden.

[24] Chapter eight has explored in detail the impact of migration on EU migrant children's academic performance more generally.

because the children of skilled EU migrants are absorbed by the private or international school sector. International schools provide the child with a uniform curriculum in all the Member States since they generally follow the universally recognised International Baccalaureate system of assessment. Foreign schools, on the other hand, enable the migrant child to follow in their mother tongue the same curriculum as that of his or her country of emigration.

This was a popular option amongst our sample of which 45 were attending or had at some point attended an international school and 47 children attended a 'foreign' school. Access to a school of this type, however, is usually only available to those with sufficient financial resources to afford the fees or where the financial burden is assumed by the school or parents' employer. For the significant proportion of those interviewed (41 per cent) who had at some point attended state school, the decision seemed, in most cases, to be motivated less by the desire to achieve full integration with nationals of the host state and more by the financial prohibitions imposed by private education. There were cases, for example, where a child attended a private foreign or international school in the host country but was subsequently transferred to the local state school due to the family's financial difficulties. The Greek schools for repatriated children referred to earlier provide a welcome solution to this in that they offer the educational provision for migrant children without the hefty price-tag attached:

> My main concern for my son was to learn English as his first language. Therefore I enrolled him in an English-speaking primary school. Unfortunately he had to stop because of financial reasons. It was too expensive for us. I was trying to find an alternative when I heard about the school for repatriated children. The lessons there could be taught in both Greek and English but he would speak English with his school mates who come from various countries and they feel more comfortable communicating in English [406].

> I could not afford to pay for a private school and the language was a problem. Their knowledge [his children's] in Greek was inadequate for a Greek state school. The only solution was the school for repatriated children. Actually, I must be grateful for its existence [410].

These schools cater specifically for migrant children at both primary and secondary level who have been residing in another country for at least two years. They follow the Greek national curriculum and students who graduate from them receive an identical qualification to that awarded by state schools. With this certificate, graduates have an option to participate either in national examinations for post-secondary studies or in the special examinations for specific categories of students. The Greek state, recognising that migrant children cannot compete on equal terms with the local children due to language difficulties and a possible lack of familiarity with the Greek education system, offers them the opportunity to compete with children of similar qualifications in separate national exams. These take place nationwide every September and are reserved for students who have attended a Greek school for no more than three years. One young interviewee highlights the merits of this system of positive discrimination:

> I will participate in the special exams for Greek returnees and migrants. These exams take place in September of each year [whereas the nation-wide exams are in June]. They are easier because the examined educational material is less in every subject and because the competition between the students is limited. Usually the proportion in the admission is 1:2 [so half of the candidates are admitted to a university of that country] ... Entitled to participate in this kind of exams are students who graduated high school or lyceum abroad, even if they have attended Greek schools a maximum of five years ago. We are lucky to have this right. Nation-wide exams are very difficult [437].[25]

Language Requirements under Directive 77/486: From Regulation to Co-operation

The findings presented so far in this chapter indicate that, in spite of half-hearted fulfilment by Member States of the requirements under Directive 77/486, EU migrant children manage to overcome many of the language-related challenges posed by migration. This in itself partly explains the Commission's tendency to turn a blind eye to non-compliance with the directive. Non-implementation of the directive may be partly attributable also to its broad personal scope – since it is not specifically confined to the education of the children of *EU* migrant children, the entitlement contained therein applies equally to the children of third country (non-EU) migrants. This necessarily encompasses a much broader range of mother languages for the Member State to support under Article 3, imposing an unreasonable and certainly impractical burden on scant national resources. Much of the language support identified in the directive, at least for third country

---

[25] For reasons already outlined in chapter eight, these schools provide only a partial solution – the historic impetus behind these schools renders them more appropriate for returning Greek migrants who already have a firm grasp of the language and culture and are not really equipped to cater for the needs of the migrant population generally.

nationals' children, has been superseded by alternative domestic provision, often as part of its anti-racism policy. The prioritisation of non-EU migrant children's educational needs over those of EU migrant children, through the implementation of more advanced programmes tailored to their needs, further supports the common presumption that the EU migrant population is relatively affluent and, therefore, consistently less needy.

A further problem associated with implementation of the directive is a pragmatic one. Any compliance with the provisions, to be cost-effective, must be proportionate to the needs of children within a given community. Provision of and access to such educational support thus depends very much on the concentration of migrants in that area. Indeed, no local education authority could be expected to fund language teaching for one or two migrant children – who may not even be of the same nationality – where these resources could be more effectively deployed for the general benefit of all children in the school. The problem with implementation lies in the fact that, unlike a lot of non-EU migrant communities which are highly concentrated in certain (usually urban) areas, the EU migrant population is, now, much more dispersed. This is particularly so in view of the fact that EU migrants are not necessarily moving for work-related reasons as previously thought, but for family, childcare or other cultural reasons which lead them to more rural areas as well as the big cities.[26]

Education and language provision also raises the issue of delineating European competence. The fact that compulsory education policy is generally perceived as falling within domestic competence in accordance with the cultural, economic, social and political context of each Member State, it is hardly surprising that Community legislation which seeks to harmonise an important aspect of education policy and which threatens to detract from domestic sovereignty has been met with reluctance. In any case, realistically, Member States can rest assured that parents are unlikely to lodge an official complaint against a local education authority or Member State for non-implementation. This, nonetheless, may be more attributable to a lack of awareness of the directive and the obligations it places upon Member States rather than the fact that they are unaffected by non-compliance.

These issues have undoubtedly fuelled domestic complacency and increasingly questioned whether imposition of the directive is the most effective means of catering for the migrant child's linguistic needs within the context of education. The Commission has thus been prompted to turn its attention in the last decade from more heavy-handed enforcement tactics

---

[26] This is discussed further in chapter three.

towards developing alternative, more acceptable programmes based on co-operation. This approach, as Chisholm (1998, p.158) argues, responds more effectively to varying contexts and differentiating populations across the EU:

> European societies respond to common problems in different ways: similar national or regional policy aims are implemented in diverse institutional contexts. Together with the impact of specific cultural traditions, these factors continue to produce different patterns of educational selection and participation.

Indeed, while European education policy measures should adapt according to the economic, social and cultural landscape of the EU, these measures could also be seen as cultivating this landscape by valorising diversity as a positive resource for enhancing integration and shared, co-operative learning. This is increasingly achievable given recent advances in information and communication technologies which offer an opportunity to introduce more innovative and, in many cases, potentially more cost-effective language teaching and learning methods. The SOCRATES action programme on educational matters, which was established in 1995 by the European Commission,[27] is one such programme of co-operation. Significantly, the notion of nurturing a sense of shared European citizenship was initially cited as one of the principal justifications for the programme. The Commission asserts in its mission statement (1994, p.1), for instance, that the principal objective of the programme is to:

> enhance quality and develop the European dimension in studies at all levels and to promote knowledge of the languages of the Community to that its citizens may take advantage of opportunities arising from the completion of the European Union, while at the same time reinforcing solidarity between the peoples of the Community .

SOCRATES concerns all types and levels of education and targets students, teachers and policy-makers as well as all educational organisations, associations and agencies at local, regional and national level. The programme was initially set up to provide a forum (but no binding obligation) for information and policy exchange with the ultimate objective of developing intercultural education across the Member States and promoting cultural and linguistic pluralism alongside equality of

---

[27] European Parliament and Council Decision 819/95/EC, 14 March 1995, (1995) OJ L87/10. Amended by European and Council Decision 98/576/EC, 23 February 1998, OJ L77, 14.03.1998).

opportunity. The first phase of SOCRATES ran from 1 January 1995 until 31 December 1999 and comprised three main areas of Community action: higher education, school education and adult education. The COMENIUS programme, in particular, was developed as a sub-programme of SOCRATES to target school education. It entails three action programmes: Action 1 concerns the organisation of transnational partnerships between pre-primary, primary and secondary schools with the aim of developing European education projects on subjects of common interest to school children in different Member States. Action 2 specifically targets the educational needs of the children of migrant workers (as well as traveller children and gypsies). This is aimed at 'promoting intercultural education to prepare schoolchildren for life in a society of ever-increasing cultural and linguistic diversity'. Action 3 involves the organisation of training activities for teachers and other educationalists with the aim of improving the quality of education generally and injecting a European dimension into teaching through experience and information exchange.

COMENIUS has been further reinforced by 'LINGUA', another programme established under SOCRATES, which funds a number of projects to improve the teaching and learning of the official languages of the EU and Member States in all sectors of education. In particular, it has developed European co-operation programmes for the training of language teachers as well as joint language-learning projects between students.

The success of the first phase of SOCRATES is highlighted by a Commission preliminary report issued on 14 March 1997 (Com (97) 99 final). The report asserts that measures suggested under SOCRATES were enthusiastically received across all the Member States and other participating countries[28] and attributed to the programme a significant increase in European co-operation in school education where little or no organised co-operation at trans-national level had existed previously. More specifically amongst its achievements the programme enabled some 80,000 young people to participate in joint projects or language exchanges, 16,000 educationalists to take part in ongoing training courses for language teaching, 1,620 partnerships and exchange agreements to be formed between 5,000 schools across the participating states and the implementation of 3,500 joint language projects.

[28] Participating countries other than the 15 Member States include the European Economic Area countries of Iceland, Norway and Liechtenstein in addition to Hungary, the Czech Republic, Romania, Poland, Slovakia and Cyprus.

A second phase of SOCRATES has now been instigated covering the period of 1 January 2000 to 31 December 2006,[29] the main goals of which include: strengthening the European dimension of education at all levels and promoting equal opportunities in all sectors of education; fostering the intercultural dimension of education by promoting enhanced knowledge of languages; encouraging and facilitating mobility in education; and encouraging new innovations in teaching methods and resources. The Commission has reiterated the fact that these objectives will be pursued in collaboration with Member States and will supplement and complement existing domestic education policies rather than conflict with or replace them.

Conclusion

The aim of this chapter has been to consider the language-related challenges facing EU migrant children. It has explored how formal education, which manifests so many of these challenges, also provides a key forum for addressing them. EC Directive 77/486 provided for a series of focused measures explicitly targeting the needs of migrant children. It went one step further than preceding legislation in this area by imposing positive requirements on Member States, rather than simply advocating passive adherence to the non-discrimination proviso. The spirit in which the directive was initially adopted, however – that is, as a very temporary, broad educational and language measure to facilitate imminent return to the country of origin – has largely influenced its less than enthusiastic reception by Member States resulting in its rather patchy and half-hearted implementation. Member States have been more proactive in funding language tuition for its nationals living in other Member States rather than assisting non-nationals within their own territory. It is hardly surprising, therefore, that such a large proportion of migrant children attend private international or foreign schools which cater specifically for their language and wider educational needs. While the experiences of children attending these schools are generally positive, they could be criticised for culturally and linguistically marginalising migrant children and reducing the level of provision available in state schools in proportion with a reduced need. This ignores, however, the obstacles facing EU migrant children living on the economic or geographical periphery for whom the need is great but provision virtually non-existent.

---

[29] Established by European Parliament and Council Decision No 253/2000/EC, of 24 January 2000.

The Commission has clearly conceded that a didactic approach to regulating Member States' education policy in respect of such a diverse population is politically problematic and ultimately ineffective. Instead, it has turned its attention towards implementing alternative, more viable and subtle means of meeting the needs of *prospective* as well as existing migrant children and young people through programmes such as LINGUA and COMENIUS. These programmes, while based on a co-operative approach, reproduce the aspirations of Articles 2 and 3 of Directive 77/486. Consequently, although Directive 77/486 has not been directly enforced across the EU, the obligations and aspirations it contains are being addressed in a more subtle and arguably more effective way through an approach based on mutual respect, voluntary information and cultural exchange. This alternative approach can be credited with reinforcing a spirit of co-operation between Member States while accommodating varying cultural, social, political and economic contexts. Moreover, it serves to safeguard domestic sovereignty in the field of education and encourages the development of notions which are central to the European citizenship agenda – that is, notions of mutual respect and participation. This provides a more positive framework within which to address the needs of EU migrant children who, as our sample indicates, represent a heterogeneous group. Their language-related experiences are, of course, influenced by a range of variables including their migration history, the level of language support they have received, the type of school they attend and their ability or willingness to receive supplementary tuition. The diversity of experience and need represented in the findings presented above both illustrates the complexities involved in regulating language provision across the Member States for this category of migrants, while highlighting the importance of enhanced intercultural exchange and mutual understanding to the European integration project.

10 Conclusion

The research reported on in this book represents an endeavour to develop further our understanding of the concept of Community citizenship. Although 'Citizenship of the Union' was only formally constituted in the Treaty on European Union, the progressive evolution of important social entitlements, for those Community nationals who move for work within the EU, has taken place since the Treaty of Rome. To that extent the now formally constituted status has been very much informed and shaped by the development and interpretation of Community law under the free movement of persons provisions. In practice the status of 'Citizenship of the Union' in Articles 17-22 EC has little real impact on those citizens who remain in their home state.[1] Based on the principle of non-discrimination (Article 12 EC), the extension of social entitlements available to Community workers exercising their right to move within the EU doubtless constitutes an important and immediately practical 'package' of benefits.

Building on previous and parallel research on the status and experience of different groups of Community migrants, this work has sought to clarify the personal scope of European citizenship raising important issues about membership and contribution which are so central to these debates.

By focusing on *Community* nationals these previous research projects have avoided the risk of conflating the interests and experiences of intra-EU migrants with that much larger group of migrants residing within the EU who hold the nationality of a third country. The intention here has not been to deflect attention from this latter group or to prioritise in any way the situation of Community nationals. In practice, there are very different groups of migrants and the tendency of migration research to use the language of 'international migration' runs the risk of generalisation both in terms of migration motivations and the consequences of moving. Rather, the objective of our cluster of projects is to unpack the notion of a simple dichotomy distinguishing the situation of Community citizens, on the one hand, from third country nationals, on the other, and the associated inference of universalism within the former group. In other words, we have

[1] This is not to deny the importance of more general developments in EU social policy in protecting the social rights of many groups in European Union societies, such as women and, more recently, children. The point here refers to the substantive scope of Articles 17-22.

attempted to challenge the assumption that all those migrants who hold Community nationality share some form of common or universal status as the 'in' group.

Indeed, analysis of Community law in the gender and migration project concluded with the suggestion of a 'tiering' of entitlement based on forms of economic contribution and family relationships (Ackers, 1998, p.111). The children and migration project has developed this suggestion further through an examination of what this situation means in practice for the children of Community migrants.

This final chapter draws together the material presented in the book to consider the extent to which the EU is evolving as a Community not only *of* but *for* its children and young people. The research has coincided with a critical and fruitful period of EU law and policy-making. In the work leading up to this project we had begun to note how, whilst there was no coherent and explicit recognition of competence in relation to families and family policy, there was evidence of an emerging approach. Driven by the logic and dynamic of the 'facilitating mobility' principle, the Commission (aided considerably by the ECJ) had begun to etch out some important material rights for the family members of Community migrant workers.

As we have seen, the Court's expansive approach has effectively drawn all dimensions of domestic social policy within the scope of the non-discrimination principle resulting in a relatively privileged status for those qualifying family members. This privileged status is not, however, universal but continues to turn on notions of contribution, membership and family relationships. An important focus of our work has thus been on the extent to which citizenship entitlement is 'tiered' or differentiated to reproduce different classes or categories of citizen with access to different levels of social entitlement. Careful analysis of the personal scope of the rights granted to Community migrants has in fact revealed the exclusive nature of Community citizenship. While in our previous and related work we have focused very much on the concept of work and the extent to which this devalues other forms of non-remunerated but socially worthwhile and economically significant activity (such as care, for example), in this project we have assumed that, on the whole, protective legislation restricting access to paid work for children is a good thing and, on this basis, extending the concept of work is not the most positive avenue for an extension of the citizenship status of children in the EU.

Instead, we have focused on the opportunity a child has to base their claims to citizenship upon their relationship to the citizen-worker parent or, indeed, to claim citizenship rights as an independent actor (on the basis of their membership of the EU). Our work has shown how a child's ability to derive rights on this basis depends on the nature of their family and their relationship with the parent. It is clear that the law privileges certain types of family and effectively excludes from full citizenship those partners and children who fall outside the 'traditional' male breadwinning, heterosexual model. Social entitlement in this context turns on the concepts of marriage and spouse in Community law and also the concepts of child and dependency. Consequently, those children and young people whose family status falls outside of the legally-recognised categories may thus be excluded entirely from Community protection and the benefits of citizenship.

Moreover, citizenship is not purely confined to material status and access to resources. It also embraces the relationship between material status and personal autonomy and the capacity to exercise choice. For those children who do qualify for material rights, the dependency requirement (and the rationale behind the very notion of derived entitlement) has meant that children have remained, to a large extent, the passive recipients of their parents' migration decisions. Their rights have largely remained coterminous with and contingent upon their parents' situation. As such, if a worker-parent decided to return home or move elsewhere the child's derived claims were potentially extinguished. Children, in common with non-working spouses, had no independent rights based upon their membership of the EU (and Community nationality). European law has, to that extent, reinforced and reproduced a dependant status for Community migrant children. We have seen how, in practice, children are given little say in migration decision-making processes (although parents' perceptions of their needs often influences these decisions). Certainly until very recently a dissenting child derived little support from the legal system to enable them to remain in the host country following a parental move. The consequences of this focus on the worker-citizen as the source of children's' citizenship entitlement has perhaps been most forcefully shown in the case of family breakdown when the removal of either parent jeopardises the material status of the family. It is in this context that the tension between the economic drivers of free movement policy and the principle of subsidiarity in relation to social policy are most evident. The failure to deal explicitly with the unintended consequences of labour migration clearly places non-working partners and children in a highly vulnerable position with no effective mechanisms to deal with issues of maintenance, custody and abduction.

As the project has evolved, so too the law has begun to change and new policy drivers have accelerated the pressure for a more coherent and principled approach to family policy and children's rights. However, the free movement framework of Regulation 1612/68 is no longer the primary context in which these developments can take place. The growing concern to draw the EU national closer to its institutions by substantiating the previously 'vacant' notion of Union citizenship has provided a further important engine driving social law and policy entitlement with more direct benefits for children and family members.

The landmark case of *Martínez Sala v Freistaat Bayern*[2] significantly enhanced the currency of Union citizenship in favour of EU nationals in this respect. The case involved a Spanish national who had been resident in Germany since 1968 and unemployed since 1986 who applied for a child-raising allowance, a non-contributory benefit granted under federal law and extended to non-nationals who are lawfully resident in Germany. The national court initially rejected the application on the basis that she was not in possession of a formal residence title. This, the claimant argued, was a direct contravention of (now) Article 12 EC that provides a general prohibition of discrimination on grounds of nationality. In order to rely on this provision Sala had to show that she fell within the scope of the free movement of persons provisions.[3]

The dilemma facing the claimant was that, as an unemployed non-national, she failed to qualify as one of the 'privileged' individuals provided for by the residence directives.[4] The Court resolved the issue by reference to Article 18 EC (then Article 8a) that endows all EU citizens with a general right of residence in all Member States. Sala's status as a *de facto* European citizen was, therefore, deemed sufficient to enable her to exercise the general right of residence.[5] Furthermore, this automatically triggered the protection of the non-discrimination proviso enshrined in Article 12 EC, a right attached to the status of Union citizenship. This decision adds considerable substance to the symbolic notion of Union citizenship and calls into question the relevance of the 'layered entitlement'

---

[2] Case C-85/96 [1998] ECR I-2691.

[3] The Court determined that child-raising allowance did fall within the material scope of the relevant secondary legislation as a 'social advantage' under Article 7(2) of Regulation 1612/68 as a 'social advantage' and as a 'family benefit' under Article 2 of Regulation 1408/71.

[4] Namely Council Directive 90/364, OJ 1990 No. L180/26; Council Directive 90/365, OJ 1990 No. L180/28; and Council Directive 93/96, OJ 1993 No. L317/59 that provide a right of residence to those of independent financial means, retired persons and students respectively.

[5] Article 18(2) EC provides the basis for this decision in that it empowers the Council to adopt provisions with a view to facilitating the exercise of Union Citizenship. This is not to suggest that there no longer exists a requirement to establish a pre-existing right to reside in the host state even though the basis of this initial right is not clearly established in *Sala*. The current position seems to be that the burden is on individual Member States to limit the general, presumed right provided for by Article 18.

previously granted according to individuals' economic value. As Fries and Shaw (1999, p.556) comment:

> It would appear that something close to a universal non-discrimination right including access to all manner of welfare benefits for all those who are Union citizens and who are lawfully resident in a Member State has now taken root in EC law.

The ruling also has potentially far-reaching consequences (and indeed benefits) if applied to the children of EU migrants. First of all, it extends the opportunities for child welfare-related claims by economically inactive parents who remain in the host state with their children. Secondly, Sala's own situation could be seen as analogous to that of many EU migrant children: on migrating to another EC country with their parents they obtain a legal right of residence by virtue of Article 10 Regulation 1612/68, in the same way that Sala obtained lawful residency by virtue of her initial status as an EU migrant worker. The decision to retain Sala's right of residence on the basis of her European citizenship, in spite of the fact that she was unemployed, could also be applied to children who wish to remain independently in the host country following their parents' departure. In this respect, they would be entitled to claim state benefits as a means of supporting themselves (Ackers and Stalford, 1999). Indeed, this is precisely what has happened in subsequent cases such as *Baumbast* [6] and *Humer*[7] (discussed in chapters four, seven and eight) which developed the principles applied in Sala in favour of children. The Advocate General in *Baumbast* referred explicitly to the application in *Sala* of Union citizenship as a (potentially directly enforceable) fundamental *individual* right to reside and remain freely within the Community (paragraphs 48-53). Certainly, it was the children's citizenship rights in this respect which were subsequently extended to the non-qualifying parents to enable them to remain as carers in the host Member State. Unlike in Sala, it is the *children* and not the parents who became the principal source of ongoing entitlement for the other family members.

Humer (discussed in chapter seven) provides a further important development of children's status as direct rights-bearers under Community free movement law. Paradoxically, while family rights under the free movement provisions remain contingent on an 'intact', legally sanctioned

---

[6] *Baumbast and R v. Secretary of State for the Home Department*, (Case C 413/99) Judgment of the Court of Justice of 17th September 2002, 2002/C274/03.

[7] *Humer* Reported 5th February 2002 (Case C-255/99) O.J. 2002/C 84/09.

relationship, the child's independent rights in *Humer* were of greatest currency once the family relationship had actually broken down.

Both of these cases confirm the ongoing potential of the free movement provisions, particularly since its formal alliance with the concept of Union citizenship following the Treaty of Maastricht. The proposals for a new, all-encompassing free movement directive (as discussed in chapter four) further illustrate this renewed commitment to developing individual rights. Yet whilst the development of rights in a mobility context might be said to have spawned the genesis of Union Citizenship, other influences have evolved to shape its character. These include pressures for procedural harmonisation, particularly in relation to cross-border family disputes, as well as political pressure to address the status of third country national migrants and their families within the EU. The new cluster of 'Brussels' Regulations described in chapter seven in addition to the proposed directive on family reunification, in particular, have served to extend family rights beyond the derived status afforded under the traditional free movement formula.

Formal recognition of the principle of non-discrimination under Article 13 EC in addition to the increasing visibility at EU level of international and European human rights norms have provided further crucial policy-drivers in this respect. The Charter of Fundamental Rights in the European Union in particular has explicitly acknowledged concerns to both protect and empower children in the resolution of family disputes (Article 24). These concerns are now likely to be incorporated into the amended European divorce and parental responsibility provisions to afford children a more active and considered voice in cross-national proceedings. While these developments may seem somewhat sporadic and unrelated, cases such as *Humer* and *Baumbast* demonstrate the ease with which the ECJ considers them together as respective strands of an evolving Union citizenship.

In another context, it is important to note how, at the start of this project, we were criticised for focusing our research interest on what were perceived to be a relatively privileged group of migrant children (the children of Community nationals). The development of social citizenship under the free movement provisions remains dependent upon nationality and, to that extent, nationality constitutes the principle axis differentiating the status of migrants within the EU. In an interesting twist, recent changes have modified this situation, placing third country nationals in a theoretically advantageous position. The proposed directive on family reunification provides an interesting illustration in this respect. Chapter four commented on how this seeks to implement a right of third country nationals to join their legally resident family members within the EU even if the latter have never moved. This contrasts with EU migrants' rights whose family members only fall within the protection of EU free movement law if the workers themselves have also moved. A second distinction between the beneficiaries of the proposed directive and traditional free movement law relates to the definition afforded to the 'family'. Article 5 of the new directive, as we have seen, presents a much wider concept of family, recognising the rights of unmarried, cohabiting parties and their children to reside and benefit from the continued social protection of the host state. As such, the more progressive interpretation of family in relation to the position of third country nationals may now highlight the limitations of the existing interpretations under the free movement provisions.

Concerns over the implementation of the UNCRC have dovetailed with a wider commitment, at Commission level, to enhance citizenship participation through the development of 'civil dialogue'. Together these two processes have succeeded in raising the issue of child-impact on the policy agenda and also generated significant pressure groups in this area. The European Commission's White Paper on Social Policy (1994) laid the foundations for a fundamental change in the whole basis of EU public policy-making. Whilst recognising the continued importance of the 'social dialogue' to labour law and policy, the persistence of 'social problems' (such as exclusion), and the emergence of new concerns in a context of demographic change, demanded a new approach to governance. The White Paper speaks of the need to:

> stimulate a new cooperative partnership between Member States, social partners, voluntary and civic organisations and European citizens...in the process of change (EC White Paper, 1994, p.7).

Greenwood (1997) similarly notes the increasing involvement of 'non-producer interests' in European public affairs over the last decade in response to concerns over the 'democratic deficit' and the remoteness of the European agenda from citizens. These changes must be seen in the light of an important symbolic development with the formalisation of the status of 'Citizenship of the Union' in Article 17EC and the Commission's desire to take Europe 'closer to the citizen'. Such concerns are also reflected in the commitment of the Economic & Social Committee to:

> … the importance of voluntary organisations in bolstering democracy … Strengthening non-parliamentary democratic structures is a way of giving

> substance and meaning to the concept of a Citizen's Europe (COM(97) 241 final, p.3).

NGOs have become an increasingly important vehicle for the promotion of children's rights across Europe (and for the monitoring of the implementation of the UNCRC). The 'civil dialogue' strategy thus constitutes a critical dimension of the strategy for the achievement of children's interests via representative NGOs across Europe. The 'link' is illustrated in the words of the Austrian Presidency's proposal on Youth Participation:

> The Council of Ministers of Youth regards the increased participation of young people as one of the central tasks to be undertaken in the process of shaping European society in political, social and economic terms (Council of Ministers, Brussels, 26/11/98).

NGO coalitions such as The European Children's Network (EURONET) and the European Forum for Child Welfare (EFCW) were thus established in the 1990s to campaign for more explicit recognition of children's rights and interests at EU level and for the implementation of more effective child-proofing mechanisms. One of their most notable achievements in this respect was the incorporation into the Charter of Fundamental Rights in the European Union, a series of focused provisions reflecting the principles of the UNCRC. Although this instrument remains decidedly aspirational at present, the regularity with which the EU institutions are already referring to the provisions of the Charter presents a promising prospect for children's rights at this level in the future.

These NGOs have also emphasised the need to engage children on a more direct level with Community policy-making and have played an important role in encouraging more active communication with children and young people about European policies that affect them. The 1999 Europe-wide consultation sessions in the advent to the White Paper on Youth Policy provides a useful illustration in this regard. It is, therefore, this political and civil engagement with children, as much as their formal legal recognition which serves to enhance both their European citizenship status and experience.

At the level of legal analysis then, the developments highlighted in this book suggest that the EU is beginning to develop a more self-conscious and explicit family policy and recognise the importance of children as individuals in their own right. The pace of change at the formal level has been remarkable as various policy drivers have dovetailed creating an important impetus for change.

Our findings in relation to migration motivations and family migration behaviour point to the complex range of issues shaping family mobility. Citizenship based on the behaviour of profit maximising male breadwinners throws a protective blanket around an increasing minority of cases and fails to respond to migration as an on-going process in which the dynamics constantly shift in response to life course events. Many parental moves are motivated by the needs of children and, in particular, concerns around educational progression highlighting the persistence of diversity within European educational systems.

Moreover, children view migration differently and often have a different concept of home to that of their parents, as well as having a very distinct life agenda. To some extent, this reinforces arguments in favour of generating individual rights for children so that they may exercise choice at some stage in their childhood in relation to their education and residence. For many this may be during their late adolescence when they may wish to remain in the host state and pursue their post-compulsory education there or, in the case of children affected by family breakdown, exercise some degree of choice in relation to custody and residence.

In many respects, it is with some optimism that we conclude this book. The situation of children and families is no doubt significantly more advanced than it was at the outset of the research and there are now many more possibilities and, indeed, a growing impetus for and expectation of further developments. Article 13 EC, for instance, has yet to be fully exploited as a legal basis for further child-related provision and there is every likelihood that the desire to enhance co-operation in 'civil and commercial' matters will yield numerous additional cross-national family provisions.

It is important, however, to remind ourselves of the very real distinction between the existence of formal rights for children and their actual implementation. Council Directive 77/486 on the education of migrant children discussed in chapters eight and nine demonstrates the many problems associated with mobilising an EU-wide commitment to honouring supra-national policies of this nature. The general failure of Member States to implement supplementary language provision effectively, coupled with the sheer diversity of national and regional systems, contributes to the problems facing these children. In reality, practices have developed which fly in the face of Community law with Member States dealing with the problems facing their own nationals resident in other Member States (by funding and regulating sponsored schools and teachers in other countries, for example) rather than developing measures to promote the integration of those Community nationals living within their territory.

In many ways this approach further compounds the overall problem by reinforcing national systems and restricting the integration of those children within the host state. Another solution, for those parents and children who lack access to this kind of system – or perhaps value a more multi-cultural approach – lies in the network of privately-funded schools known as the international school system. For those families who have the material resources (or benefit from financial support from employers) to send their children to these schools, it is often a preferred option, enabling children to have access to a wide range of language support and well-resourced schools with extensive extra-curricular activities providing some form of multi-cultural 'bubble'. Whilst these schools also restrict the integration of children within the host state (save perhaps some of the very wealthy host nationals or nationals who have themselves experienced or anticipated mobility), they play a particularly important role in supporting children in families who move repeatedly, on a trans-European or international scale, providing some continuity of curricular and style.

Education and concerns around progression emerged as major factors shaping migration decisions and also the experiences of migrant children. Diversity in the educational provision, curricula and examination systems coupled with language problems often make it difficult for parents and children to consider using statutory provision. The ability to tap into supplementary provision is profoundly uneven with different children receiving very different levels of support depending on where they live and the policies of their host and home country. Recourse to international schooling reflects the occupational status and financial situation of the parents.

These issues illustrate the point that European law only delivers tangible benefits through its engagement with domestic welfare systems. Linked to that is the fact that the simple application of the non-discrimination principle fails to deliver a more harmonised and predictable Social Europe since it fails to address the challenges created by territorial injustice or the 'postcode lottery' both between and within countries. In the absence of any move in the direction of harmonisation in some key areas of social policy (at least in terms of admissions policies and principle progression systems), the non-discrimination principle is unlikely to smooth the transition of families moving throughout the EU and will, indeed, become even more marked in the post-accession era.

Similar problems of ensuring Member State compliance with and enforcement of supra-national policy is already evident in relation to the cross-national family provisions such as Regulation 1347/2000 (discussed in chapter seven). Many domestic family practitioners have yet to acknowledge that such measures have effectively supplanted pre-existing international law and there is still much work to be done to ensure more effective cross-judicial and cross-administrative co-operation to ensure ongoing compliance by private parties with any agreements reached. Concerns have also been raised over the potential injustice created by the new Brussels provisions. The abolition of 'forum conveniens' and the 'race' to secure jurisdiction in particular have been identified by practitioners as hampering mediation and encouraging forum shopping. Clearly this raises concerns not only in relation to the prejudicial impact this may have on the party with less resources or know-how to avail him or herself of other more favourable jurisdictions, but also in relation to the impact of such practices (which encourage haste rather than a more considered conciliatory approach) on children's welfare and participation in proceedings.

As such, whilst recent progressive developments at European level to support migrant families and mitigate the consequences of migration are to be welcomed, it is important to recognise the limits of the law in this respect.

The material presented in chapter six reflects the impact of migration on families. Managing kin relationships transnationally is by no means easy, particularly when families move repeatedly and linguistic competency restricts communication. Whereas some of our adult respondents acknowledged a positive side to this, perhaps because their relationships were more developed and 'mature' prior to migration, children often reported a sense of loss and a desire for more 'everyday' relationships with their wider family. In more extreme circumstances, reported in this chapter and also in our other work, the emergence of care crises present serious challenges to the migrant family resulting in short or long term return moves and tensions between sibling carers.

Our work with migrant families and children has drawn attention to both the positive aspects of mobility but also some of the policy externalities associated with peripatetic careers. While caring responsibilities in the 'home' country often precipitated a review of location, and in some circumstances separation within the nuclear family, so too did the tensions associated with dual careers. The increasing labour market participation and career progression of women in the EU is likely to accentuate these 'tensions' as the career demands of both parents pull families in different directions.

The research has thus identified some of the policy 'exhausts' of EU employment policy with its emphasis upon supporting and promoting mobility in terms of the impact of repeated mobility on the lives of children, on their relationships with family (the 'doing' of transnational kinship), and on their social integration.

Migration and international partnering and parenting constitutes the basis of a vibrant and stimulating childhood for many children. However, the increased incidence of family breakdown, both in general across Europe but also particularly in response to the many tensions experienced by migrant families, represents a real concern. It is to be hoped that developments in the law will increase access to and the speed with which decisions around maintenance and custody can be resolved and that they also promote the active involvement of children in these processes. Nevertheless, the social consequences of family breakdown for this group of children should not be underestimated as parents and extended family are geographically dispersed limiting the possibility of effective co-parenting and the development of strong relationships with grandparents and wider family.

Promoting 'Critical Responsibility' in Socio-Legal Research

The principles (of equality and inclusivity) we have referred to above are relevant not only in terms of EU law and policy but also in terms of research policy and practice. We talked at length in chapter two about our approach to comparative enquiry and the importance of involving children in research. Finally, we would like to end the book with a note about the social and moral responsibilities of researchers and of the socio-legal research community in particular in relation to their critical engagement with policy and user groups.

Bottoms and colleagues (2002) in a recent and to our knowledge unique book on the values and methods of socio-legal enquiry, identify the gulf between the work generated by academic research on the one hand and the development and exercise of the law by legal professionals and practitioners on the other. In the book Melton (2002, p.450) interestingly describes how the use of social science was a:

> common feature in the panoply of children's cases in the [American] appellate courts. Indeed, the ostensible reliance on social science in children's cases has become so widely accepted that whether such work is cited is no longer so much to do with judges' ideology.

It is important to remember that he is speaking here in the specific context of American juvenile courts. In that context, Melton (2002) highlights two of the most formidable challenges faced by socio-legal research. Firstly, he contends that the generalisability of social scientists' research to legal issues is often severely limited by inappropriate methodology and, secondly, that the Courts' intuitions about human behaviour are often more persuasive than empirical research.

In relation to the first point, Melton points to the limitations of social science research. On the one hand he suggests that research cited is often methodologically weak and the findings consequently inaccurate. On the other, the tendency of researchers to focus their research on questions that easily fit their research methods and professional concerns limits the public utility of the research which is rarely closely linked to the legal arguments involved.

Notwithstanding the quality and relevance of social science research, Melton also refers in his second point to the relative weight attached to social science evidence. The Courts, he suggests, have:

> ... often found the "pages of human experience" – an intuitive assessment of social reality based on the way that the Court believes that the world ought to be ordered – to be more persuasive than empirical research in drawing factual conclusions to underlie its reasoning about matters pertaining to children and families (Melton, 2002, p.451).

Using the language of 'critical responsibilities', Bottoms and colleagues (2002, p.1) suggest that researchers have:

> ... an obligation to understand child-relevant law and policy so that they are prepared to conduct research that is useful to courts, policy-makers, and practitioners.

Legal professionals and practitioners then have a responsibility to 'understand and use that research' (Bottoms et al, 2002, p.1). The underlying objective is thus to 'produce scientifically sound research that will have a real impact on children's lives' (Bottoms et al, 2002, p.3).

This view is reiterated in the Socio-Legal Studies Association (SLSA) code of ethical practice which notes the importance to the integrity of the discipline of ensuring that outcomes are widely disseminated 'for the benefit of the community' and, in particular to 'those they have researched' (SLSA, 2002, sub-section 2.1). In keeping with the notion of 'critical responsibilities' referred to above, the SLSA code (Principle 8) also emphasises the importance of 'social obligations' in socio-legal research.

Socio-legal research, as a variant of evaluation research, has an enormous contribution to make to the development of evidence-based law and policy through the promotion of a more active engagement of academic research and policy-making. It is important that we build into our research mechanisms to ensure maximum impact in the potential user and policy-making community. In the word of Bottoms and colleagues (2002, p.10), we 'must find successful ways to disseminate the results to policy and law makers'.

Our study has focused on the status and experiences of migrant children in families in which at least one parent holds Community nationality. As such, the children, as European citizens, fell within the protective cloak of the free movement provisions. Whilst we have shown that this cloak is of uneven quality and a little threadbare in places, we also believe that the research has wider application and symbolic importance supporting an impetus for change. The empirical reality of peripatetic lives implying repeated mobility together with the unpredictable evolution of life-courses and family relationships presented in our work leads us to question the validity and necessity of such narrowly defined and fixed forms of status differentiation. As such it leads us to support moves in the direction of a more holistic approach to citizenship for all Community nationals whether migrant or not and also for those third country nationals legally residing within the EU.

Turner (1997) has described citizenship as, 'a platform for interdisciplinary research on the problems of social membership in advanced societies' (cited in Lister, 1997, p.7). The research reported on in this book is concerned precisely with the evolution of social membership in the EU and has sought to evaluate, in as holistic a way as possible, the scope and quality of that membership in the context of children as citizens. In so doing we hope that our findings are both relevant and accessible to those in a position to influence the future development of European citizenship.

Bibliography

Ackers, H. L. (1994), 'Women, Citizenship and EC Law: The Gender Implications of the Free Movement Provisions', *Journal of Social Welfare and Family Law*, vol. 16, no. 4, pp.391-406.

Ackers, H. L. (1996), 'Citizenship, Gender and Dependence in the European Union: Women and Internal Migration', *Social Politics*, vol. 3, no. 2-3, pp.316-330.

Ackers, H. L. (1998), *Shifting Spaces: Women, Citizenship and Migration within the European Union*, Policy Press, Bristol.

Ackers, H. L. (1999), 'Context, Culture and Values in Migration Research with Children within the European Union', *International Journal of Social Research Methodology*, vol. 2, pp.171-183.

Ackers, H. L. (2000), 'From 'Best Interests' to Participatory Rights: Children's Involvement in Family Migration Decisions', *Child and Family Law Quarterly*, vol. 12, no. 2, pp.167-184.

Ackers, H. L. (2001), *The Participation of Women Researchers in the TMR Programme of the European Commission: An Evaluation*, European Commission (DG Research), Brussels.

Ackers, H. L. and Abbott, P. (1996), *Social Policy for Nurses and the Caring Professions*, Open University Press, Buckingham.

Ackers, H. L. and Dwyer, P. (2002), *Senior Citizenship? Retirement, Migration and Welfare in the European Union*, Policy Press, Bristol.

Ackers, H. L. and Perista, H. (1998), 'Citizenship and Paid Work: the Impact of Migration on Employment Status', in H. L. Ackers (1998) *Shifting Spaces: Women, Citizenship and Migration within the European Union*, Policy Press, Bristol, pp.183-223.

Ackers, H. L and Stalford, H. (1999), 'Children Migration and Citizenship in the European Union: Intra-Community Mobility and the Status of Children in EC Law', *Children and Youth Services Review*, 21 (Nos. 11/12), pp.987-1010.

Alcock, P. (2001), 'The Comparative Context', in P. Alcock and G. Craig (eds), *International Social Policy*, Palgrave, Basingstoke.

Alcock, P. and Craig, G. (2001) (eds), *International Social Policy*, Palgrave, Basingstoke.

Alcock, P. (2001), 'The Comparative Context', in P. Alcock and G. Craig (eds.), *International Social Policy*, Palgrave, Basingstoke.

Alderson, P. (1995), *Listening to Children: Children, Ethics and Social Research*, Barnardos, Ilford.

Alston, P. (1999) (ed.), *The EU and Human Rights*, Oxford University Press, New York.

Anderson, B. (2001), 'Different Roots in Common Ground: Transnationalism and Migrant Domestic Workers in London', *Journal of Ethnic and Migration Studies*, vol. 27, no. 4, pp.673-683.

Anwar, M (1979), *Myth of Return: Pakistanis in Britain*, Heinemann, London.

Archard, D. (1993), *Children: Rights and Childhood*, Routledge, London.

Bainham, A. (1998), *Children: The Modern Law*, Jordan Publishing, Bristol.

Baldassar, L. and Baldock, C, (2000), 'Linking Migration and Family Studies: Transnational Migrants and the Care of Ageing Parents,' in B. Agozino, (ed.) *Theoretical and Methodological Issues in Migration Research: Interdisciplinary, Intergenerational and International Perspectives*, Ashgate, Aldershot and Brookfield, VT, pp.61-89.

Barnard, C. (1995), 'The Treaty on European Union, Education and Vocational Training', *Oxford Studies in Comparative Education*, vol. 5, no. 2, p.13.

Basch, L., Glick Schiller, N. and Blanc-Szanton, C. (1994) (eds), *Nations Unbound*, Gordon and Breach, Pennsylvania.

Bernstein, B. and Brannen, J. (1996) (eds), *Children, Research and Policy*, Taylor & Francis, London.

Betten, L. and MacDevitt, D. (1996) (eds), *The Protection of Fundamental Social Rights in the European Union,* Kluwer Law International, The Hague.

Boh, K. et al (1989) (eds), *Changing Patterns of European Family Life: A Comparative Analysis of 14 European Countries*, Routledge, London.

Bonney, N. and Love, J. (1991), 'Gender and Migration: Geographical Mobility and the Wife's Sacrifice', *The Sociological Review*, vol. 39, no. 2, pp.335-348.

Bottoms, B. L., Bull Kovera, M. and McAuliff, B. D., (2002), 'Children, Social Science and the Law: An Introduction to the Issues', in B.L Bottoms, M. Bull Kovera, and B. D. McAuliff, (eds) *Children, Social Science and the Law*, Cambridge University Press, Cambridge, pp.1-14.

Boyle, P., Halfacree, K. and Robinson, V. (1998), *Exploring Contemporary Migration*, Longman, Harlow.

Bradshaw, J. et al (1996), *The Employment of Lone Parents: A Comparison of Policy in 20 Countries*, Family Policy Studies Centre, London.

Brannen, J. and O'Brien, M. (1996) (eds), *Children in Families*, Falmer Press, London.

Brinkmann, G. (2000), 'Family Reunion: Third Country Nationals and the Community's New Powers', in Guild, E. and Harlow, C. (eds) *Implementing Amsterdam*, Oxford: Hart, pp. 241-266.

Brown, A. L. and de Loache, J. S. (1978), 'Skills, Plans and Self-Regulation', in R. J. Siegler (ed.), *Children's Thing: What Develops?*, Lawrence Erlbaum, Hillsdale, NJ.

Brown, L. N. and Kennedy, T. (2000), *The Court of Justice of the European Communities* (5th Edition), Sweet and Maxwell, London.

Camilleri, C. (1986), *Cultural Anthropology and Education*, Kogan Page in association with UNESCO, Guilford.

Cantwell, B., Roberts, J. and Young, V. (1999), 'Presumption of Contact in Private Law – An Interdisciplinary Issue', *Family Law*, vol. 17, no. 3, pp.226-232.

Castles, F. and Mitchell, D. (1992), 'Identifying Welfare State Regimes: The Links Between Politics, Instruments and Outcomes', *Governance*, vol. 5, no. 1, pp.1-26.

Cavaco, C. (1993), 'A Place in the Sun: Return Migration and Rural Change in Portugal', in King, R. (ed.) *Mass Migration in Europe*, Belhaven Press, Chichester.

CEC (1990), *Report on Childcare in the European Communities 1985 to 1990*, no.31, August 1990, Brussels.

CEC (2000), *Communication From the Commission to The Council*: 'Towards a European Research Area' COM (2000) 6 final, Brussels.

CEC (2001), *New Labour Markets, Open to All with Access for All*, COM 2001, Brussels.

CEC (2002), *Communication From the Commission to The Council: Commission's Action Plan for Skills and Mobility*, COM (2002) 72, Brussels.

Chamberlayne, P. and King, A. (1996), 'Biographical Approaches in Comparative Work: the 'Cultures of Care' Project', in L. Hantrais and S. Mangen (eds.), *Cross-National Research Methods in the Social Sciences*, Pinter, London.

Cochrane, A. and Clarke, J. (1993), *Comparing Welfare States*, Sage, London.

Cornwell, J (1984), *Hard Earned Lives: Accounts of Health and Illness from East London*, Tavistock, London.

Costa, P. (1997), 'Intercultural Education and Teacher Training', in Woodrow et.al. (eds), *Intercultural Education: Theories, Policies and Practice*, Ashgate, London.

CEC (2001), Council of European Professional and Managerial Staff (EUROCADRES).

Craig, P. and de Búrca, C. (1998), *EU Law: Text, Cases and Materials* (2nd Edition), Oxford University Press, Oxford.

Craig, P. and de Búrca, C. (2002), *EU Law: Text, Cases and Materials* (3rd Edition), Oxford University Press, Oxford.

Cullen, H. (1996), 'From Migrants to Citizens? European Community Policy on Intercultural Education', *International and Comparative Law Quarterly*, vol. 45, Jan, pp.109-129.

Cullen, H. (2003), 'Children's Rights and the Charter', in A. Ward, P. Carroza and S. Peers (eds), *The European Union Charter of Fundamental Rights: Context and Possibilities*, Oxford University Press, Oxford.

D'Oliveira, J. (1995), 'Union Citizenship: Pie in the Sky?', in A. Rosas and E. Antola (eds) *A Citizen's Europe: In Search of a New Order*, Sage, London.

Dalichow, F. (1987), 'Academic Recognition Within the European Community', *European Journal of Education*, vol. 22, no. 1, pp.39-58.

Daycare Trust and National Childcare Campaign (1994) *Childcare Now*, vol. 14, No's 1 and 2, available at: www.nationalchildcaremonth.com

de Búrca, G. (1998), 'The Principle of Subsidiarity and the Court of Justice as an Institutional Actor', *Journal of Common Market Studies*, vol. 36, issue 2, pp.217-235.

de Búrca, G. (2001), 'The Drafting of the EU Charter of Fundamental Rights', *European Law Review*, vol. 26, pp.126-138.

Department for Education and Employment (DfEE) (1981) (Circular No 5/81).

Ditch, J., et al (1998), *A Synthesis of National Family Policies in 1996: Report of the European Observatory on National Family Policies*, SPRU, University of York.

Doek, J., Van Loon, H., and Vlaardingerbroek, P. (1998), *Children on the Move: How to Implement their Right to Family Life*, Martinus Nijhoff Publishers, London.

Murch, M., Douglas, G., Scanlan, L. et al (2000), 'Safeguarding Children's Welfare in Non-Contentious Divorce: Towards a New Conception of the Legal Process?', *The Modern Law Review*, vol. 63, pp.177-196.

Drew E., Emerek, R. & Mahon, E. (1998) (eds), *Women, Work and the Family in Europe*, Routledge, London.

Edwards, R. and Alldred, P. (1999), 'Children and Young people's Views of Social Research: the Case of Research on Home-School Relations', *Childhood*, vol. 6, no. 2, pp.261-281.

Eekelaar, J. (1986), 'The Emergence of Children's Rights', *Oxford Journal of Legal Studies*, vol. 6, p.161.

Eekelaar, J. (1994), 'The Interests of the Child and the Child's Wishes: The Role of Dynamic Self-Determinism', in P. Alston (ed.), *The Best Interests of the Child*, Clarendon, Oxford, pp.42-61.

European Commission (1973), 'For a Community Policy on Education', *Bulletin of the European Communities Supplement*, vol. 10, no. 73, p.11.

European Commission (1988), *Report on the Implementation of Directive 77/486*, COM (88) 787 Final, Brussels.

European Commission (2000), 'The Education of Migrants' Children', available at: www.europa.eu.int/scadplus/leg/en/cha/c11034.htm.

European Commission Network on Child Care (1996), *School Age Childcare in the European Union*, European Commission, Brussels.

European Forum for Child Welfare (EFCW) (2002), *Child Justice: Equal Justice? The Right to be Heard and the Issue of Discrimination Against Children*', EFCW, Brussels.

The European Union Migrants Forum (2000) *Migrants Forum Courier*, September-October, Issue 1.

EUROSTAT (1996), *Key Data on Education in the European Union 95*, Luxembourg Office for Official Publications of the European Community, Brussels: European Commission.

EUROSTAT (2000), *Key Data on Education in the European Union 1999-2000*, DGXXII on Education Training and Youth, Brussels.

Faist, T. (2001), 'Social Citizenship in the European Union: Nested Membership', *Journal of Common Market Studies*, vol. 39, no. 1, pp.37-58.

Finch, J. (1989), *Family Obligations and Social Change*, Polity Press, Cambridge.

Finch, J. and Groves, D. (1983) (eds), *A Labour of Love: Women, Work and Caring*, Routledge and Kegan Paul, London.

Finch, J and Mason, J. (1993), *Negotiating Family Responsibilities*, Routledge, London.

Franklin, B. (1995), 'The Case for Children's Rights: A Progress Report', in B. Franklin (ed.), *The Handbook of Children's Rights: Comparative Policy and Practice*, Routledge, London, pp.3-24.

Freeman, M. D. A (1983), *The Rights and Wrongs of Children*, Frances Pinter, London.

Fries, S. and Shaw, J. (1999), 'Citizenship of the Union: First Steps in the European Court of Justice', *European Public Law*, vol. 4, issue 4, pp.533-559.

Freeman, M. (1996) (ed.), *Children's Rights: A Comparative Perspective*, Dartmouth Publishing Company, Aldershot.

Glendenning, C. (1992), *The Costs of Informal Care: Looking Inside the Household*, HMSO, London.

Graham, H. (1983), 'Caring: A Labour of Love?', in Finch, J. and Groves, D. (eds) *A Labour of Love: Women, Work and Caring*, Routledge and Kegan Paul, London.

Grodin, M. A., and Glantz, L. H. (1994), *Children as Research Subjects: Science, Ethics and Law*, Oxford University Press, Oxford.

Hadley, T. (1998), 'Practical Obstacles to Mobility: Employee Mobility and the Business Context' paper to the UK seminar on the implementation of Regulation 1408/71EC, 'Free Movement and Social Security in Europe', Brunel University, June 1998.

Hantrais, L. (1996), 'Comparative Research Methods', *Social Research Update*, issue 13, pp.1-8.

Hantrais, L. (1997), 'What is a Family or Family Life in the European Union?', in Guild, E. (ed.) *The Legal Framework and Social Consequences of Free Movement of Persons in the European Union*, Kluwer Law International, The Hague.

Hantrais, L. (1999), 'Contextualisation in Cross-National Comparative Research', *International Journal of Social Research Methodology*, vol. 2, no. 2, pp.93-109.

Hantrais, L. and Mangen, S. (1996) (eds), *Cross-National Research Methods in the Social Sciences*, Pinter, London and New York.

Hantrais, L. & Mangen, S. (eds) (1999), 'Cross-national Research', *International Journal of Social Research Methodology: Theory and Practice*, vol. 2, no. 2.

Hart, R. (1992),'Children's Participation from Tokenism to Citizenship', *Innocenti Essays*, no. 4, UNICEF, London.

Hervey, T. (1998), *European Social Law and Policy*, Longman, London.

Hill, M. and Tisdall, K. (1997), *Children and Society*, Longman, New York.

Hodson, D. and Green, M. (2001), 'Has the SFLA Code met its Waterloo?', *Solicitor's Journal*, March, p.241.

Hood, S., Kelley, P. and Mayall, B. (1996), 'Children as Research Subjects: A Risky Enterprise?', *Children & Society*, vol. 10, no. 2, pp. 117-128.

James, A. and Prout, A. (1990), *Constructing and Reconstructing Childhood*, Falmer Press, London.

James, A. and Prout, A. (1995), 'Hierarchy, Boundary and Agency: Toward a Theoretical Perspective on Childhood', *Sociological Studies of Children*, vol.7, pp.77-99.

Jensen, A. M. (1989), 'Reproduction in Norway: An Area of Non-Responsibility', in P. Close (ed.), *Family Divisions and Inequalities in Modern Society*, Macmillan, Basingstoke.

Jones, H. and Millar, J. (1996) (eds), *The Politics of the Family*, Aldershot: Avebury.

Kelson, G. A. and DeLaet, D. L. (1999), *Gender and Immigration*, Macmillan, London.

Kiernan, K. (1999a), 'The Changing Demography of Partnership', *Centre for Research on Family, Kinship and Childhood Working Paper*, no. 14, University of Leeds.

Kiernan, K. (1999b), 'Cohabitation in Western Europe', *Population Trends*, vol. 96, pp.25-32.

Kiernan, K. (2001), 'The Rise Of Cohabitation And Childbearing Outside Marriage In Western Europe' *International Journal of Law Policy and the Family*, vol. 15, no. 1, pp.1-21.

Kilkelly, U. (1999), *The Child and the European Convention on Human Rights*, Ashgate, Aldershot.

Kofman, E. (2000), 'The Invisibility of Skilled Female Migrants and Gender Relations in Studies of Skilled Migration in Europe', *International Journal of Population Geography*, vol. 6, pp. 45-59.

Kornhaber, A. and Woodward, K. L. (1981), *Grandparents/Grandchildren: The Vital Connection*, Anchor Press, New York.

Koser, K. and Salt, J. (1997), 'The Geography of Highly Skilled International Migration', *International Journal of Population Geography*, Vol.3, pp.285-303.

Kostakopolou, T. (2002), 'Integrating Non-EU Migrants in the European Union: Ambivalent Legacies and Mutating Paradigms', *Columbia Journal of European Law*, vol. 8, pp.1-21.

Langan, M. and Ostner, I. (1991), 'Gender and Welfare: Towards a Comparative Perspective', in G. Room (ed.), *Towards a European Welfare State*, SAUS Publications, Bristol.

Lansdown, G. (1992), 'Key Right is the Child's Right to be Heard', *Childright*, vol. 91, no. 4, p.4.

Lansdown, G. (1994), 'Children's Rights', in B. Mayall (ed.) *Children's Childhoods: Observed and Experienced*, Falmer Press, London.

Lenaerts, K. (2000), 'Fundamental Rights in the European Union', *European Law Review,* vol. 25, pp.575-600.

Levitas, R. and Guy, W. (1996) (eds), *Interpreting Official Statistics*, Routledge, London.

Lewis, J. (1997), 'Gender and Welfare Regimes: Further Thoughts', *Social Politics*, vol. 4, pp.160-177.

Lewis, J., Datta, J. and Sarre, S. (1999), 'Individualism and Commitment in Marriage and Cohabitation', *LCD Research Series* No 8/99.

Liddy, J. (1998), 'Current Topic: The Concept of Family Life under the ECHR', *E.H.R.L.R.*, Issue 1, pp.15-25.

Lin, G. and Rogerson, P. A. (1995), 'Elderly Parents and the Geographic Availability of their Adult Children', *Research on Ageing*, vol. 17, no. 3, pp.303-332.

Lister, R. (1997), *Citizenship: Feminist Perspectives*, Macmillan, London.

Lowe, N. (2001), 'New International Conventions Affecting the Law Relating to Children – A Cause for Concern', November Issue, *International Family Law*, pp.171-181.

Lowe, N. and Murch, M. (2001), 'Children's Participation in the Family Justice System: Translating Principles into Practice', *Child and Family Law Quarterly*, vol.13, no. 2, pp.137-158.

Lundström, K. (1996), 'Family Life and the Freedom of Movement of Workers in the European Union', *International Journal of Law, Policy and the Family*, vol. 10, pp.250-280.

Mabbett, D. and Bolderson, H. (1999), 'Theories and Methods in Comparative Social Policy', in J. Clasen (ed.), *Comparative Social Policy: Concepts, Theories and Methods*, Blackwell Publishers, Oxford, pp.34-56.

Malcolm, E. (1996), *Elderly Return Migration from Britain to Ireland: A Preliminary Study*, Report No. 44, National Council for the Elderly, Dublin.

Mallick, K. (1999), 'Language, Diversity and Intercultural Education', in Verma, G. and Mallick, K. (eds) *Researching Education: Perspectives and Techniques*, Falmer Press, London.

Mason, J. (1998,) 'Living Away from Kin: Kinship and Geographical Reasoning' *Centre for Research on Family, Kinship and Childhood Working Paper*, no. 7, University of Leeds.

Mayall, B. (1999), 'Children and Childhood', in S. Hood, B. Mayall, and S. Oliver (eds), *Critical Issues in Social Research: Power and Prejudice*, Open University Press, Buckingham.

Maclean, M. (1995), 'The European Union and the Curriculum', *Oxford Studies in Comparative Education*, vol. 5, no.2.

McGlynn, C. (2000), 'A Family Law for the European Union?' in J. Shaw, (ed.), *Social Law and Policy in an Evolving European Union*, Hart, Oxford, pp.223-241.

McGlynn, C. (2001a), 'Families and the European Union Charter of Fundamental Rights: Progressive Change or Entrenching the Status Quo?', *European Law Review*, vol. 26, pp.582-597.

McGlynn, C. (2001b), 'The Europeanisation of Family Law', *Child and Family Law Quarterly,* vol. 35, no.1, pp.35-49.

Meehan, E. (1993), *Citizenship and the European Community*, Sage, London.

Melton, G. B. (2002), 'Starting a New Generation of Research', in B. L. Bottoms, M. Bull Kovera, and B. D. McAuliff (eds), *Children, Social Science and the Law*, Cambridge University Press, Cambridge, pp.449-454.

Minow, M. (1987), 'Interpreting Rights: An Essay for Robert Cover', *Yale Law Journal*, vol. 96, no. 8, pp.1860-2017.

Mitchell, K. (1984), 'Protecting Children's Rights During Research', *Paediatric Nursing*, vol. 10, no. 1, pp.9-10.

Mnookin, R. H. (1981), 'Thinking about Children's Rights – Beyond Kiddie Libbers and Child Savers', *Stanford Law Review*, 24.

Moebius, I. and Szyszczak. E. (1998), 'Of Raising Pigs and Children', *Yearbook of European Law*, vol. 18, pp.125-156.

Morrow, V. and Richards, M. (1996), 'The Ethics of Social Research with Children: An Overview', *Children & Society*, vol. 10, no.2, pp.90-105.

Nicholas Mostyn QC (2001), 'Brussels II - The Impact on Forum Disputes', *Family Law*, May Issue, p.364.

Neale, B. and Smart, C. (1998), 'Agents or Dependants? Struggling to Listen to Children in Family Law and Family Research', *Centre for Research on Family, Kinship & Childhood Working Paper*, no. 3, University of Leeds.

Neuwahl, N. and Rosas, A. (1995) (eds), *The European Union and Human Rights*, Nijhoff, The Hague.

Nielsen, R. and Szyszczak, E. (1994), *The Social Dimension of the European Union*, 2nd edition, Handelshøjskolens Forlag, Copenhagen.

Nuthall, K (1999), 'Uni Backs Student in Fight for Job', *The Times Higher Education Supplement*, 19th November.

O'Connor, J. S. (1993), 'Gender Class and Citizenship in the Comparative Analysis of Welfare States; Theoretical and Methodological Issues', *British Journal of Sociology*, vol. 44, no. 3, pp.501-519.

O'Donnell, K. (1995), 'Protection of Family Life: Positive Approaches and the ECHR', *Journal of Social Welfare and Family Law*, vol. 17, no. 3, pp.261-280.

Oakley, A. (1993), 'Women and Children First and Last: Parallels and Differences Between Children's and Women's Studies', in J. Qvortrup (ed.), *Childhood as a Social Phenomenon: Lessons from an International Project*, European Centre for Social Welfare Policy and Research, Vienna.

OECD (2002), International Mobility of the Highly Skilled, Paris: Organisation for Economic Co-operation and Development (OECD) Proceedings.

Orsi, R. (1985), *The Madonna of 115th Street: Faith and Community in Italian Harlem, 1880-1950*, Yale University Press, New Haven.

Penn, H. (1998), 'Is Comparative Research a Way Forward?', in T. David (ed.), *Researching Early Childhood Education: European Perspectives*, Paul Chapman Publishing, London, pp.7-24.

Peck, B .T. (1997), *Teaching and Educating for a New Europe: A Challenge for the Countries of the European Union*, Nova Science Publishers Inc.

Perista, H. (2002), 'Trabalho, família e usos do tempo - uma questão de género', *Sociedade e Trabalho*, no. 6.

Phizacklea, A. (2000), 'The Politics of Belonging: Sex Work, Domestic Work – Transnational Household Strategies', in S. Westwood and A. Phizacklea, (eds) *Transnationalism and the Politics of Belonging*, Routledge, London.

Piper, C. (1999), 'Barriers to Seeing and Hearing Children in Private Law Proceedings', *Family Law*, pp.394-398

Piper, C. (2000), 'Assumptions about Children's Best Interests', *Journal of Social Welfare and Family Law*, vol.22, no. 3, pp.261-276.

Porter, J. P. (1985), 'Regulatory Considerations When Children are Involved as Subjects in Research', *Journal of School Health*, vol. 55, no. 5, pp.175-178.

Pringle, K. (1998), *Children and Social Welfare in Europe*, Open University Press, Buckingham.

Raghuram, P. (2003), 'The Difference that Skills Make: Gender, Family Migration Strategies and Regulated Labour Markets', *Journal of Ethnic and Migration Studies*, forthcoming.

Reynolds, C. and Bennett, R. (1991), 'The Career Couple Challenge', *Personnel Journal*, vol. 70, pp.46-49.

Roche, M. (1992), *Rethinking Citizenship: Welfare, Ideology and Change in Modern Society*, Polity Press, Cambridge.

Roche, J. (1996), 'Children's Rights: A Lawyer's View', in M. John (ed.), *Children in our Charge: The Child's Right to Resources*, Jessica Kingsley, London, pp.23-38.

Roche, J. (1999), 'Children: Rights, Participation and Citizenship', *Childhood*, vol. 6, no. 4, pp.475-493.

Rodgers, B. and Pryor, J. (1998), *Divorce and Separation: the Outcomes for Children*, Joseph Rowntree Foundation, York.

Rogerson, P. A., Burr, J. A. and Lin, G. (1997), 'Changes in Geographic Proximity between parents and their Adult Children', *International Journal of Population Geography*, vol. 3, pp.121-136.

Rosenblatt, J. and Lewis, I. (1997), *Children and Immigration*, Cavendish Publishing Limited, London.

Ruxton, S. (1996), *Children in Europe*, NCH Action for Children, London.

Ruxton, S. (1999), 'A Children's Policy for the 21st Century: First Steps', EURONET, Brussels.

Salt, J. and Ford, R. (1993), 'Skilled International Migration in Europe: The Shape of Things to Come?', in R. King (ed.) *Mass Migration in Europe*, Belhaven Press, London.

Save the Children (1995), *Towards a Children's Agenda*, Save the Children Fund (UK), London.

Scheiwe, K. (1994), 'EC Law's Unequal Treatment of the Family: The Case Law of the European Court of Justice on Rules Prohibiting Discrimination on Grounds of Sex and Nationality', *Social And Legal Studies*, vol. 3, pp.243-265.

Schunk, M. (1996), 'Constructing Models of the Welfare Mix: Care Options of Frail Elders', in L. Hantrais and S. Mangen (eds), *Cross-National Research Methods*, Pinter, London, pp.84-94.

Shaw, J. (1998), 'The Nature and Extent of Educational Rights under EC Law: A Review', *Journal of Social Welfare and Family Law*, vol. 20, no. 2, pp.203-210.

Shelley, J. (2001), 'Gay Couples Wed for the First Time in Germany on 1st August 2001', *European Voice,* 2nd-5th September, vol.7, no. 31.

Simpson, R. and Walker, R (1993) (eds), *Europe: For Richer for Poorer?*, CPAG, London.

Singleton, A. (1999), 'Combining Quantitative and Qualitative Research Methods in the Study of International Migration', *International Journal of Social Research Methodology*, vol. 2, pp.151-157.

Skolverket [The National Agency for Education in Sweden] (1998), Skolan i siffror 1998: Del 2. Skolverkets rapport nr. 148.

Smart, C. and Neale, B. (1999), *Family Fragments?*, Polity Press, Cambridge.

Smart, C. and Neale, B. (2000), ''It's my life too': Children's Perspectives on Post-Divorce Parenting', *Family Law*, March Issue, pp.163-169.

Solberg, A. (1996), 'The Challenge in Child Research: From 'Being' to 'Doing'', in, J. Brannen and M. O'Brien (eds), *Children in Families*, Falmer Press, London, pp 53-66.

Spicker, P. (1991), 'The Principle of Subsidiarity and the Social Policy of the European Community', *Journal of European Social Policy*, vol. 1, no. 3, pp.3-14.

Stalford, H. E. (2000a), 'The Developing European Agenda on Children's Rights', *Journal of Social Welfare and Family Law*, vol. 22, pp.229-236.

Stalford, H. (2000b), 'The Citizenship Status of Children in the European Union', *International Journal of Children's Rights*, vol. 8, no. 2, pp.101-131.

Stalford, H (2002), 'Concepts of Family Under EU Law: Lessons from the ECHR', *International Journal of Law, Policy and the Family*, vol. 16, no. 3, pp.410-434.

Stalford, H. (2003a), 'Regulating Family Life in Post-Amsterdam Europe', *European Law Review*, vol. 28, no. 1, pp.39-52.

Stalford, H. (2003b), 'Old Problems, New Solutions? European Union Regulation of Cross-National Child Maintenance', *Child and Family Law Quarterly*, vol. 15, no. 3, pp.269-278.

Stalford, H. (2003c), 'European Family Law and the Voice of the Child', *International Family Law*, June Issue, pp.68-74.

Stalford, H. (2003d), 'Brussels and Beyond: A Better Deal for Children in the European Union?', in Boele-Woelki, K. (ed) *Perspectives for the Unification and Harmonisation of Family Law in Europe*, Commission for European Family Law, Oxford: Intersentia, pp.471-487.

Stalford, H. and Donnelly, E. (2002), 'Brussels II Revisited: An Overview of Proposed Amendments', *Family Law*, issue 32, pp.904-907.

Stanley, L. and Wise, S. (1993), *Breaking Out Again: Feminist Ontology and Epistemology*, Routledge, London.

Steiner (1996), *Textbook On EC Law*, (5th edition) Blackstone Press, London.

Stychin, C. (2000) 'Consumption, Capitalism and the Citizen: Sexuality and Equality Rights Discourse in the European Union', in J. Shaw (ed.), *Social Policy in an Evolving European Union*, Hart, London pp.259-276.

Sumner (2002), 'The European Charter of Fundamental Rights and Sexual Orientation', paper to the International Society of Family Law 11th World Conference, August 2002, Oslo.

Treseder, P. (1997), *Empowering Children and Young People: A Training Manual*, Save the Children, London.

Trinder, L. (1997), 'Competing Constructions of Childhood: Children's Rights and Children's Wishes in Divorce', *Journal of Social Welfare and Family Law*, vol.19, no. 3, pp.291-305.

Truex, D. (2001), 'Brussels II – It's Here', *International Family Law*, April Issue, p.7.

Twigg, J. and Atkin, K. (1994), *Carers Perceived: Policy and Practice in Informal Care*, Open University Press, Buckingham.

Tymchuk, A. J. (1992), 'Assent Processes', in B. Stanley and J. E. Sieber (eds), *Social Research on Children and Adolescents: Ethical Issues*, Sage, London.

Ungerson, C. (1987), *Policy is Personal: Sex, Gender and Informal Care*, Tavistock, London.

Veil, S. (1997), *Report of the High Level Panel on the Free Movement of Persons*, European Commission, Brussels.

Verma, G. (1997), 'Pluralism and the Future of Multicultural Education', in Woodrow et. al (eds), *Intercultural Education: Theories, Policies and Practice*, Ashgate, Aldershot.

Wallace, C. (1993), 'The Concept of Citizenship: An Overview', *Slovak Sociological Review*, March, p.1.

Wallace, C. and Fine, K. (1996), 'Gender, Citizenship and Transition: Introduction to Special Issue', *Social Politics*, vol. 3, pp.237-242.

Warnes, A. (1984), Residential Separation and Visiting Between Retired Parents and their Sons and Daughters', in D. B. Bromley (ed.) *Gerontology: Social and Behavioural Perspectives*, Croom Helm, Kent, pp.213-219.

Warnes, A. (1986), 'The Residential Mobility Histories of Parents and Children and Relationships to Present Proximity and Social Integration', *Environment and Planning A*, vol. 18, pp.1581-1594.

Warnes, A. M. (2002), 'The Challenge of Intra-Union Migration to Social Europe', *Journal of Ethnic and Migration Studies*, vol. 28, no. 1, pp.135-152.

Wilk, L. (2000), 'Intergenerational Relationships: Grandparents and Grandchildren', in *Family Issues between Gender and Generations*, European Observatory on Family Matters, Directorate-General for Employment and Social Affairs, European Commission.

Wintemute, R. and Andenæs, M. (2001) (eds), *Legal Recognition of Same-Sex Partnerships*, Hart Publishing, Oxford.

Woods, L. (1999), 'Family Rights in the EU – Disadvantaging the Disadvantaged', *Child and Family Law Quarterly*, vol. 11, no. 1, p.17.

Yeandle, S. (1984), *Women's Working Lives: Patterns and Strategies*, Tavistock, London.

Index